The Transatlantic Era (1989–2020) in Documents and Speeches

This accessible textbook uses key documents embedded in a clear narrative to chart the post-Cold War rise and decline of transatlantic relations. It provides a novel interpretive framework by proposing that the three decades between 1989 and 2020 represent a distinct "transatlantic era".

Providing a unique new look at the recent history and politics of transatlantic relations, the book argues that three key phases can be identified:

- 1989–1999: victory?
- 2000–2010: divergence?
- 2011–2020: disarray?

Each period defines a particular set of political, economic, and security dynamics, with the trend being a gradual undermining of the strengths on which transatlantic unity once relied. These three decades therefore represent both the high point of the transatlantic region's power and potential, and its gradual decline in a global context. Presenting students with a critical perspective of US and European transatlantic policies through annotated key documents covering central aspects of security, political, economic, and cultural affairs, it will be essential reading on all International Relations courses as well as of great interest to scholars and students of US and European Studies, Foreign Policy, and Security Studies.

Bram Boxhoorn is director of the Netherlands Atlantic Association (The Hague), a non-partisan organization that focuses on transatlantic security issues, such as the role of NATO in the Euro–Atlantic security framework, EU–US relations, and NATO–Russian relations.

Giles Scott-Smith holds the Roosevelt Chair in New Diplomatic History at Leiden University, the Netherlands.

"A fascinating look at three decades' worth of transatlantic security cooperation. Boxhoorn and Scott-Smith offer insights and thought provoking questions for everyone interested in the changing political fortunes of the West and the prospect of a global power shift."

Sten Rynning, *University of Southern Denmark*

The Transatlantic Era (1989–2020) in Documents and Speeches

Edited by
Bram Boxhoorn and Giles Scott-Smith

Routledge
Taylor & Francis Group

LONDON AND NEW YORK

First published 2022
by Routledge
2 Park Square, Milton Park, Abingdon, Oxon OX14 4RN

and by Routledge
605 Third Avenue, New York, NY 10158

Routledge is an imprint of the Taylor & Francis Group, an informa business

British Library Cataloguing-in-Publication Data
A catalogue record for this book is available from the British Library

Library of Congress Cataloging-in-Publication Data
Names: Boxhoorn, Bram, author. | Scott-Smith, Giles, 1968– author.
Title: The transatlantic era (1989–2020) in documents and speeches /
Bram Boxhoorn and Giles Scott-Smith.
Description: First Edition. | New York: Routledge, 2022. |
Includes bibliographical references and index.
Identifiers: LCCN 2021021586 (print) | LCCN 2021021587 (ebook) |
ISBN 9780367747855 (Hardback) | ISBN 9780367747862 (Paperback) |
ISBN 9781003159551 (eBook)
Subjects: LCSH: United States—Foreign relations—1989– | Europe—Foreign
relations—1989– | United States—Foreign relations—Europe—Textbooks. |
Europe—Foreign relations—United States—Textbooks. | World politics—1989–
Classification: LCC JZ1480 .B645 2022 (print) | LCC JZ1480 (ebook) |
DDC 327.4073—dc23
LC record available at https://lccn.loc.gov/2021021586
LC ebook record available at https://lccn.loc.gov/2021021587

ISBN: 978-0-367-74785-5 (hbk)
ISBN: 978-0-367-74786-2 (pbk)
ISBN: 978-1-003-15955-1 (ebk)

DOI: 10.4324/9781003159551

Typeset in Times New Roman
by codeMantra

Contents

Authors

Bram Boxhoorn is director of the Netherlands Atlantic Association (The Hague), a non-partisan organisation that focuses on transatlantic security issues, such as the role of NATO in the Euro–Atlantic security framework, EU–US relations, and NATO–Russian relations. Before that he was assistant professor at the University of Amsterdam where he read European history and international relations. He received his Ph.D. in history at the University of Amsterdam in 1992. From 1988 until today he is associated as a lecturer on international relations at Webster University (Leiden). He is a regular commentator in Dutch media on issues concerning NATO, US foreign policy, and European history and politics.

Giles Scott-Smith holds the Roosevelt Chair in New Diplomatic History at Leiden University, and is also attached to the Roosevelt Institute for American Studies in Middelburg, the Netherlands. From 2013 to 2016, he was Chair of the Transatlantic Studies Association. In 2018, as one of the organisers of the New Diplomatic History network (http://www.newdiplomatichistory.com), he was a founding editor of *Diplomatica: A Journal of Diplomacy and Society* (Brill). He is also co-editor for the *Key Studies in Diplomacy* series with Manchester University Press.

Acknowledgements

The editors would like to thank Kate Delaney for the translation of Hans van Mierlo, 'The Vitality of the Nation-State and Europe in the 21st Century' (Part II Document 10). The editors would also like to thank Dario Fazzi for his contribution to this project.

Introduction
The transatlantic era

This collection of documents charts the development of transatlantic relations in the post-Cold War era. It puts forward an interpretive framework for this period, by proposing that the three decades between 1989 and 2020 represented the rise and decline of what we call the *transatlantic era*. In the early 1990s there existed a moment of possibility for the North American and European allies to shape international politics according to their shared values and interests, centred on democracy and the free market. Their principal rival, the Soviet Union, was no longer present as a challenger state. The People's Republic of China was not yet a great power, and was temporarily isolated following the violent suppression of the Tiananmen Square pro-democracy protests in 1989. The end of the Cold War appeared to present an opportunity for establishing a world order based on international law, democratic principles, free-market capitalism, and Western leadership, grounded on the fundamental relationship between North America and Europe. It was, in many ways, a repeat of the "1945 moment" when the United States possessed unparalleled power and influence, only this time with greater European involvement. The era of transatlantic dominance in global governance seemed at hand.

Fast forward 30 years and this post-Cold War opportunity seems a distant dream. Under the combined pressures of the presidency of President Trump, Brexit, underwhelming European Union (EU) leadership, widespread polarisation and populist politics across the North Atlantic region, a belligerent Russia under Vladimir Putin, a rising China, and social-cultural challenges posed by immigration, by 2020 US-European relations had reached their lowest ebb. Reporting on the Munich Security Conference in February 2019, the *New York Times* commented that "The Rift between Trump and Europe is now Open and Angry."[1] In the late 2010s it became commonplace for articles to claim the end of the transatlantic relationship, the end of the liberal order, and even the end of the United States as a great power.[2] The arrival of the Covid-19 global pandemic only further exposed the inability of the United States and Europe to work together against a common threat, leading to what one Dutch commentator referred to as "Coronationalism."[3] Although the election of Joe Biden as US President in 2020 revived a sense of normalcy in transatlantic relations, the arrival of a single leader could not overcome the deeper structural fissures and centrifugal pressures that had arisen over the preceding decades. As Biden looked to Europe at the end of 2020 for a common stance towards a rising China, the EU instead signed a major Comprehensive Agreement on Investment that demonstrated far less willingness to confront Beijing on prickly issues such as human rights.[4]

The argument put forward by this volume is that this does not simply represent a temporary decline that can be easily reversed by new leadership. The *transatlantic era* instead represents an argument that the 30-year period after 1989 was a unique moment of potential for securing and extending systems of global governance on Western principles

DOI: 10.4324/9781003159551-1

and on a global scale, but that this period has instead seen the gradual unravelling of the transatlantic relationship along lines of fundamental political, economic, and cultural divergence. These forces of divergence have involved as much internal dynamics (changing political patterns, economic and financial stresses, and cultural identities) as they have external pressures (new threats, rising powers). Transatlantic relations will of course continue to be vital in global governance, but the "transatlantic era" – a definable era when those nations had the potential to define the contours of that global governance in their own image – is now under stress. Certainly, transatlantic political, economic, and cultural forces will still seize the initiative at particular times, as was seen with the way the cause of the Black Lives Matter (BLM) movement crossed the Atlantic in force in 2020. And improved coordination in crucial policy fields such as combating climate change could still position the transatlantic at the centre of global developments. Nevertheless, we are already in a transition towards a new multipolar era of global governance, the contours of which are still unclear.

The state of the art

Transatlantic relations have of course already generated a large bibliography, but a handful of titles stand out as defining the field. In particular, the works by Lundestad and Hanhimaki et.al. provide comprehensive overviews and analysis of the post-World War II period, with both of them focusing on the key political and economic developments.[5] In contrast, Nolan provided a longer analysis of transatlantic relations through the 20th century, and also incorporated greater attention for cultural developments.[6] Yet all three, while foundational in insight, still face two principal drawbacks. First, they were all written towards the end of or just after the first decade of the 21st century, and are therefore rather dated. Second, the post-Cold War era was for these works not a period that could be clearly defined separate from the Cold War – it was already possible to discern some key trends, but no more. Nolan went the furthest by focusing on fundamental differences between the United States and Europe on issues such as neoliberalism, religion, and war, going so far as to conclude with the statement that "The American Century in Europe is over."[7] This volume agrees with this assessment, but shifts the emphasis away from US-centrism by claiming that a distinct *transatlantic era* existed after 1989 that cannot be simply treated as an addendum to narratives of American dominance.

Analyses of post-Cold War international relations have often been framed around the notion of a "unipolar moment" in US foreign policy, such that the overwhelming dominance of American political, economic, and security interests (not to mention culture) shaped the passage of events to a great extent. Writing at the end of the Cold War, Charles Krauthammer could exclaim that "The center of world power is the unchallenged superpower, the United States, attended by its Western allies."[8] The argument put forward by the transatlantic era is that this is too US-centric an interpretation of the post-Cold War period. It is undoubtedly the case that the United States was the dominant power in terms of the scale of its economy, its security establishment, its ability to coerce others with a variety of foreign policy instruments, and its soft power. Yet the context for this unipolar moment was still an American hegemony embedded in a system of global governance and expecting a network of allies and international organisations to maintain its rules and norms. At the centre of this was the transatlantic relationship, with its dense layers of political, economic, and cultural ties and its overarching security architecture of NATO. But as the unipolar became the unilateral gradually through the 1990s (missile defence, Kyoto) and increasing into the 2000s (especially following 9/11 and the Global War on Terror), it was exactly the transatlantic dimension that started to fragment, due to the opening up of major differences not only over policies, but also over threat perceptions and values.[9] It is also important to recognise the place of Russia in this process, since the rise and demise of the transatlantic era can be neatly charted from the ambitious hopes for a democratised, marketised Russia in the 1990s, to the resurgence of Russian nationalism and a rejection of US-European influence from the late 2000s onwards.[10] Since then Vladimir Putin has aimed to recreate the previous Soviet sphere of influence through Russian foreign policy in its "near abroad" and the Arctic.[11] China has only in the last decade started to play a similar role, as the United States and Europe follow different paths – the one belligerent, the other accommodating – to deal with Beijing's increasing assertiveness and challenge to the Western liberal world order. For this reason, the "transatlantic era" is chosen in place of a more general designator such as "the West," since the latter would include US relations with a wider and more disparate circle of allies including Japan and Australia (for instance, as represented in the 37 nations that are members of the Organisation for Economic Cooperation and Development).[12]

Whereas narratives ascertaining to the rise and decline of the West must necessarily adopt a longer historical context along the lines of Lundestad and Nolan, the transatlantic era instead lays claim to clarifying how we can understand the awkward 30-year period that lay between the end of the American Century and the rise of a new phase in international relations, be that the Multipolar, or the Chinese Millennium, or whatever.[13] Some commentators have pointed to tectonic shifts in democratic systems, brought on by neoliberal marketisation and post-9/11 security regimes, as the guiding theme for understanding the transformation of the West in recent decades.[14] Economically, the transatlantic region was still globally dominant in terms of foreign direct investment and the EU and the United States were still each other's largest trading partners in 2020, but this was not enough to secure global leadership.[15] Presciently, the Atlantic Council concluded in 2004 that "only under the most favourable economic conditions could one expect the joint global leadership provided by the transatlantic relationship since the end of World War II to survive in its current form through 2020."[16] That did not come to pass. Hence, this volume presents a unique interpretation of recent history. It argues that while the EU-US relationship will remain crucial for future world orders in the decades to come, the *pivotal* function and the ability to shape those orders according to their own designs have now passed. Our book therefore argues against Jussi Hanhimäki's claim that transatlantic relations will continue largely unchanged. In contrast to his optimism, we point to structural shifts that indicate the need to reconsider what these relations mean in the context of global politics.[17]

The *transatlantic era* was defined by a belief in liberal internationalism – the argument that American hegemonic power rested on the multilateral structure of international organisations and the rules and norms of global governance that they maintain. When coercive power was required to force challengers to desist, Europe provided the principal allies. The US-European relationship has been fundamental for making American hegemony function, and hence, a focus on the unipolar or the West is not sufficient. And the turning away from liberal internationalism – or, rather, the inability of the United States and Europe to find sufficient common ground to continue to make it work, due to the United States' unilateral interests and the EU's growing regulatory powers, aspirations, international identity, and political malaise – is what, partly, has also defined the end of that era.

The transatlantic era was thus not simply a period defined by US hegemony – it was also a period of European designs to shape its own strategic, political, and economic future. Europe came out of the Cold War in a euphoric mood, but was soon confronted with the limits to its power when Yugoslavia imploded into civil war, something that only US military power could bring to an end. NATO and EU expansion in irregular tandem created overlapping spheres of influence, one for Washington and one for Brussels, with uneven coordination between the two. Efforts to clarify the European governance structure with a Treaty establishing a Constitution for Europe were undermined by two referenda defeats in France and the Netherlands in 2005, indicating the distance that had opened up between the Union's planners and the citizens they were supposed to be planning for. The result was a typical EU compromise, involving top-down political management in the crafting of the Treaty of Lisbon. Strategically the EU has produced its first Security Strategy in 2003 and a follow-up Global Strategy in 2016, the latter talking ambitiously of the goal of "strategic autonomy." But it took the shocks of the Trump presidency and the Brexit referendum in that same year to generate serious thinking on Europe's security, fuelled mainly by a French desire to distance itself from US interests, and Angela Merkel declared in 2017 that "we Europeans truly have to take our fate into our own hands." Yet this did not result in any immediate or significant moves to increase defence spending, with most NATO members remaining below the 2% of GDP margin. The relationship between the United States and Europe has always been unbalanced, but the transatlantic era was marked by a growing European desire for greater autonomy without the political will or cooperation to actually deliver the assets required to achieve it. This produced a volatile basis for transatlantic security cooperation, evolving from a situation of agenda-setting in the 1990s to one of uncertainty and fragility as the 2020s began.

Various works have chronicled elements of this narrative since 2010, focusing on divergent threat perceptions and security relations,[18] the consequences of the EU's crises and US political shifts,[19] and a lack of coordinated leadership in responding to a changing global environment.[20] In 2020, spurred on by the prospect of either a Trump second term or a Biden presidency, think tanks on both sides of the Atlantic were searching for ways forward, be that the need for greater "strategic autonomy" for Europe,[21] or through a call for a "New Deal" "joining in common action a more globally committed America with a more self-reliant and capable Europe to meet the challenges to our health, security, prosperity and way of life."[22] But just as President Trump did not single-handedly signal the end of the transatlantic era,[23] so too does President Biden not signal its revival. The Carnegie Endowment recognised that

> Looking back, 1989 was a momentous year that ushered in the modern era of transatlantic relations. It was also the year that Cher released her international hit single "If I Could Turn Back Time." She couldn't then, and we can't now – the only direction to look is forward.[24]

But forward to what? Following the violent storming of the US Capitol by Trump supporters on 6 January 2021, foreign policy cognoscenti lined up to argue that the United States had to fix its democratic system at home before it could once again endeavour to promote democracy abroad.[25] Walter Russell Mead talked of a "Wilsonian recession" – the belief in a Wilsonian liberal international order was "deeply implanted in American political culture," but the context in which it could be realised was now radically altered.[26] Perhaps climate is providing the game-changer. The new agenda for the "greening" of the transatlantic economy by both the US and the EU gained momentum during the first year of Biden's presidency, with both actors pledging to achieve net-zero emissions by 2050.[27] At the US-EU Summit in June 2021, it was announced that a High-Level Climate Action Group would be created to ensure compliance with the 2015 Paris Agreement. The foundations may have been laid for increased transatlantic participation, coordination, and perhaps global leadership on combating climate change, but this will only become clear in the coming decade.

Meanwhile, some social developments, such as the Occupy movement's opposition to neoliberalism,[28] #MeToo against sexual harassment, and the protests of BLM against racial violence towards black people, have provided the basis for new forms of transatlantic cooperation at the grassroots level. The connections made between BLM and the protests against the legacies of colonialism in Europe following the death of George Floyd in Minneapolis on 25 May 2020 demonstrated a significant joining of transatlantic social forces. Hence, while for its advocates the passing of the transatlantic era is a moment of crisis for the democratic-capitalist order, some critics may not mourn the end of what they consider to be a hypocritical and unjust power structure.

The transatlantic era, 1989–2020: three phases

This collection of documents presents the transatlantic era in the form of three decade-long sections, each one chronicling a particular phase of the era in the post-Cold War period. It draws on a wide variety of sources covering politics, economics, and debates in the public realm to build a coherent image of the evolution of the era from optimism to pessimism and decline, making use of policy statements, international agreements, speeches, and public commentary. The selection of documents was based on three broad criteria. First, documents that mark important moments in political decision-making or trends in politics and political economy. Second, documents that set out important developments in security assessment and strategic thinking. Third, documents from the public sphere that indicate important trends in the transatlantic zeitgeist. From these three sources a coherent picture of transatlantic transition can be drawn.

Part I: 1989–1999 - Victory?

This section covers the 1990s, when the apparatus of transatlantic governance seemed to possess the most potential for creating an era of peace and prosperity. The United States did not face any single challenger to its primacy. Globalisation was the keyword for the decade, and the United States was promoting the expansion of free market economics and democracy across the globe. With the demise of the Soviet Union, it appeared as if the nations of the transatlantic region, built on intensive security and economic cooperation and now expanded to include much of Central and Eastern Europe, would be able to determine the future agenda for global governance. Efforts were made to solidify the relationship with the New Transatlantic Agenda, and NATO revised its Strategic Concept twice, each time expanding the scope and the tasks for the organisation. From this perspective, the 1990s appear as a decade of enormous potential. The Rio Summit of 1992 (the UN's Conference on the Environment and Development) seemed to herald a new age of cooperation towards greater sustainability, the protection of biodiversity, and reduced carbon emissions, but the subsequent transatlantic divide that opened up only a few years later in Kyoto soon undermined that optimism. The break-up of Yugoslavia, US military predominance and the awkward ambition of the EU to develop a substantial security apparatus of its own, and the arrival of the Euro as a new reserve currency all led to transatlantic frictions. By the end of the decade, NATO's mission in Kosovo had given the alliance a new impetus as a force for humanitarian intervention, but the fractures this caused with Russia were a harbinger of what was to come, and NATO itself was increasingly suffering from a divide in capabilities between the United States and the rest. The EU was consolidating its role as an economic and financial powerhouse, with the introduction of the Euro seen by some as a direct challenge to the unique role of the US$ in the global system. But alongside that, Europe's capabilities in the security field still lagged behind.

Part II: 2001–2010 - Divergence?

The decade of the 2000s was encapsulated by 9/11 and the Iraq war at one end, and the financial crisis at the other. During this period there was a strong sense expressed on both sides of the Atlantic that diverging security concerns were leading to a breakdown in consensus on fundamental policies. The US "Global War on Terror" was not accepted by all European allies, and the military response to this security threat by the United States was balanced by a European perspective more geared to terrorism as a crime. Nevertheless, NATO was still able to run its largest operation to date in Afghanistan, albeit with mixed long-term results, and with deep divides opening up in terms of the willingness and capabilities of various allies to take responsibility for large-scale security operations. Explanatory analyses pointed to different strategic outlooks and levels of ambition between the United States and Europe, suggesting that the divergence was not so much a temporary obstacle as a long-term trend that may be irreversible. The EU's moves to develop its own security identity and strategy did not result in any significant reduction in reliance on the United States. US "hyperpower" divided Europe and generated increasing friction with Russia under the leadership of Vladimir Putin. The designation of "terrorism" as the number one threat, and the determination of the George W. Bush administration to push the boundaries of the law in response, caused major rifts on issues such as rendition and Guantanamo Bay. Then from 2007 a series of bank and insurance company failures, encapsulated by Lehman Brothers in September 2008, challenged the capabilities of democratic systems to respond and maintain financial stability. In the United States, grassroots anger was channelled into the Tea Party on the right and Occupy on the left, and with the election of Barack Obama, transatlantic responses to the financial crunch in the banking world entered a period of distinct divergence. While the Americans pumped billions into sustaining the banking system, in Europe the electoral victories for centre-right and rightist political forces initiated policies of austerity in public spending. Obama would continue to be overwhelmingly popular in Europe, but already in his first term the announcement of a "Pivot to Asia" pointed to the United States distancing itself from European issues. Geopolitically and economically the Atlantic space was gradually losing its pr9dominance as the Pacific and the Indian Oceans became key areas of growth and trade.[29]

Part III: 2011–2020 - Disarray?

The second decade of the 21st century saw growing divergence across all areas of transatlantic exchange, most notably in security policy and economic and financial management, to the point where policy-level cooperation was seriously undermined. The socio-economic effects of the financial crisis led to a further weakening of the middle classes across the transatlantic region, and a substantial growth in the rich-poor divide. New social movements such as Occupy and BLM came to define the struggles at the heart of transatlantic societies. Obama's "Pivot to Asia" was combined with an apparent reduced interest in European affairs, although the belligerence of Russia, particularly concerning the annexation of the Crimea in 2014, did lead to a stronger US response compared to an EU – and particularly Germany – more closely involved with Russian energy supplies. Nevertheless, even under Obama Europeans were questioning where the continent stood in the US view on world order. The "Arab Spring" seemed like an opportunity to support the democratic transformation of the Middle East, but instead the political infrastructure of several nations proved too fragile and a return to authoritarianism and sectarianism was the result. The collapse of Syria into civil war and the fragmentation of Libya following the fall of Gaddafi also generated a sustained migration across the Mediterranean from 2015 onwards, driven by conflict, economic gain, and climate change, that strained the abilities of the EU to coordinate national responses and share the burden. NATO's mission in Libya further illustrated the strains within the alliance, this time between a United States unwilling to lead and a Europe unable to act decisively without it. The Syrian civil war also exposed the lack of transatlantic political will to either intervene militarily or force a diplomatic solution, and instead, the field was left open for others, in particular Russia, Turkey, and Iran, to act in support of their respective allies. Politically, the combined effects of economic downturn, austerity, and refugees have also heavily contributed to the rise of political forces loosely referred to as "populism" that promote various forms of ethnic nationalism. The EU became the focus of this discontent, most notably in the Brexit referendum of 2016 where the "Leave" campaign cleverly directed social anger on to the Brussels bureaucracy. This was coupled with the election of Donald Trump in 2016, which for the first time placed a leader in the White House who was deeply sceptical of the merits of the transatlantic alliance. Trump's complaints about a relative lack of European investment in defence were not new, but they had never been expressed so bluntly or with so much nefarious intent. Political changes in Hungary, Italy, Poland, and Turkey placed equal stress on the assumptions of the EU as an apparatus of consensus, and at the end of the decade the Eurozone was still struggling to regain its former levels of growth. The onset of the Covid-19 pandemic in early 2020 only exposed further the transatlantic rifts in public policy and the inability of the EU to coordinate the interests of its Member States.

As a result, the 2010s were marked by both political forces from within (populism, Brexit, effects of austerity policies) and from without (Russian foreign policy, Syrian and Libyan turmoil, migration) that fundamentally challenged what was once taken for granted as a transatlantic alliance. Crucially, the transatlantic space became increasingly divided on the grounds of identity as well as interests. Several documents in this collection point in this direction, with religion acting as a key source of divergence between American and European views of the world.[30] But religion has also been a factor of division within the United States and Europe themselves. The continuing influence of the religious right in US politics was evident during the Trump presidency, with Vice-President Mike Pence the designated spokesperson. In Europe, Catholicism fuelled the populism of the Law and Justice party in Poland, while Islam provided the basis for Recep Erdogan's new direction away from Europe for Turkey. Immigration has added to this trend, mainly through the rise of an anti-Islamic populism, but also in relation to the "hispanification" of the United States, something that Samuel Huntington focused on in his post-9/11 book *Who Are We?*[31] US Secretary of Defence Robert Gates raised the alarm on this issue in a farewell speech in 2011 when he called on Europeans to recognise the changes occurring in the US Congress – it would soon no longer be possible to assume that the transatlantic relationship was central for US foreign relations.[32]

A transatlantic era, when the United States and Europe seemed to have the post-Cold War opportunity to shape global politics in their interests, is therefore passing. New challenges and rising challengers are testing transatlantic unity. The trends point to either the transatlantic losing its prominent role and becoming simply one region among many, or its fragmentation as other North-South and/or East-West forces of integration begin to overlap and "distort" the transatlantic space.

The risk of putting forward such a collection of documents as this is that it becomes self-referential, missing a global context and lacking attention for global developments that have also led to changes in the transatlantic environment. While this is true up to a point, it is also the case that such a collection can only be convincing if it presents a coherent narrative and if it maintains its focus on developments within the transatlantic space. There are no documents here, for instance, from the G20 or the BRICS, and while the evolution of NATO is covered in detail, the debate on its possible extension to the Asia-Pacific region has been left out.[33] In this way the evolution of EU-US relations can be tracked in an accessible way, while still giving attention to wider developments when required. This also avoids the trap of trying to provide too much context, and so ultimately becoming another text on "global politics," of which there is already a sufficient number.

The rise of China is an important contextual element in the narrative of the transatlantic era. Differing approaches towards Beijing – the United States seeing a strategic rival to its global hegemony, the EU seeing an increasingly important trading partner – prevented the emergence of a joint response. Added to this was the increasingly influential role of China within the spaces of European governance itself. The transcontinental Belt and Road Initiative launched in 2013 had the potential to revolutionise China-EU trade. Investments in the wake of the 2008 financial crisis, in particular the Greek port of Piraeus, solidified China's presence in Europe's infrastructure networks. Joint military exercises with Russia in the Mediterranean in 2015 and the Baltic in 2017 brought the Chinese military to Europe's vicinity, while ambitious Arctic strategies saw Beijing also demanding a say in the governance of Europe's high north. Even within the EU itself, Beijing's close involvement with Central and Eastern European countries via the "17+1" arrangement was seen by some critics as a means to split the Union and prevent a united front against China's growing economic power. For all of these reasons, the role of China generated very different calculations on both sides of the Atlantic. The signing of a major EU-China trade deal at the end of 2020 confirmed the trend that the EU, driven in particular by the sizeable German stake in China as an export market, was not going to follow Washington's line. Hence, China, somewhat similar to Russia, also has a significant role in defining the rise and demise of the transatlantic era.

The documents gathered here chart how the post-Cold War ambitions of the United States and Europe gradually foundered on lack of coordination, lack of coherence, and/or lack of resources. By including political, economic, and security documents as well as cultural commentary, the collection provocatively identifies the moments when the diverging interests of the United States and Europe gradually became more apparent. It is not intended to be a comprehensive collection – it would be simple to propose any number of additions, based on alternative conceptions of the transatlantic, for instance. Nevertheless, the documents presented here provide a unique and foundational educational resource for identifying, clarifying, and exploring the rise and demise of the transatlantic era since the end of the Cold War.

Notes

1 'Rift between Trump and Europe is now open and angry,' *New York Times*, 17 February 2019.
2 M. Schwartz, 'The end of Atlanticism: Has Trump killed the ideology that won the Cold War?' *The Guardian*, 4 September 2018; P. Goodman, 'The post-war order is under assault from the powers that built it,' *New York Times*, 26 March 2018; Graham Allison, "The myth of the liberal order", *Foreign Affairs* 97 (July/August 2018); T. Wood, 'NATO and the myth of the liberal international order,' *New York Review of Books*, 21 August 2018.

3 Ko Colijn, 'Coronationalisme,' 18 March 2020, Clingendael Institute, <https://spectator.cling-endael.org/nl/publicatie/coronationalisme>

4 See https://trade.ec.europa.eu/doclib/press/index.cfm?id=2233.

5 Geir Lundestad, *The United States and Western Europe since 1945* (Oxford: Oxford University Press, 2005); Jussi Hanhimaki, Benedikt Schoenborn, and Barbara Zanchetta, *Transatlantic Relations since 1945: An Introduction* (London: Routledge, 2012).

6 Mary Nolan, *The Transatlantic Century: Europe and America 1890–2010* (Cambridge: Cambridge University Press, 2012).

7 Ibid., p. 373.

8 Charles Krauthammer, 'The Unipolar Moment,' *Foreign Affairs* 70 (1990–1991), 23. See also Hal Brands, *Making the Unipolar Moment: US Foreign Policy and the Rise of the Post-Cold War Order* (Ithaca: Cornell University Press, 2016)

9 Ruud Janssens and Rob Kroes (eds.), *Post-Cold War Europe, Post-Cold War America* (Amsterdam: VU University Press, 2004); Sergio Fabbrini (ed.), *The United States Contested: American Unilateralism and European Discontent* (London: Routledge, 2006).

10 Frances Burwell and Svante Cornell (eds.), *The Transatlantic Partnership and Relations with Russia* (Stockholm: Institute for Security and Development Policy, 2012).

11 See Robert Donaldson and Vidya Nadkarni, *The Foreign Policy of Russia: Changing Systems, Enduring Interests* (London: Routledge, 2019).

12 Matthias Schmelzer, *The Hegemony of Growth: The OECD and the Making of the Economic Growth Paradigm* (Cambridge: Cambridge University Press, 2016). On the debate surrounding 'the West' see the introduction to Valerie Aubourg, Gerard Bossuat, and Giles Scott-Smith (eds.), *European Community, Atlantic Community?* (Paris: Soleb, 2008).

13 See for instance Jeffrey Anderson, G. John Ikenberry, and Thomas Risse, *The End of the West: Crisis and Change in the Atlantic Order* (Ithaca: Cornell University Press, 2008). For an early attempt to define the post-Cold War period as a distinctive transition phase: Michael Cox, Ken Booth, and Timothy Dunne (eds.), *The Interregnum: Controversies in World Politics* (Cambridge: Cambridge University Press, 1999).

14 Simon Reid-Henry, *Empire of Democracy: The Remaking of the West since the Cold War 1971–2017* (London: John Murray, 2019). Reid-Henry dates his study from the onset of neoliberalism in the early 1970s, tracking its sustained influence on democratic systems worldwide. The book also lacks a definitive end-point regarding a distinct 'era', and is more focused on democratic transformations as a global phenomenon rather that specific regional dynamics within the West itself, in contrast to this volume.

15 Daniel Hamilton and Joseph Quinlan, *The Transatlantic Economy 2020* (Johns Hopkins University: Foreign Policy Institute, 2020), p. vii.

16 *The Transatlantic Economy in 2020: A Partnership for the Future?* Policy Paper, Atlantic Council, 1 November 2004.

17 Jussi Hanhimäki, *Pax Transatlantica: America and Europe in the Post-Cold War Era* (Oxford: Oxford University Press, 2021).

18 Mary Hampton, *A Thorn in Transatlantic Relations: American and European Perceptions of Threat and Security* (Basingstoke: Palgrave, 2013); Michele Testoni, *NATO and Transatlantic Relations in the 21st Century: Foreign and Security Policy Perspectives* (London: Routledge, 2020).

19 Marianne Riddervold and Akasemi Newsome (eds.), *Transatlantic Relations in Times of Uncertainty: Crises and EU-US Relations* (London: Routledge, 2020).

20 Riccardo Alcaro, John Peterson, and Ettore Greco (eds.), *The West and the Global Power Shift: Transatlantic Relations and Global Governance* (Basingstoke: Palgrave Macmillan, 2016).

21 Sophia Besch and Luigi Scazzieri, *European Strategic Autonomy and a New Transatlantic Bargain,* Centre for European Reform, December 2020.

22 Project on Europe and the Transatlantic Relationship, *Stronger Together: A Strategy to Revitalize Transatlantic Power*, Belfer Center for Science and International Affairs, December 2020.

23 See the useful discussion on this point: Anna Dimitrova, 'The State of the Transatlantic Relationship in the Trump Era,' 3 February 2020, Robert Schuman Centre, <https://www.robert-schuman.eu/en/european-issues/0545-the-state-of-the-transatlantic-relationship-in-the-trump-era>

24 Erik Brattberg and Dan Baer, 'Introduction,' in Brattberg and Baer (eds.), *Reimagining Transatlantic Relations*, Carnegie Endowment, 6 October 2020, <https://carnegieendowment.org/2020/10/06/reimagining-transatlantic-relations-pub-82848>

25 Emma Ashford (Atlantic Council), 'America can't promote democracy abroad. It can't even protect it at home,' *Foreign Policy*, 7 January 2021; James Goldgeier and Bruce Jentleson, 'The

United States needs a democracy summit at home,' *Foreign Affairs*, 9 January 2021; Thomas Wright (Brookings Institution), 'The US must now repair democracy at home and abroad,' *The Atlantic*, 10 January 2021.

26 Walter Russell Mead, 'The end of the Wilsonian Era: Why liberal internationalism failed," ' *Foreign Affairs*, January/February 2021.

27 Morena Skalamera, '"Greening" over the Transatlantic Divide – Domestic constraints and the possibility of renewed cooperation,' *Perry World House*, Spring 2021, <https://global.upenn.edu/sites/default/files/perry-world-house/SkalameraTransatlantic.pdf >.

28 See 'The Global May manifesto' of the International Occupy assembly,' *The Guardian*, 11 May 2012, <https://www.theguardian.com/commentisfree/2012/may/11/occupy-globalmay-manifesto>.

29 See, for an example of this trend, Robert Kaplan, *Monsoon: The Indian Ocean and the Future of American Power* (New York: Random House, 2011).

30 On the importance of religion (or the 'God gap') see Nolan, *The Transatlantic Century*, and Hampton, *A Thorn in Transatlantic Relations*.

31 Samuel Huntington, *Who Are We? The Challenges to America's National Identity* (New York: Simon & Schuster, 2005).

32 See Part III, Document 2.

33 See, for instance, Alexander Moens and Brooke Smith-Windsor (eds.), *NATO and Asia-Pacific*, Forum Paper 25, NATO Defence College, 2016.

Part I
1989–1999: victory?

Document 1

President George H.W. Bush, Remarks to the Citizens in Mainz, Federal Republic of Germany, 31 May 1989

George H.W. Bush had been elected President of the United States in November 1988, having served as President Reagan's Vice-President from 1980–88) and directly involved in formulating US foreign policy during that period. During those previous eight years, the relationship between the United States and the Soviet Union had changed from one of outright hostility to one of mutual recognition, opening the way for arms control agreements and a reduction in nuclear weapons on both sides. This remarkable shift had much to do with the more moderate stance of Reagan during his second term as President (1984–88), and the arrival of a new leader of the Soviet Union, Mikhail Gorbachev, in March 1985. Gorbachev was especially keen to strike deals with the United States in order to lower Soviet military spending and allow him time to restructure the Soviet system without the threat of a US military challenge. Gorbachev made it clear he was aiming to reshape European security by reducing the number of nuclear weapons and withdrawing Soviet support for Eastern bloc regimes. In these circumstances there were many questions surrounding the attitude of the United States towards this radically changing transatlantic relationship. President Bush used his official visit to Western Europe in May 1989 to outline his own vision for a peaceful Europe beyond the East-West divide. Using the 40th anniversary of the formation of NATO, Bush claimed the mantle for change by insisting that the West's collective determination to defend democracy was the real basis for a positive shift in international affairs. In doing so Bush made it clear that the negotiations over the future of Europe would not be made between equals. A 'Europe whole and free' would be based on Western ideals and it would not involve any competition between different systems. Bush therefore declared that the end of the Cold War would come about through the strength and superiority of the Western democratic capitalist system, and this would be the standard line adopted by the United States into the 1990s. It would have far-reaching consequences regarding the future role of the United States in European security arrangements and the attempt at the same time to normalize relations with post-Soviet Russia.

[This is an excerpt from the full document]

As you know best, this is not just the 40th birthday of the alliance, it's also the 40th birthday of the Federal Republic: a republic born in hope, tempered by challenge. And at the height of the Berlin crisis in 1948, Ernst Reuter called on Germans to stand firm and confident, and you did – courageously, magnificently.

And the historic genius of the German people has flourished in this age of peace, and your nation has become a leader in technology and the fourth largest economy on Earth. But more important, you have inspired the world by forcefully promoting the principles of human rights, democracy, and freedom. The United States and the Federal Republic

DOI: 10.4324/9781003159551-3

have always been firm friends and allies, but today we share an added role: partners in leadership.

Of course, leadership has a constant companion: responsibility. And our responsibility is to look ahead and grasp the promise of the future. I said recently that we're at the end of one era and at the beginning of another. And I noted that in regard to the Soviet Union, our policy is to move beyond containment. For 40 years, the seeds of democracy in Eastern Europe lay dormant, buried under the frozen tundra of the Cold War. And for 40 years, the world has waited for the Cold War to end. And decade after decade, time after time, the flowering human spirit withered from the chill of conflict and oppression; and again, the world waited. But the passion for freedom cannot be denied forever. The world has waited long enough. The time is right. Let Europe be whole and free.

And in this same spirit, I set forth four proposals to heal Europe's tragic division, to help Europe become whole and free.

First, I propose we strengthen and broaden the Helsinki process to promote free elections and political pluralism in Eastern Europe. As the forces of freedom and democracy rise in the East, so should our expectations. And weaving together the slender threads of freedom in the East will require much from the Western democracies.

In particular, the great political parties of the West must assume an historic responsibility to lend counsel and support to those brave men and women who are trying to form the first truly representative political parties in the East, to advance freedom and democracy, to part the Iron Curtain.

In fact, it's already begun to part. The frontier of barbed wire and minefields between Hungary and Austria is being removed, foot by foot, mile by mile. Just as the barriers are coming down in Hungary, so must they fall throughout all of Eastern Europe. Let Berlin be next – let Berlin be next! Nowhere is the division between East and West seen more clearly than in Berlin. And there this brutal wall cuts neighbor from neighbor, brother from brother. And that wall stands as a monument to the failure of communism. It must come down.

Now, glasnost may be a Russian word, but "openness" is a Western concept. West Berlin has always enjoyed the openness of a free city, and our proposal would make all Berlin a center of commerce between East and West – a place of cooperation, not a point of confrontation. And we rededicate ourselves to the 1987 allied initiative to strengthen freedom and security in that divided city. And this, then, is my second proposal: Bring glasnost to East Berlin.

My generation remembers a Europe ravaged by war. And of course, Europe has long since rebuilt its proud cities and restored its majestic cathedrals. But what a tragedy it would be if your continent was again spoiled, this time by a more subtle and insidious danger – Chancellor referred to – that of poisoned rivers and acid rain. America's faced an environmental tragedy in Alaska. Countries from France to Finland suffered after Chernobyl. West Germany is struggling to save the Black Forest today. And throughout, we have all learned a terrible lesson: Environmental destruction respects no borders.

So, my third proposal is to work together on these environmental problems, with the United States and Western Europe extending a hand to the East. Since much remains to be done in both East and West, we ask Eastern Europe to join us in this common struggle. We can offer technical training, and assistance in drafting laws and regulations, and new technologies for tackling these awesome problems. And I invite the environmentalists and engineers of the East to visit the West, to share knowledge so we can succeed in this great cause.

My fourth proposal, actually a set of proposals, concerns a less militarized Europe, the most heavily armed continent in the world. Nowhere is this more important than in the two Germanys. And that's why our quest to safely reduce armament has a special significance for the German people.

To those who are impatient with our measured pace in arms reductions, I respectfully suggest that history teaches us a lesson: that unity and strength are the catalyst and prerequisite to arms control. We've always believed that a strong Western defense is the best road to peace. Forty years of experience have proven us right. But we've done more than just keep the peace. By standing together, we have convinced the Soviets that their arms buildup has been costly and pointless. Let us not give them incentives to return to the policies of the past. Let us give them every reason to abandon the arms race for the sake of the human race.

Questions

What is "the Helsinki process" that Bush refers to in his first proposition?
How far do you think that Bush's vision for a post-Cold War Europe has been realized?

Reference

https://usa.usembassy.de/etexts/ga6-890531.htm

Document 2

Mikhail Gorbachev, Address before the Parliamentary Assembly of the Council of Europe, 6 July 1989

Mikhail Gorbachev was the last General Secretary of the Soviet Communist Party, from March 1985 to August 1991. Committed to preserving the Soviet Union, Gorbachev had initiated far-reaching reforms to liberalise Soviet Society (glasnost) and make the economy more decentralized and efficient (perestroika). He also sought a normalization of relations with the West, holding summits with President Reagan in Geneva in 1985 and Reykjavik in 1986, where major reductions in nuclear arsenals were discussed. The Intermediate-Range Nuclear Forces (INF) Treaty of 1987 was a crucial measure for reducing tensions in Europe and laying a path towards the end of the forty-year Cold War between the United States and the Soviet Union. With relations between the superpowers improving, the future of a divided Europe, and in particular the future of the two Germanies, was of immediate importance. By early 1989 major changes were occurring in the Eastern bloc, with Poland having talks that would eventually lead to a government led by the Solidarity trade unionist Tadeusz Mazowiecki, and Hungary demilitarizing its border with Austria, allowing East Germans to flee unhindered to the West. In this rapidly changing context, Gorbachev travelled to Strasbourg to outline his idea of "a common European home" where security concerns would be replaced by a peaceful competition between different socio-economic systems. A reduction in nuclear weapons in both East and West would allow for a greater concentration of effort in satisfying basic needs for all of the peoples of the continent. As part of his plan for resuscitating the Soviet economy, Gorbachev hoped to achieve a general settlement on European security issues so that he could reduce the burden of military spending and gradually redirect resources towards civilian needs. Instead, Gorbachev's glasnost and perestroika triggered nationalist secessionism among the Soviet republics, particularly in the Baltic states and the Caucasus, and these movements, combined with his introduction of democratic reforms, led ultimately to the demise of the Soviet Union in December 1991.

[This is an excerpt from the full document]

Mr. President, ladies and gentlemen, I thank you for the invitation to make an address here—in one of the epicentres of European politics and of the European Idea.

This meeting could, perhaps, be viewed both as evidence of the fact that the pan-European process is a reality and of the fact that it continues to evolve.

Now that the twentieth century is entering a concluding phase and both the post-war period and the cold war are becoming a thing of the past, the Europeans have a truly unique chance—to play a role in building a new world, one that would be worthy of their past, of their economic and spiritual potential.

Now more than ever before, the world community is experiencing profound changes. Many of its components are currently at the turning point of destinies.

DOI: 10.4324/9781003159551-4

The material foundation of life is changing drastically as are its spiritual parameters. There are new, and increasingly more powerful factors of progress emerging.

But alongside these factors and in their wake, there continue to persist and even escalate the threats emanating from this very progress.

There is an inevitable need to do everything within the power of modern intellect so that Man would be able to continue the role assigned to him on this earth, perhaps in the universe at large, so that he would be able to adapt himself to the stress-inducing newness of modern existence and win the fight for the survival of the present and succeeding generations.

This applies to all mankind. But it applies three times as much to Europe—both in the sense of its historic responsibility and in the sense of the urgency and immediacy of problems and tasks at hand, and in the sense of opportunities.

It is also the specific feature of the situation in Europe that it can cope with all this, live up to the expectations of its peoples and do its international duty at the new stage of world history, only by recognising its wholeness and by making the right conclusions.

The 1920s saw the theory of "a declining Europe" gain wide currency. But that theme seems to be in vogue with some people even today. As far as we are concerned, we do not share the pessimism regarding the future of Europe.

Europe experienced, before everyone else, the consequences of the internationalisation first and foremost of economic and subsequently of the whole public life.

The interdependence of countries, as a higher stage of the process of internationalisation, made itself felt here before it did in other parts of the world.

Europe experienced more than once the attempts at unification by force. But it also experienced lofty dreams of a voluntary democratic community of European peoples.

Victor Hugo said that the day would come when you, France, you, Russia, you, Italy, you, England, you Germany—all of you, all the nations of the continent—will, without losing your distinguishing features and your splendid distinctiveness, merge inseparably into some high society and form a European brotherhood. The day would come when the only battlefield would be markets open for trade and minds open to ideas.

Nowadays it is no longer enough merely to ascertain the commonality of destiny and interdependence of European states.

The idea of European unification should be collectively thought over once again in the process of the co-creation of all nations—large, medium and small.

Is it realistic to raise the question in these terms? I know that many people in the West perceive that the main difficulty lies in the existence of two social systems.

Yet the difficulty lies elsewhere—it lies in the rather widespread belief (or even in the political objective) that what is meant by overcoming the division of Europe is actually overcoming socialism.

But this is a course for confrontation, if not something worse. There will be no European unity along these lines.

The fact that the states of Europe belong to different social systems is a reality. The recognition of this historical fact and respect for the sovereign right of each people to choose their social system at their own discretion are the most important prerequisite for a normal European process.

The social and political order in some particular countries did change in the past, and it can change in the future as well. But this is exclusively a matter for the peoples themselves and of their choice.

Any interference in internal affairs, any attempts to limit the sovereignty of states—whether of friends and allies or anybody else—are inadmissible.

Differences between states cannot be eliminated. In fact, they are even salutary, as we have said on more than one occasion—provided, of course, that the competition between different types of society is aimed at creating better material and spiritual conditions of life for people.

Thanks to *perestroika*, the Soviet Union will be in a position to take full part in such an honest, equal and constructive competition. For all our present shortcomings and lagging behind, we know full well the strong points of our social system which follow from its essential characteristics.

And, we are confident that we shall be able to make use of them both to the benefit of ourselves and of Europe.

It is time to consign to oblivion the cold war postulates when Europe was viewed as an arena of confrontation divided into "spheres of influence" and someone else's "forward-based defences", as an object of military confrontation—namely a theatre of war.

In today's interdependent world the geopolitical notions, brought forth by a different epoch, turn out to be just as helpless in real politics as the laws of classical mechanics in the quantum theory.

In the meantime, it is precisely on the basis of the outmoded stereotypes that the Soviet Union continues—although less than in the past—to be suspected of hegemonistic designs and of the intention to decouple the United States from Europe.

There are even some people who are not unwilling to put the USSR outside of Europe from the Atlantic to the Urals by confining it to the space "from Brest to Brest". To them, the Soviet Union is ostensibly too big for joint living: the others will not feel very comfortable next to it, or so they say.

The realities of today and the prospects for the foreseeable future are obvious: the Soviet Union and the United States are a natural part of the European international and political structure.

Their involvement in its evolution is not only justified, but also historically conditioned. No other approach is acceptable. In fact, it will even be counterproductive.

The philosophy of the concept of a common European home rules out the probability of an armed clash and the very possibility of the use or threat of force, above all military force, by an alliance against another alliance, inside alliances or wherever it may be.

It suggests a doctrine of restraint to replace the doctrine of deterrence. This is not just a play on notions, but a logic of European development imposed by life itself.

Questions

Was Gorbachev right that the Soviet Union should have been seen as an equal partner in a post-Cold War Europe?

Are we any closer to Victor Hugo's ideal of a "European brotherhood"?

References

© Council of Europe; Source: Centre for Contemporary and Digital History (C2DH), UNIVERSITÉ DU LUXEMBOURG

https://www.cvce.eu/content/publication/2002/9/20/4c021687-98f9-4727-9e8b-836e0bc1f6fb/publishable_en.pdf

Document 3

Charter of Paris for a New Europe, Conference on Security and Co-operation in Europe (CSCE), 19–21 November 1990

During 1990–1991 the configurations of Europe were dramatically re-drawn. The with-drawal of Soviet forces from Eastern Europe and the winding up of the Warsaw Pact heralded a new era where Europe would need to craft a post-Cold War security apparatus. At the time there seemed to be three possibilities for a future European security architecture. Regarding NATO, there was no guarantee that it would continue now that Soviet forces had withdrawn from Central Europe, a move which seemed to take away its very reason for existence. The expansion of NATO to include former members of the Warsaw Pact and the Soviet Union was certainly not anticipated by the Soviet leadership in 1990–1991. The Treaty on European Union signed in early 1992 (see Document 6) expanded European competences with the am-bition of a Common Foreign and Security Policy (CFSP). This raised the issue of greater European autonomy in security affairs, and introduced a new debate as to the most appro-priate and effective cooperation between CFSP and NATO. Alongside the continuation of NATO and the expansion of EU competences was a third model. The Conference on Security and Cooperation in Europe (CSCE) stemmed from the 35-nation conference held in Helsinki in July–August 1975 that produced the Helsinki Accords. From then on the CSCE process had worked towards greater cooperation between East and West, linking security concerns with issues of freedom of movement and human rights. The CSCE model offered a prospective post-Cold War security architecture because of its broad agenda (social and economic issues as well as security), its established record as a forum for East-West dialogue, and because it involved all European nations (except Andorra and Albania), together with the United States, Canada, and the Soviet Union (soon to be Russia), on an equal basis. For this reason it was supported by Moscow as a preferable alternative to either NATO or the EU, and others – particularly France – saw in the CSCE an opportunity for a new North American-Eurasian security model that would shift the focus more towards democratization, protection of minor-ities, and human rights. Agreed soon after the re-unification of Germany, the Paris Charter looked towards establishing a post-Cold War Europe free of superpower tensions where ma-jor issues would be dealt with on through multilateral diplomacy. However, the CSCE model was of no interest to a United States that did not regard a post-Soviet Russia as an equal, and by the early 1990s this alternative blueprint for post-Cold War security 'from Vancouver to Vladivostok' had been edged aside in favour of maintaining – and expanding – NATO. The CSCE has nevertheless continued in the form of the permanent Organisation for Security and Cooperation in Europe, established in 1995.

[This is an excerpt from the full document]

Unity

Europe whole and free is calling for a new beginning. We invite our peoples to join in this great endeavour.

DOI: 10.4324/9781003159551-5

We note with great satisfaction the Treaty on the Final Settlement with respect to Germany signed in Moscow on 12 September 1990 and sincerely welcome the fact that the German people have united to become one State in accordance with the principles of the Final Act of the Conference on Security and Co-operation in Europe and in full accord with their neighbours. The establishment of the national unity of Germany is an important contribution to a just and lasting order of peace for a united, democratic Europe aware of its responsibility for stability, peace and co-operation.

The participation of both North American and European States is a fundamental characteristic of the CSCE; it underlies its past achievements and is essential to the future of the CSCE process. An abiding adherence to shared values and our common heritage are the ties which bind us together. With all the rich diversity of our nations, we are united in our commitment to expand our co-operation in all fields. The challenges confronting us can only be met by common action, co-operation and solidarity.

Guidelines for the future

Proceeding from our firm commitment to the full implementation of all CSCE principles and provisions, we now resolve to give a new impetus to a balanced and comprehensive development of our co-operation in order to address the needs and aspirations of our peoples.

Human Dimension

We declare our respect for human rights and fundamental freedoms to be irrevocable.

We will fully implement and build upon the provisions relating to the human dimension of the CSCE.

Proceeding from the Document of the Copenhagen Meeting of the Conference on the Human Dimension, we will cooperate to strengthen democratic institutions and to promote the application of the rule of law. To that end, we decide to convene a seminar of experts in Oslo from 4 to 15 November 1991.

Determined to foster the rich contribution of national minorities to the life of our societies, we undertake further to improve their situation. We reaffirm our deep conviction that friendly relations among our peoples, as well as peace, justice, stability and democracy, require that the ethnic, cultural, linguistic and religious identity of national minorities be protected and conditions for the promotion of that identity be created. We declare that questions related to national minorities can only be satisfactorily resolved in a democratic political framework. We further acknowledge that the rights of persons belonging to national minorities must be fully respected as part of universal human rights. Being aware of the urgent need for increased cooperation on, as well as better protection of, national minorities, we decide to convene a meeting of experts on national minorities to be held in Geneva from 1 to 19 July 1991.

We express our determination to combat all forms of racial and ethnic hatred, antisemitism, xenophobia and discrimination against anyone as well as persecution on religious and ideological grounds.

In accordance with our CSCE commitments, we stress that free movement and contacts among our citizens as well as the free flow of information and ideas are crucial for the maintenance and development of free societies and flourishing cultures. We welcome increased tourism and visits among our countries.

The human dimension mechanism has proved its usefulness, and we are consequently determined to expand it to include new procedures involving, inter alia, the services of experts or a roster of eminent persons experienced in human rights issues which could be raised under the mechanism. We shall provide, in the context of the mechanism, for individuals to be involved in the protection of their rights. Therefore, we undertake to develop further our commitments in this respect, in particular at the Moscow Meeting of the Conference on the Human Dimension, without prejudice to obligations under existing international instruments to which our States may be parties.

We recognize the important contribution of the Council of Europe to the promotion of human rights and the principles of democracy and the rule of law as well as to the development of cultural co-operation. We welcome moves by several participating States to join the Council of Europe and adhere to its European Convention on Human Rights. We welcome as well the readiness of the Council of Europe to make its experience available to the CSCE.

Questions

Was the Charter in some ways a challenge to President Bush's vision of a Europe "whole and free," or Gorbachev's "common European home"?

How did the "human dimension" of the Charter contrast with other ways of interpreting European futures?

Reference

https://www.csce.gov/international-impact/publications/charter-paris-new-europe

Document 4

President George H.W. Bush, Address before a Joint Session of Congress on the End of the Gulf War, 6 March 1991

On 2 August 1990 the Iraqi army invaded and occupied neighbouring Kuwait. The reasons for Iraqi leader Saddam Hussein's decision to invade stemmed from the effects of the 1980–1988 Iran-Iraq war, which Iraq had withstood at great cost, owing creditor states in the Gulf region around $37bn by the end of the decade. The refusal of Kuwait, Saudi Arabia, and the United Arab Emirates to cancel Iraqi debt led Hussein to begin pressuring Kuwait to obtain territory along their disputed border (drawn in 1922 by the UK) and also accuse the Kuwaitis of over-production in oil, which was contributing to keeping the oil price low. Following an ultimatum for the recovery of lost revenues, Iraq invaded Kuwait and secured it within 12 hours, the royal family fleeing across the border to Saudi Arabia. The US immediately moved to secure UN backing for a strong response, involving Resolution 660 condemning the invasion, Resolution 661 placing sanctions on Iraq, and Resolution 665 introducing a naval blockade. With strong pressure from UK prime minister Margaret Thatcher "not to go wobbly," US President George H.W. Bush moved towards a stronger response with UN Resolution 678, which authorized "all necessary means" to remove Iraqi forces from Kuwait if they were still present on 15 January 1991. On 14 January France attempted a last-minute mediation via the UN by linking Iraqi withdrawal to an international effort to resolve the Israel-Palestine conflict, but although gathering some European support it was rejected by the US, the UK, and the USSR. The level of agreement between the US and the USSR in the run-up to the Gulf War seemed to herald the opening of a new phase in international politics. Cooperation in the United Nations Security Council enabled a remarkable international coalition of forces under US leadership to eject Iraqi forces from Kuwait with an effective, devastating military campaign. Speaking to Congress at the end of the six-week war, President Bush outlined four main issues to focus on in order to ensure lasting peace in the Middle East. He mentioned the phrase "new world order" in several speeches during 1990–91 to mark the end of Cold War antagonisms and the hope that the international states system could be managed more according to justice and international law. It subsequently became a catch-phrase for the ensuing decade, both positively (in terms of a UN-led search for peace) and negatively (in terms of the increasing use of unilateral US power). Saddam Hussein would remain in power until the invasion of Iraq by the US and its "Coalition of the Willing" in February 2003 (this time not sanctioned by the UN).

[This is an excerpt from the full document]

The war is over

This is a victory for every country in the coalition, for the United Nations. A victory for unprecedented international cooperation and diplomacy, so well led by our Secretary of State, James Baker. It is a victory for the rule of law and for what is right.

DOI: 10.4324/9781003159551-6

Tonight, I come to this House to speak about the world—the world after war. The recent challenge could not have been clearer. Saddam Hussein was the villain; Kuwait, the victim. To the aid of this small country came nations from North America and Europe, from Asia and South America, from Africa and the Arab world, all united against aggression. Our uncommon coalition must now work in common purpose: to forge a future that should never again be held hostage to the darker side of human nature.

So, tonight let me outline four key challenges to be met.

First, we must work together to create shared security arrangements in the region. Our friends and allies in the Middle East recognize that they will bear the bulk of the responsibility for regional security. But we want them to know that just as we stood with them to repel aggression, so now America stands ready to work with them to secure the peace. This does not mean stationing U.S. ground forces in the Arabian Peninsula, but it does mean American participation in joint exercises involving both air and ground forces. It means maintaining a capable U.S. naval presence in the region, just as we have for over 40 years. Let it be clear: Our vital national interests depend on a stable and secure Gulf.

Second, we must act to control the proliferation of weapons of mass destruction and the missiles used to deliver them. It would be tragic if the nations of the Middle East and Persian Gulf were now, in the wake of war, to embark on a new arms race. Iraq requires special vigilance. Until Iraq convinces the world of its peaceful intentions—that its leaders will not use new revenues to rearm and rebuild its menacing war machine—Iraq must not have access to the instruments of war.

And third, we must work to create new opportunities for peace and stability in the Middle East. On the night I announced Operation Desert Storm, I expressed my hope that out of the horrors of war might come new momentum for peace. We've learned in the modern age geography cannot guarantee security, and security does not come from military power alone.

Fourth, we must foster economic development for the sake of peace and progress. The Persian Gulf and Middle East form a region rich in natural resources with a wealth of untapped human potential. Resources once squandered on military might must be redirected to more peaceful ends. We are already addressing the immediate economic consequences of Iraq's aggression. Now, the challenge is to reach higher, to foster economic freedom and prosperity for all the people of the region.

By meeting these four challenges we can build a framework for peace. I've asked Secretary of State Baker to go to the Middle East to begin the process. He will go to listen, to probe, to offer suggestions—to advance the search for peace and stability. I've also asked him to raise the plight of the hostages held in Lebanon. We have not forgotten them, and we will not forget them.

To all the challenges that confront this region of the world there is no single solution, no solely American answer. But we can make a difference. America will work tirelessly as a catalyst for positive change.

But we cannot lead a new world abroad if, at home, it's politics as usual on American defense and diplomacy. It's time to turn away from the temptation to protect unneeded weapons systems and obsolete bases. It's time to put an end to micromanagement of foreign and security assistance programs—micromanagement that humiliates our friends and allies and hamstrings our diplomacy. It's time to rise above the parochial and the pork barrel, to do what is necessary, what's right, and what will enable this nation to play the leadership role required of us.

The consequences of the conflict in the Gulf reach far beyond the confines of the Middle East. Twice before in this century, an entire world was convulsed by war. Twice this century, out of the horrors of war hope emerged for enduring peace. Twice before, those hopes proved to be a distant dream, beyond the grasp of man. Until now, the world we've known has been a world divided—a world of barbed wire and concrete block, conflict, and cold war.

Now, we can see a new world coming into view. A world in which there is the very real prospect of a new world order. In the words of Winston Churchill, a world order in which "the principles of justice and fair play protect the weak against the strong..." A world where the United Nations, freed from cold war stalemate, is poised to fulfill the historic vision of its founders. A world in which freedom and respect for human rights find a home among all nations. The Gulf war put this new world to its first test. And my fellow Americans, we passed that test.

For the sake of our principles, for the sake of the Kuwaiti people, we stood our ground. Because the world would not look the other way, Ambassador al-Sabah, tonight Kuwait is free. And we're very happy about that.

Tonight, as our troops begin to come home, let us recognize that the hard work of freedom still calls us forward. We've learned the hard lessons of history. The victory over Iraq was not waged as "a war to end all wars." Even the new world order cannot guarantee an era of perpetual peace. But enduring peace must be our mission. Our success in the Gulf will shape not only the new world order we seek but our mission here at home.

In the war just ended, there were clear-cut objectives—timetables—and, above all, an overriding imperative to achieve results. We must bring that same sense of self-discipline, that same sense of urgency, to the way we meet challenges here at home. In my State of the Union Address and in my budget, I defined a comprehensive agenda to prepare for the next American century.

Questions

How does Bush merge US and global interests in this speech?
Why and how has Bush's proposal for a "new world order" been criticized since 1991?

Reference

https://millercenter.org/the-presidency/presidential-speeches/march-6-1991-address-joint-session-congress-end-gulf-war

Document 5
NATO Strategic Concept, 8 November 1991

During the Cold War, NATO compiled four Strategic Concepts, all classified, in 1949, 1952, 1957, and 1968. Each one outlined the military strategy for the Alliance in response to the evolving threat from Warsaw Pact forces. At the NATO Summit in London in July 1990, with the peaceful re-unification of Germany in process and antagonism between the two superpowers declining, the Alliance's leaders laid out a new post-Cold War vision. While reaffirming the basic principles on which the Alliance has rested since its inception, they also recognised the changing threat environment caused by a withdrawal of Soviet forces from Central Europe. Nationalist antagonisms were returning, notably among the former republics of Yugoslavia, where war had broken out in May–June 1991. The first NATO Strategic Concept to be made public immediately on release, the document was agreed by the North Atlantic Council in Rome in November 1991. It expressed optimism at the end of the Cold War but also a realization that NATO would need to adapt in order to meet the increasingly irregular challenges to regional stability and transatlantic security. The Concept considered NATO vital for the post-Cold War security environment, but saw its role as more multi-functional in the years to come, moving away from a focus on nuclear forces and being open to arms reduction initiatives such as the Strategic Arms Reduction Talks (START). Following the Harmel Report of 1968, NATO had sought arms reduction agreements with the Warsaw Pact, and the landmark Treaty on Conventional Armed Forces in Europe (CFE) in 1990 secured the large-scale withdrawal of military personnel and hardware from Europe by both sides. While at the time of issue the Strategic Concept still saw the Soviet military as a potential adversary, threats to security were now regarded as most likely to come from ethnic tensions and boundary disputes within Eastern Europe, and more global challenges such as the proliferation of weapons of mass destruction, terrorism, and the disruption of natural resource supplies.

[This is an excerpt from the full document]

Part I – The Strategic Context

The new strategic environment

1   Since 1989, profound political changes have taken place in Central and Eastern Europe which have radically improved the security environment in which the North Atlantic Alliance seeks to achieve its objectives. The USSR's former satellites have fully recovered their sovereignty. The Soviet Union and its Republics are undergoing radical change. The three Baltic Republics have regained their independence. Soviet forces have left Hungary and Czechoslovakia and are due to complete their withdrawal from Poland and Germany by 1994. All the countries that were formerly

DOI: 10.4324/9781003159551-7

adversaries of NATO have dismantled the Warsaw Pact and rejected ideological hostility to the West. They have, in varying degrees, embraced and begun to implement policies aimed at achieving pluralistic democracy, the rule of law, respect for human rights and a market economy. The political division of Europe that was the source of the military confrontation of the Cold War period has thus been overcome.

2   In the West, there have also been significant changes. Germany has been united and remains a full member of the Alliance and of European institutions. The fact that the countries of the European Community are working towards the goal of political union, including the development of a European security identity, and the enhancement of the role of the WEU [Western European Union] are important factors for European security. The strengthening of the security dimension in the process of European integration, and the enhancement of the role and responsibilities of European members of the Alliance are positive and mutually reinforcing. The development of a European security identity and defence role, reflected in the strengthening of the European pillar within the Alliance, will not only serve the interests of the European states but also reinforce the integrity and effectiveness of the Alliance as a whole.

3   Substantial progress in arms control has already enhanced stability and security by lowering arms levels and increasing military transparency and mutual confidence (including through the Stockholm CDE agreement [Confidence- and security-building measures and Disarmament in Europe] of 1986, the INF Treaty [Intermediate-range Nuclear Forces] of 1987 and the CSCE agreements [Conference on Security and Cooperation in Europe] and confidence and security-building measures of 1990). Implementation of the 1991 START Treaty will lead to increased stability through substantial and balanced reductions in the field of strategic nuclear arms. Further far-reaching changes and reductions in the nuclear forces of the United States and the Soviet Union will be pursued following President Bush's September 1991 initiative. Also of great importance is the Treaty on Conventional Armed Forces in Europe (CFE), signed at the 1990 Paris Summit; its implementation will remove the Alliance's numerical inferiority in key conventional weapon systems and provide for effective verification procedures. All these developments will also result in an unprecedented degree of military transparency in Europe, thus increasing predictability and mutual confidence. Such transparency would be further enhanced by the achievement of an Open Skies regime. There are welcome prospects for further advances in arms control in conventional and nuclear forces, and for the achievement of a global ban on chemical weapons, as well as restricting de-stabilising arms exports and the proliferation of certain weapons technologies.

4   The CSCE process, which began in Helsinki in 1975, has already contributed significantly to overcoming the division of Europe. As a result of the Paris Summit, it now includes new institutional arrangements and provides a contractual framework for consultation and cooperation that can play a constructive role, complementary to that of NATO and the process of European integration, in preserving peace.

5   The historic changes that have occurred in Europe, which have led to the fulfilment of a number of objectives set out in the Harmel Report, have significantly improved the overall security of the Allies. The monolithic, massive and potentially immediate threat which was the principal concern of the Alliance in its first forty years has disappeared. On the other hand, a great deal of uncertainty about the future and risks to the security of the Alliance remain.

6   The new Strategic Concept looks forward to a security environment in which the positive changes referred to above have come to fruition. In particular, it assumes both the completion of the planned withdrawal of Soviet military forces from Central and Eastern Europe and the full implementation by all parties of the 1990 CFE Treaty.

The implementation of the Strategic Concept will thus be kept under review in the light of the evolving security environment and in particular progress in fulfilling these assumptions. Further adaptation will be made to the extent necessary.

Security challenges and risks

7   The security challenges and risks which NATO faces are different in nature from what they were in the past. The threat of a simultaneous, full-scale attack on all of NATO's European fronts has effectively been removed and thus no longer provides the focus for Allied strategy. Particularly in Central Europe, the risk of a surprise attack has been substantially reduced, and minimum Allied warning time has increased accordingly.

8   In contrast with the predominant threat of the past, the risks to Allied security that remain are multi-faceted in nature and multi-directional, which makes them hard to predict and assess. NATO must be capable of responding to such risks if stability in Europe and the security of Alliance members are to be preserved. These risks can arise in various ways.

9   Risks to Allied security are less likely to result from calculated aggression against the territory of the Allies, but rather from the adverse consequences of instabilities that may arise from the serious economic, social and political difficulties, including ethnic rivalries and territorial disputes, which are faced by many countries in central and eastern Europe. The tensions which may result, as long as they remain limited, should not directly threaten the security and territorial integrity of members of the Alliance. They could, however, lead to crises inimical to European stability and even to armed conflicts, which could involve outside powers or spill over into NATO countries, having a direct effect on the security of the Alliance.

10   In the particular case of the Soviet Union, the risks and uncertainties that accompany the process of change cannot be seen in isolation from the fact that its conventional forces are significantly larger than those of any other European State and its large nuclear arsenal comparable only with that of the United States. These capabilities have to be taken into account if stability and security in Europe are to be preserved.

11   The Allies also wish to maintain peaceful and non-adversarial relations with the countries in the Southern Mediterranean and Middle East. The stability and peace of the countries on the southern periphery of Europe are important for the security of the Alliance, as the 1991 Gulf war has shown. This is all the more so because of the build-up of military power and the proliferation of weapons technologies in the area, including weapons of mass destruction and ballistic missiles capable of reaching the territory of some member states of the Alliance.

12   Any armed attack on the territory of the Allies, from whatever direction, would be covered by Articles 5 and 6 of the Washington Treaty. However, Alliance security must also take account of the global context. Alliance security interests can be affected by other risks of a wider nature, including proliferation of weapons of mass destruction, disruption of the flow of vital resources and actions of terrorism and sabotage. Arrangements exist within the Alliance for consultation among the Allies under Article 4 of the Washington Treaty and, where appropriate, coordination of their efforts including their responses to such risks.

13   From the point of view of Alliance strategy, these different risks have to be seen in different ways. Even in a non-adversarial and cooperative relationship, Soviet military capability and build-up potential, including its nuclear dimension, still constitute the most significant factor of which the Alliance has to take account in maintaining the

strategic balance in Europe. The end of East-West confrontation has, however, greatly reduced the risk of major conflict in Europe. On the other hand, there is a greater risk of different crises arising, which could develop quickly and would require a rapid response, but they are likely to be of a lesser magnitude.

14 Two conclusions can be drawn from this analysis of the strategic context. The first is that the new environment does not change the purpose or the security functions of the Alliance, but rather underlines their enduring validity. The second, on the other hand, is that the changed environment offers new opportunities for the Alliance to frame its strategy within a broad approach to security.

Questions

How has the position of the Soviet Union changed in NATO's strategic calculations?
In what ways did this Strategic Concept change the purpose of NATO from a Cold War to a post-Cold War alliance?

Reference

https://www.nato.int/cps/en/natohq/official_texts_23847.htm

Document 6
Treaty on European Union, 7 February 1992

The Treaty on European Union, commonly known as the Maastricht Treaty, laid out the future development of European integration based on three pillars: the European Community, Common Foreign and Security Policy (CFSP), and Justice and Home Affairs. The CFSP was a means to incorporate the moribund Western European Union (WEU) into the EU as the core institution for building a new security architecture. It was also a step towards developing the existing inter-governmental mechanisms of European Political Cooperation (EPC), in operation since the 1970s to achieve greater coordination of member state foreign policies to promote a common outlook for the (then) European Community (EC). The weaknesses of the EPC framework were already evident long before the outbreak of the Yugoslav wars in early 1991, but it was the Balkans conflict that provided the catalyst for a more concerted effort at foreign policy coordination. In particular, the debate over whether or not to recognize Slovenia and Croatia (but not Bosnia-Herzegovina) as independent republics had divided the EC between Germany (which saw this as an essential move to block Serbian aggression) and others (which considered it a provocative move that would lead to further escalation). Germany eventually succeeded in obtaining agreement and went ahead with recognition in December 1991, but it did not lead to a more concerted effort on the part of European nations to resolve the conflict (See Part I Document 11). During the Maastricht negotiations it was clear that a compromise had to be reached between those member states who wanted to further more supranational institution-building, and those, such as the United Kingdom, that wanted to keep national prerogatives such as foreign policy out of the competence of the European Commission and other EU bodies. Nevertheless, the CFSP provisions did provoke a running transatlantic debate through the 1990s as to how a more capable European defence and security apparatus would fit next to the existing obligations of NATO. At the NATO summit in 1998, US Secretary of State Madeleine Albright set out "three Ds" that for her were essential in this debate: "no diminution of NATO, no discrimination and no duplication" (see Document 16). This signaled the difficulties for the EU to develop its own credible security apparatus without still relying on US forces and infrastructure for conducting missions. In 2009 the EU's Lisbon Treaty created the position of High Representative for the CFSP to increase coordination among member states. 21 nations belonged to both NATO and the EU by 2020, and various agreements have strengthened cooperation, but larger questions about a distinct European security apparatus and its relationship with the US still remained.

[This is an excerpt from the full document]

Title V: Provisions on a Common Foreign and Security Policy

Article J

A common foreign and security policy is hereby established which shall be governed by the following provisions.

DOI: 10.4324/9781003159551-8

Article J.1

1   The Union and its Member States shall define and implement a common foreign and security policy, governed by the provisions of this Title and covering all areas of foreign and security policy.

2   The objectives of the common foreign and security policy shall be:

   –   to safeguard the common values, fundamental interests and independence of the Union;
   –   to strengthen the security of the Union and its Member States in all ways;
   –   to preserve peace and strengthen international security, in accordance with the principles of the United Nations Charter as well as the principles of the Helsinki Final Act and the objectives of the Paris Charter;
   –   to promote international cooperation;
   –   to develop and consolidate democracy and the rule of law, and respect for human rights and fundamental freedoms.

3   The Union shall pursue these objectives:

   –   by establishing systematic cooperation between Member States in the conduct of policy, in accordance with Article J.2;
   –   by gradually implementing, in accordance with Article J.3, joint action in the areas in which the Member States have important interests in common.

The Member States shall support the Union's external and security policy actively and unreservedly in a spirit of loyalty and mutual solidarity. They shall refrain from any action which is contrary to the interests of the Union or likely to impair its effectiveness as a cohesive force in international relations. The Council shall ensure that these principles are complied with.

Article J.2

1   Member States shall inform and consult one another within the Council on any matter of foreign and security policy of general interest in order to ensure that their combined influence is exerted as effectively as possible by means of concerted and convergent action.

2   Whenever it deems it necessary, the Council shall define a common position. Member States shall ensure that their national policies conform to the common positions.

3   Member States shall coordinate their action in international organizations and at international conferences. They shall uphold the common positions in such forums. In international organizations and at international conferences where not all the Member States participate, those which do take part shall uphold the common positions.

Article J.4

1   The common foreign and security policy shall include all questions related to the security of the Union, including the eventual framing of a common defence policy, which might in time lead to a common defence.

2   The Union requests the Western European Union (WEU), which is an integral part of the development of the Union, to elaborate and implement decisions and actions of the Union which have defence implications. The Council shall, in agreement with the institutions of the WEU, adopt the necessary practical arrangements.

3   Issues having defence implications dealt with under this Article shall not be subject to the procedures set out in Article J.3.
4   The policy of the Union in accordance with this Article shall not prejudice the specific character of the security and defence policy of certain Member States and shall respect the obligations of certain Member States under the North Atlantic Treaty and be compatible with the common security and defence policy established within that framework.
5   The provisions of this Article shall not prevent the development of closer cooperation between two or more Member States on a bilateral level, in the framework of the WEU and the Atlantic Alliance, provided such cooperation does not run counter to or impede that provided for in this Title.
6   With a view to furthering the objective of this Treaty, and having in view the date of 1998 in the context of Article XII of the Brussels Treaty, the provisions of this Article may be revised as provided for in Article N(2) on the basis of a report to be presented in 1996 by the Council to the European Council, which shall include an evaluation of the progress made and the experience gained until then.

Questions

Why did the Maastricht Treaty represent a challenge to ongoing US dominance in European security affairs through NATO?
How far do you think the EU has come in developing a CFSP?

References

https://eur-lex.europa.eu/legal-content/EN/TXT/?uri=CELEX:11992M/TXT

Document 7

Defense Planning Guidance FY 1994–1999, April 1992

The DPG document is widely regarded as an early statement of neoconservative goals for post-Cold War US foreign policy. Compiled by I. Lewis 'Scooter' Libby, Paul Wolfowitz, and Zalmay Khalilzad for then Defense Secretary Dick Cheney, the Guidance was a classified document used to outline US military strategy and so provide reasoning for the future defense budget. Since the administration of George H.W. Bush had few neoconservatives among its senior staffers, Libby, Wolfowitz and Khalilzad sought further advice from outsiders such as Richard Perle, Albert Wohlstetter, and Andrew Marshall, the futurologist chief of the Pentagon's Office of Net Assessment. The DPG put forward several key positions that became the mainstay for neoconservative thinking on US foreign policy, such as the determined projection of power as the lone superpower, the prevention of regional rivals to US dominance, the sanctioning of pre-emptive force to eliminate immediate threats, and the rejection of multilateralism if it did not suit US interests. With the demise of the Soviet Union fresh in their minds, the authors emphasized that "Our first objective is to prevent the re-emergence of a new rival," and the document effectively placed the US as the arbiter of global order for the forceable future. When a draft version of the Guidance was leaked to the New York Times *it triggered such a negative response that President Bush himself publicly retracted it. Nevertheless, some commentators such as Charles Krauthammer praised its clear-headed assessment of the US role as the only superpower, and the DPG outlined the grounds for what would become known as the "unipolar moment" in international relations. Cheney also saw its merits, and while a slightly watered-down version was approved, the original's intent would provide the basis for the developing neoconservative world-view in the coming decade. Libby, Wolfowitz, and Khalilzad would go on to join the Project for a New American Century (PNAC), established by neoconservative public intellectuals William Kristol and Robert Kagan in 1997, which argued for reviving the Reaganite stance of military and moral superiority that many on the Right felt had won the Cold War. In an article in* Foreign Affairs *in 1996 entitled "Toward a Neo-Reaganite Foreign Policy," Kristol and Kagan had argued that the US should aim for a "benevolent global hegemony." Several of the Project's members – Dick Cheney, Peter Rodman, Elliott Abrams, Lewis 'Scooter' Libby, Zalmay Khalilzad, Donald Rumsfeld, Paul Wolfowitz, Richard Perle, and Paula Dobriansky – took up positions in the George W. Bush administration in 2001, and the DPG unquestionably acted as a blueprint for the post-9/11 National Security Strategy of 2002.*

[This is an excerpt from the full document]

This Defense Planning Guidance addresses the fundamentally new situation which has been created by the collapse of the Soviet Union – the disintegration of the internal as well as the external empire, and the discrediting of Communism as an ideology with global pretensions and influence. The new international environment has also been shaped by

DOI: 10.4324/9781003159551-9

the victory of the United States and its Coalition allies over Iraqi aggression – the first post-Cold War conflict and a defining event in U.S. global leadership. In addition to these two great successes, there has been a less visible one, the integration of the leading democracies into a U.S.-led system of collective security and the creation of a democratic "zone of peace."

Our fundamental strategic position and choices are therefore very different from those we have faced in the past. The policies that we adopt in this new situation will set the nation's direction for the next century. Guided by a fundamentally new defense strategy, we have today a compelling opportunity to meet our defense needs at lower cost. As we do so, we must not squander the position of security we achieved at great sacrifice through the Cold War, nor eliminate our ability to shape the future security environment in ways favorable to us and those who share our values.

DEFENSE POLICY GOALS

The national security interests of the United States are enduring, as outlined in the President's 1991 National Security Strategy Report: the survival of the United States as a free and independent nation, with its fundamental values intact and its institutions and people secure; a healthy and growing U.S. economy to ensure opportunity for individual prosperity and resources for national endeavors at home and abroad; healthy, cooperative and politically vigorous relations with allies and friendly nations; and a stable and secure world, where political and economic freedom, human rights and democratic institutions flourish.

These national security interests can be translated into four mutually supportive strategic goals that guide our overall defense efforts:

> Our most fundamental goal is·to deter or defeat attack from whatever source, against the United States, its citizens and forces, and to honor our historic and treaty commitments.

The second goal is to strengthen and extend the system of defense arrangements that binds democratic and like-minded nations together in common defense against aggression, builds habits of cooperation, avoids the renationalization of security policies, and provides security at lower costs and with lower risks for all. Our preference for a collective response to preclude threats or, if necessary to deal with them is a key feature of our regional defense strategy.

The third goal is to preclude any hostile power from dominating a region critical to our interests, and also thereby to strengthen the barriers against the reemergence of a global threat to the interests of the U.S. and our allies. These regions include Europe, East Asia, the Middle East/Persian Gulf, and Latin America. Consolidated, nondemocratic control of the resources of such a critical region could generate a significant threat to our security.

The fourth goal is to reduce sources of regional instability and limit violence should conflict occur, by encouraging the spread and consolidation of democratic government and open economic systems and discouraging the spread of destructive technology, particularly of weapons of mass destruction [and the means to deliver them]. To this end, we must encourage other nations to respect the rule of law and each other's economic, social, ethnic, and political interests.

To reach these goals, the United States must show the leadership necessary to encourage sustained cooperation among major democratic powers. The alternative would be to leave our critical interests and the security of our friends dependent upon individual efforts that could be duplicative, competitive, or ineffective. We must also encourage and assist Russia, Ukraine, and the other new republics of the former Soviet Union in establishing democratic political systems and free markets so they too can join the democratic "zone of peace."

A collective response will not always be timely and, in the absence of U.S. leadership, may not gel. While the United States cannot become the world's policeman and assume responsibility for solving every international security problem, neither can we allow our critical interests to depend solely on international mechanisms that can be blocked by countries whose interests may be very different from our own. Where our allies interests are directly affected, we must expect them to take an appropriate share of the responsibility, and in some cases play the leading role; but we must maintain the capabilities for addressing selectively those security problems that threaten our own interests. Such capabilities are essential to our ability to lead, and should international support prove sluggish or inadequate, to act independently, as necessary, to protect our critical interests. [Moreover, history suggests that effective international, multilateral action is most likely to come about as a response to U.S. leadership, <u>not</u> as an alternative to it.]

We cannot lead if we fail to maintain the high quality of our forces as we reduce and restructure them. As a nation we have never before succeeded in pacing reductions without endangering our interests. We must proceed expeditiously, but at a pace that avoids breaking the force or sending misleading signals about our intentions to friends or potential aggressors. An effective reconstitution capability is important as well, since it signals that no potential rival could quickly or easily gain a predominant military position.

At the end of World War I, and again to a lesser extent at the end of World War II, the United States as a nation made the mistake of believing that we had achieved a kind of permanent security, that a transformation of the security order achieved through extraordinary American sacrifice could be sustained without our leadership and significant American forces. Today, a great challenge has passed; but other threats endure, and new ones will arise. If we reduce our forces carefully, we will be left with a force capable of implementing the new defense strategy. We will have given ourselves the means to lead common efforts to meet future challenges and to shape the future environment in ways that will give us greater security at lower cost.

Questions

Why was the Gulf War of 1991 so important for framing this document's arguments?
What is the principal message of the DPG to America's European allies?

Reference

https://www.archives.gov/files/declassification/iscap/pdf/2008-003-docs1-12.pdf

Document 8

Richard Lugar, "NATO: Out of Area or Out of Business. A Call for U.S. Leadership to Revive and Redefine the Alliance," Remarks Delivered to the Open Forum of the U.S. State Department, 2 August 1993

Richard Lugar served as Republican Senator for Indiana from 1976–2012, including as chairman of the Senate Foreign Relations Committee from 1985–87 and 2003–2007. Lugar had a special interest in nuclear weapons and, with Senator Sam Nunn, was responsible for the vital Cooperative Threat Reduction Program (the Nunn-Lugar Act) of 1991, which led to the securing and dismantling of weapons of mass destruction in the former Soviet Union. Lugar's speech in August 1993 was more than a plea for securing NATO action in the Yugoslavia wars. The failure of both the UN's peacekeeping missions and the EU's attempts to establish itself as a credible security provider via the CFSP had led to a power vacuum in which the conflict could drag on with no end in sight. At the same time, the United States was undergoing a transition away from the Cold War security dynamic of two superpowers towards a still undefined post-Cold War security environment that required a new interpretation of national interest and strategic goals. Lugar's call for a regenerated NATO was a call to the Clinton administration to recognize the continuing centrality of Europe for American well-being, both internationally in terms of security and domestically in terms of economic growth. Although NATO's 1991 Strategic Concept had expanded the focus of the alliance, Lugar felt that a lack of political will, coupled with the forces of "re-nationalization," were now threatening to undermine its very purpose. A new "strategic bargain" would require both clear US leadership and a greater commitment on the part of NATO's European members to organize their military capabilities for power projection beyond their immediate territory. Relations with France needed to be repaired to allow for French re-entry to NATO's command structures (De Gaulle had withdrawn French military involvement in 1966). A newly re-united Germany needed to grasp the need for a greater investment in collective security. And crucially, NATO membership needed to be extended eastwards, with particular focus on Poland, Hungary, and the Czech Republic to begin with. Lugar was cautious regarding Ukraine, seeing it as "not an easy call" and yet still "the key variable in the entire Eastern security equation." Prophetically, Lugar stated that "A key question is how far the West is willing to go in tailoring its policies to assuage Russian concerns." NATO enlargement through the 1990s and 2000s would become the central issue that prevented a full rapprochement between Russia and the West following the Cold War.

[This is an excerpt from the full document]

I want to share some thoughts on the need for a new strategic bargain between Europe and the United States to deal with the new challenges emerging throughout Europe, challenges that could directly impact vital American national interest.

The policy dispute over Bosnia is no longer just about Bosnia, but rather about allied unity and the willingness of Europeans and Americans to adjust their Cold War political and security institutions and missions to the changing geo-strategic circumstances in and

DOI: 10.4324/9781003159551-10

around Europe. In some ways, the details of such adjustments are less important than the pressing need to demonstrate and convince politicians and publics on both sides of the Atlantic that American leadership on European security issues is both possible <u>and</u> advantageous for Europeans as well as for Americans.

The Bosnian Legacy

As much as some would hope that Bosnia would disappear from the front pages, it has not. Bosnia will not go away. When it came to the crunch, it was the West that blinked, not the Bosnian Serbs. We have been seeking to recover from that temporary blindness ever since.

Western leaders know that their current foreign policy toward Bosnia has become that of the lowest common denominator, a policy that is little more than a fig leaf designed to cover their trans-Atlantic dispute. The so-called 'peace formula' was designed primarily to preserve a modicum of agreement between the allies and with Russia. But the new 'policy' offers havens that are not safe, promises of protection that may not be kept, and encourages the combatants to violate truces and ceasefires.

The 'new' policy reflected the abandonment of United States leadership and decisiveness in favor of 'multilateralism' and the desire to pursue consensus. But there has been a great act of collective failure in Europe. An entire political class has sought refuge behind the idea that nothing could be done. In the end, Bosnia was treated as a Third-World civil war, not a tragedy at the heart of the European continent. But the consequences go wider. How many potential aggressors, within central and eastern Europe and beyond, will now feel they can defy the international community with impunity – that the West is all bark and no bite?

What can be more vital to America's national security than Europe's future? Yet the Clinton administration – after suggesting that it planned to pursue lifting the arms embargo on the Bosnian Muslims and selective air strikes on Serb military targets – gave up that plan with little struggle in the face of European opposition. The administration instead accepted a weak alternative of protecting safe havens for the Bosnian Muslims. But what was worse, there appeared to be an inclination to turn that policy <u>mistake</u> into a policy doctrine, a <u>doctrine</u> of diminished U.S. leadership cloaked in 'multilateralism' at a time when the number of security threats are increasing.

Vital Interests Redefined

Part 1: Europe – The Emerging Strategic Landscape

Many are inclined to see a new U.S. engagement in Europe and/or of extending NATO's reach in terms of costs and risks. The restructuring of Western security mechanisms to deal with the new strategic challenges in Europe is difficult. But the leap is worth taking because the alternatives are very dangerous.

Identifying 'the problem' is crucial. The problem is not just the tragedy of Bosnia or even that Eastern Europe might unravel. The danger is that Europe as a whole could again come apart. There is no stable security order in Europe today. The revolutions of 1989 overturned not only communism but the peace orders established after the Second World War.

This is true due to the nature of these conflicts, i.e., the two nationalisms – that is, the difference between healthy national pride and destructive xenophobic nationalism. The key is the struggle between the forces of integration and disintegration, and this conflict is not limited geographically but runs through Europe.

The crisis, therefore, is not a Balkan crisis or a potential East European or Russian-Ukrainian crisis. It is a European crisis – the danger that Europe could again come apart at the seams. The current crises may be on Europe's periphery but they are not peripheral to European security. This is where Europe's future will be decided and underscores the link between what happens in the East and the future of the West. It is not a question of geography but of the nature of conflict, the rise of anti-Western forces, and two competing forms of nationalism.

Without overdoing the theme of a 'clash of civilizations,' I think Samuel Huntington, writing in Foreign Affairs, and Bob Kaplan, writing in the New Republic, have it about right. The Balkans – the fault line between east and west since Roman-Byzantine days – is the strategic heart of the world. It is the place where the vectors of conflict in the Middle East, the Caucasus and the towns of Germany interact. In short, it is the intersection of the two 'arcs of crisis' shaping Europe's future.

In an era of civilization clash, Bosnia is turning out to be, for the West, the Berlin crisis of the 1990s. The Muslim enclaves have come to symbolize the Islamic world in the latter's conflict with the Christian world. As Bosnia has been carved up like a piece of meat, Islamic fundamentalists have been handed an issue far more incendiary than Palestine: the systematic destruction of the Muslim civilization with the open complicity of the West. That is why I argue that post-Cold War Europe is being defined not so much by the Maastricht Treaty as by what is occurring in the Balkans.

Defining the current problems in terms of the future of Europe as a whole helps clarify the issue of vital American interests. There are three common-sense arguments that suggest the need for U.S. leadership and engagement in Europe:

- The U.S. cannot allow Europe to unravel for the third time in this century. Not only did the U.S. fight two world wars but it spent trillions of dollars on the Cold War. A modest investment not to stabilize and secure the peace is only prudent.
- The U.S. will not be able to pursue domestic reconstruction successfully without peace and stability in Europe. Crises in Europe could derail the Clinton presidency and his economic plan. Getting it wrong in Europe will cost the U.S. a great deal more in the long run – for example, it will push defense spending back up and disrupt commercial trade.
- The U.S. needs a new bargain with Europe not only to stabilize the continent but also to induce Europe to become the outward-looking and meaningful ally Washington needs to reduce its own global burden. Creating this new partnership is one of the key objectives of the new NATO bargain.

Part II: NATO and a New Transatlantic Strategic Bargain

What is needed is nothing less than a new trans-Atlantic strategic bargain. This bargain must extend collective defense and security arrangements to those areas in the east and south where the seeds of future conflict in Europe lie and address the new security challenges facing post-Cold War Europe.

Forging a new trans-Atlantic bargain is not only necessary for European security; it is a precondition for American domestic renewal. Without a stable, prosperous and strong Europe, it will be impossible to reduce American defense burdens or to successfully reinvigorate the American economy.

But forging this bargain requires a clear understanding of the new strategic challenges to Western interests in Europe. The possible resurgence of anti-democratic and anti-Western political movements in and between the arcs of crisis to the east and the south is but one side of the security problem in the new Europe.

The West needs a strategy to project democracy and security into the two arcs of crisis. Such a strategy must of course contain political and economic components to promote the transition to democracy in the East. But equally if not more important, the West must also establish a security framework for these regions. In short, strategically, we need to reorganize and revitalize the West in order to deal with the East and the South. [...]

The common denominator of all the new security problems in Europe is that they all lie beyond NATO's current borders and it is clear that they cannot be dealt with effectively by any single country in isolation. The only mechanism capable of this task is NATO; not the European Community. Not CSCE, not the WEU, but NATO. And if NATO does not do it, it will not be done.

[If]f NATO doesn't deal with them, it will become irrelevant. While NATO is increasingly pushed into dicey conflicts, such as Bosnia, it is a long way from having the strategy and structure necessary to meet the new strategic challenges. Even though the phrase 'out of area' is increasingly anachronistic, NATO will either develop the strategy and structure to go 'out of area' or it will 'go out of business.'

NATO at present is divided between those intent on preserving the status quo while avoiding new commitments and those who believe that the alliance must confront the new challenges in Europe or become irrelevant. The status quo is neither desirable not sustainable. The choice is not between the current NATO and a New NATO but rather between a New NATO or no NATO. If NATO is to survive, then it must be transformed from an alliance for collective defense against a specific threat into an alliance in the service of shared values and common strategic interests.

Questions

Has the expansion of NATO membership turned out as Lugar anticipated?
What would a new "transatlantic strategic bargain" look like today?

Reference

The Richard G. Lugar Senatorial Papers, Indiana University Libraries, Modern Political Papers: http://collections.libraries.indiana.edu/lugar/items/show/342

Document 9

North American Free Trade Agreement (NAFTA), 1 January 1994

NAFTA was a major step towards creating a North American trade bloc, bringing in a set of regulations for Canada, Mexico, and the United States. The idea for a North America free trade zone had been launched by Ronald Reagan as part of his 1980 presidential campaign, and the first result of this proposal was the Canada-United States Free Trade Agreement of 1988. The creation of the European Single Market and the EU's plans in the Maastricht Treaty of 1992 for a Single Currency increased the sense in the United States that a further response was needed. NAFTA was intended to bring the benefits of increased employment and investment for all three parties, but in particular for Mexico, which had the advantage of cheap labour for US manufacturing companies and which sought to attract foreign direct investment following the debt crisis of the 1980s. NAFTA was controversial for its weakening of labour laws and environmental protections, leading to political opposition in both Canada and the United States. President Bush attempted to bypass labour restrictions but was held up through 1992 and was forced to pass the issue on to his successor, President Clinton. To persuade congressional doubters, Clinton added two supplementary agreements, the North American Agreement on Labor Cooperation (NAALC) and the North American Agreement on Environmental Cooperation (NAAEC). In November 1993 the Act passed the House by 234-200 and the Senate by 61-38, splitting both parties along free trade and protectionist lines. The results of NAFTA were mixed. While trade volumes between the US and Mexico did increase due to tariff reductions, particularly in agricultural products, Canada saw fewer direct benefits. Although the US Chamber of Commerce claimed an increase in the export of goods and services, US labour unions countered that hundreds of thousands of jobs had been lost in the manufacturing heartland states such as Michigan, Ohio, Wisconsin, and Pennsylvania. Presidential candidate Ross Perot had gained fame in the second candidates' debate in 1992 for describing the "giant sucking sound" of US jobs that would be displaced to Mexico due to NAFTA, and this negative sentiment was part of Donald Trump's own presidential campaign in 2016 as he blamed others for the size of the US trade deficit. New negotiations eventually led to the United States-Mexico-Canada Agreement (USMCA) that came into effect on 1 July 2020. However, attempts to deepen the transatlantic link by joining NAFTA with the EU through a Transatlantic Trade and Investment Partnership (TTIP) during the 2010s were ultimately halted in 2019 when the EU saw no grounds for agreement with the Trump administration.

[This is an excerpt from the full document]

Article 101: Establishment of the Free Trade Area

The Parties to this Agreement, consistent with Article XXIV of the *General Agreement on Tariffs and Trade*, hereby establish a free trade area.

DOI: 10.4324/9781003159551-11

Article 102: Objectives

1   The objectives of this Agreement, as elaborated more specifically through its principles and rules, including national treatment, most-favored-nation treatment and transparency, are to:

   a   eliminate barriers to trade in, and facilitate the cross-border movement of, goods and services between the territories of the Parties;
   b   promote conditions of fair competition in the free trade area;
   c   increase substantially investment opportunities in the territories of the Parties;
   d   provide adequate and effective protection and enforcement of intellectual property rights in each Party's territory;
   e   create effective procedures for the implementation and application of this Agreement, for its joint administration and for the resolution of disputes; and
   f   establish a framework for further trilateral, regional and multilateral cooperation to expand and enhance the benefits of this Agreement.

2   The Parties shall interpret and apply the provisions of this Agreement in the light of its objectives set out in paragraph 1 and in accordance with applicable rules of international law.

Article 103: Relation to Other Agreements

1   The Parties affirm their existing rights and obligations with respect to each other under the *General Agreement on Tariffs and Trade* and other agreements to which such Parties are party.
2   In the event of any inconsistency between this Agreement and such other agreements, this Agreement shall prevail to the extent of the inconsistency, except as otherwise provided in this Agreement.

Article 104: Relation to Environmental and Conservation Agreements

1   In the event of any inconsistency between this Agreement and the specific trade obligations set out in:

   a   the Convention on International Trade in Endangered Species of Wild Fauna and Flora, done at Washington, March 3, 1973, as amended June 22, 1979,
   b   the Montreal Protocol on Substances that Deplete the Ozone Layer, done at Montreal, September 16, 1987, as amended June 29, 1990,
   c   the Basel Convention on the Control of Transboundary Movements of Hazardous Wastes and Their Disposal, done at Basel, March 22, 1989, on its entry into force for Canada, Mexico and the United States, or
   d   the agreements set out in Annex 104.1,

such obligations shall prevail to the extent of the inconsistency, provided that where a Party has a choice among equally effective and reasonably available means of complying with such obligations, the Party chooses the alternative that is the least inconsistent with the other provisions of this Agreement.

2   The Parties may agree in writing to modify Annex 104.1 to include any amendment to an agreement referred to in paragraph 1, and any other environmental or conservation agreement.

Article 105: Extent of Obligations

The Parties shall ensure that all necessary measures are taken in order to give effect to the provisions of this Agreement, including their observance, except as otherwise provided in this Agreement, by state and provincial governments.

Questions

What are some of the basic advantages and disadvantages of free trade?
Why did the proposed Transatlantic Trade and Investment Partnership generate such resistance in the 2010s?

Reference

https://www.congress.gov/bill/103rd-congress/house-bill/3450/text

Document 10

New Transatlantic Agenda, announced at the US-EU Summit, Madrid, 3 December 1995

The combined effects of the Maastricht Treaty and the continuing US commitment to European security meant that a new framework for transatlantic cooperation needed to be laid out for the post-Cold War world. Following on from the Transatlantic Declaration on EC-US Relations adopted in November 1990, the New Transatlantic Agenda was signed by President Bill Clinton, Spanish Prime Minister Felipe Gonzalez (president of the European Union), and European Commission President Jacques Santer in December 1995. It put forward a broad agenda with the aim to move from consultation to joint action, cementing the US-European axis as the driving force for global governance, political consensus, and security provision. At the time the EU was the largest investment partner of the US, with over $315m of assets, while the US possessed $320m of investments in the EU. The incentives for securing a common strategy for the post-Cold War world were therefore strong. The Agenda outlined an Action Plan for the following issues: promoting peace, democracy and development around the world; responding to global challenges (international crime, environmental decline, diseases such as Ebola); expanding world trade (including a Multilateral Agreement on Investment); and strengthening "the commercial, social, cultural, scientific and educational ties among our people." The Agenda represented a bold call to both deepen transatlantic economic integration through a common regulatory and customs apparatus, and solidify the leading role of the transatlantic region in the organisations of global governance such as the World Trade Organization, the G7, and the UN. Specific attention was given to solving continuing regional conflicts such as those between the Arab states and Israel, Turkey, Greece and Cyprus, and Russia and the Ukraine. In short, the Agenda was an ambitious document that in many ways represents the high point of the search for a common post-Cold War strategic agenda for the transatlantic region. It did lead to a greater institutionalization of contacts between US and EU officials at all levels of their respective administrations, which may not have removed all the disagreements but which did make dialogue much easier when trade disputes arose, and did generate the sense of a shared purpose for joint action on a wide range of issues. Further deepening of the relationship was pursued through a host of new initiatives: a Transatlantic Business Dialogue, Transatlantic Consumer Dialogue, Transatlantic Policy Network, Transatlantic Environmental Dialogue, and the Transatlantic Legislators Dialogue. Most importantly, the ambition of the Agenda was global rather than regional. Diverging approaches to the Arab-Israeli dispute and even Russia had split the US and Europe many times before. Nevertheless, in the following decade US-European relations would diverge due to the introduction of the Euro, continuing imbalances within NATO, ongoing trade disputes, and conflicting responses to the terrorist threat.

[This is an excerpt from the full document]

We, the United States of America and the European Union, affirm our conviction that the ties which bind our people are as strong today as they have been for the past half

DOI: 10.4324/9781003159551-12

century. For over fifty years, the transatlantic partnership has been the leading force for peace and prosperity for ourselves and for the world. Together, we helped transform adversaries into allies and dictatorships into democracies. Together, we built institutions and patterns of cooperation that ensured our security and economic strength. These are epic achievements.

Today we face new challenges at home and abroad. To meet them, we must further strengthen and adapt the partnership that has served us so well. Domestic challenges are not an excuse to turn inward; we can learn from each other's experiences and build new transatlantic bridges. We must first of all seize the opportunity presented by Europe's historic transformation to consolidate democracy and free-market economies throughout the continent.

We share a common strategic vision of Europe's future security. Together, we have charted a course for ensuring continuing peace in Europe into the next century. We are committed to the construction of a new European security architecture in which the North Atlantic Treaty Organisation, the European Union, the Western European Union, the Organisation for Security and Cooperation in Europe and the Council of Europe have complementary and mutually reinforcing roles to play.

We reaffirm the indivisibility of transatlantic security. NATO remains, for its members, the centrepiece of transatlantic security, providing the indispensable link between North America and Europe. Further adaptation of the Alliance's political and military structures to reflect both the full spectrum of its roles and the development of the emerging European Security and Defence Identity will strengthen the European pillar of the Alliance.

As to the accession of new members to NATO and to the EU, these processes, autonomous but complementary, should contribute significantly to the extension of security, stability and prosperity in the whole of Europe. Furthering the work of Partnership for Peace and the North Atlantic Cooperation Council and establishing a security partnership between NATO and Russia and between NATO and Ukraine will lead to unprecedented cooperation on security issues.

We are strengthening the OSCE [Organisation for Security and Cooperation in Europe] so that it can fulfil its potential to prevent destabilising regional conflicts and advance the prospect of peace, security, prosperity, and democracy for all.

Increasingly, our common security is further enhanced by strengthening and reaffirming the ties between the European Union and the United States within the existing network of relationships which join us together.

Our economic relationship sustains our security and increases our prosperity. We share the largest two-way trade and investment relationship in the world. We bear a special responsibility to lead multilateral efforts towards a more open world system of trade and investment. Our cooperation has made possible every global trade agreement, from the Kennedy Round to the Uruguay Round.

Through the G-7, we work to stimulate global growth. And at the Organisation for Economic Cooperation and Development, we are developing strategies to overcome structural unemployment and adapt to demographic change.

We are determined to create a New Transatlantic Marketplace, which will expand trade and investment opportunities and multiply jobs on both sides of the Atlantic. This initiative will also contribute to the dynamism of the global economy.

At the threshold of a new century, there is a new world to shape – full of opportunities but with challenges no less critical than those faced by previous generations. These challenges can be met and opportunities fully realised only by the whole international community working together. We will work with others bilaterally, at the United Nations and in other multilateral fora.

We are determined to reinforce our political and economic partnership as a powerful force for good in the world. To this end, we will build on the extensive consultations established by the 1990 Transatlantic Declaration and the conclusions of our June 1995 Summit and move to common action.

Today we adopt a New Transatlantic Agenda based on a Framework for Action with four major goals:

- Promoting peace and stability, democracy and development around the world. Together, we will work for an increasingly stable and prosperous Europe; foster democracy and economic reform in Central and Eastern Europe as well as in Russia, Ukraine and other new independent states; secure peace in the Middle East; advance human rights; promote non-proliferation and cooperate on development and humanitarian assistance.
- Responding to global challenges. Together, we will fight international crime, drug-trafficking and terrorism; address the needs of refugees and displaced persons; protect the environment and combat disease.
- Contributing to the expansion of world trade and closer economic relations. Together, we will strengthen the multilateral trading system and take concrete, practical steps to promote closer economic relations between us.
- Building bridges across the Atlantic. Together, we will work with our business people, scientists, educators and others to improve communication and to ensure that future generations remain as committed as we are to developing a full and equal partnership.

For the last fifty years, the transatlantic relationship has been central to the security and prosperity of our people. Our aspirations for the future must surpass our achievements in the past.

Questions

In what ways is the NTA important for laying out a global strategy for the transatlantic region?

Why do you think many observers have considered the results of the NTA to be disappointing?

Reference

https://www.europarl.europa.eu/summits/mad3_en.htm#annex10

Document 11

The General Framework Agreement for Peace in Bosnia and Herzegovina (Dayton Accords), 14 December 1995

The conflict in former Yugoslavia had various phases, all of them connected to Slobodan Milosevic's plans for a 'Greater Serbia' and the use of both Serb regular and paramilitary forces to occupy territory in Croatia and Bosnia Herzegovina during 1991–1995. From 1992 the epicentre of the conflict was Bosnia, which became divided into Croat-, Bosnian Serb-, and Bosnian-controlled territory and the capital Sarajevo subjected to constant bombardment by Bosnian Serb forces. In support of UN peace-keeping operations (UNPROFOR), NATO had initiated Operation Deny Flight in April 1993 to enforce a no-fly zone over Bosnia, and the mandate was later expanded to provide air support for UN forces. Deny Flight resulted in the first combat engagement in NATO's history with a dogfight over Banja Luka on 28 February 1994, and was also the first mission for the German Luftwaffe in a combat zone since 1945. The situation escalated following the catastrophe of Srebrenica, where Bosnian Serb forces under Ratko Mladic overran this UN-protected 'safe haven' and proceeded to massacre up to 8000 Bosnian Muslims. NATO responded with Operation Deliberate Force in August-September 1995 that involved large-scale attacks against Bosnian Serb targets around Sarajevo. Combined with a Croatian military offensive and pressure from the US and Russia, the Serbian leadership was eventually forced to the negotiating table at Wright-Patterson Air Force Base near Dayton, Ohio. Talks were held between 1–21 November 1995, and the agreement was signed in Paris on 14 December 1995. The fact that a US military installation was chosen as the site for the most important European conflict resolution negotiations since World War II indicated the continuing centrality of the US in all matters related to European peace and security. The Accords allowed for the establishment of an Implementation Force (IFOR), comprising eventually of military personnel from 32 nations, including Russia, but coordinated by NATO under a UN mandate. In December 1996 IFOR was replaced by a Stabilisation Force (SFOR), and in 2004 responsibility was passed from NATO to the EU in the form of the EUFOR Althea mission. Responsibility for security provision in post-conflict Bosnia therefore transitioned from a transatlantic to a European framework within a decade.

[This is an excerpt from the full document]

Annex 1-A: Agreement on the Military Aspects of the Peace Settlement

The Republic of Bosnia and Herzegovina, the Federation of Bosnia and Herzegovina, and the Republika Srpska (hereinafter the "Parties") have agreed as follows:

Article I: General Obligations

1   The Parties undertake to recreate as quickly as possible normal conditions of life in Bosnia and Herzegovina. They understand that this requires a major contribution

DOI: 10.4324/9781003159551-13

on their part in which they will make strenuous efforts to cooperate with each other and with the international organisations and agencies which are assisting them on the ground. They welcome the willingness of the international community to send to the region, for a period of approximately one year, a force to assist in implementation of the territorial and other militarily-related provisions of the agreement as described herein.

a   The United Nations Security Council is invited to adopt a resolution by which it will authorize Member States or regional organizations and arrangements to establish a multinational military Implementation Force (hereinafter "IFOR"). The Parties understand and agree that this Implementation Force may be composed of ground, air and maritime units from NATO and non-NATO nations, deployed to Bosnia and Herzegovina to help ensure compliance with the provisions of this Agreement (hereinafter "Annex"). The Parties understand and agree that the IFOR will begin the implementation of the military aspects of this Annex upon the transfer of authority from the UNPROFOR Commander to the IFOR Commander (hereinafter "Transfer of Authority"), and that until the Transfer of Authority, UNPROFOR will continue to exercise its mandate.

b   It is understood and agreed that NATO may establish such a force, which will operate under the authority and subject to the direction and political control of the North Atlantic Council ("NAC") through the NATO chain of command. They undertake to facilitate its operations. The Parties, therefore, hereby agree and freely undertake to fully comply with all obligations set forth in this Annex.

c   It is understood and agreed that other States may assist in implementing the military aspects of this Annex. The Parties understand and agree that the modalities of those States' participation will be the subject of agreement between such participating States and NATO.

2   The purposes of these obligations are as follows:

a   to establish a durable cessation of hostilities. Neither Entity shall threaten or use force against the other Entity, and under no circumstances shall any armed forces of either Entity enter into or stay within the territory of the other Entity without the consent of the government of the latter and of the Presidency of Bosnia and Herzegovina. All armed forces in Bosnia and Herzegovina shall operate consistently with the sovereignty and territorial integrity of Bosnia and Herzegovina;

b   to provide for the support and authorization of the IFOR and in particular to authorize the IFOR to take such actions as required, including the use of necessary force, to ensure compliance with this Annex, and to ensure its own protection; and

c   to establish lasting security and arms control measures as outlined in Annex 1-B to the General Framework Agreement, which aim to promote a permanent reconciliation between all Parties and to facilitate the achievement of all political arrangements agreed to in the General Framework Agreement.

3   The Parties understand and agree that within Bosnia and Herzegovina the obligations undertaken in this Annex shall be applied equally within both Entities. Both Entities shall be held equally responsible for compliance herewith, and both shall be equally subject to such enforcement action by the IFOR as may be necessary to ensure implementation of this Annex and the protection of the IFOR.

Questions

Why did it take so long for NATO to intervene in the Yugoslav conflict?
Do you think NATO should play a greater role as a UN peace-keeping force in general?

Reference

https://www.osce.org/files/f/Referencess/e/0/126173.pdf

Document 12

President Clinton, Speech to the People of Detroit, 22 October 1996

After the end of the Cold War, a debate on the future security arrangements for Europe did temporarily raise the issue of the continuing validity of NATO following the demise of the Soviet Union. In the early 1990s, alternatives involving the Russians through the Organisation for Security and Cooperation in Europe (see Part I Document 3), and the development of European capabilities through the EU's CFSP (see Part I Document 6), were put forward. The decision by the United States in 1994 to pursue the expansion of NATO by adding former Warsaw Pact members, beginning with Poland, the Czech Republic, and Hungary, was a far-reaching move that gave the Organisation a leading role in defining the continent's post-Cold War architecture. The three eventually joined the Alliance in 1999. The expansion of NATO eastwards had always been a contentious issue in relations between the West and Russia, dating from the negotiations on the unification of Germany in 1990 that included apparent verbal commitments that such expansion would not occur in order to mollify the Soviet side and pave the way to an agreement. While Russian leader Boris Yeltsin was able to maintain power, the issue could be managed (see Part I Document 13), but the subsequent presidencies of Vladimir Putin after 2000 increasingly pointed to NATO expansion as a betrayal of post-Cold War commitments to build a new security architecture that would not be antagonistic towards Russia. Bill Clinton had first been elected in 1991 on the back of a campaign that prioritised domestic issues and economic interests, and foreign affairs were decidedly secondary. Clinton's National Security Advisor Anthony Lake (1993–1997) eventually outlined a policy of 'enlargement' whereby the United States pursued the promotion of democracy and free market capitalism around the world, and this provided the context for pursuing the expansion of NATO to include former Warsaw Pact members. The Republican Party's winning of both houses of Congress in the 1994 mid-term elections also boosted the NATO plan, since a majority of them were in favour of extending US power in this way. In this speech during his re-election campaign, Clinton outlined his vision for a peaceful Europe secured through the gradual expansion of NATO membership and a close working relationship with Russia through the Partnership for Peace.

[This is an excerpt from the full document]

The bedrock of our common security remains NATO. When President Truman signed the North Atlantic Treaty 47 years ago, he expressed the goal of its founders plainly, but powerfully: to preserve their present peaceful situation and to protect it in the future. All of us here today, every single one of us, are the beneficiaries of NATO's extraordinary success in doing just that.

NATO defended the West by deterring aggression. Even more, through NATO, Western Europe became a source of stability instead of hostility. France and Germany moved from conflict to cooperation. Democracy took permanent root in countries where fascism

DOI: 10.4324/9781003159551-14

once ruled. I came to office convinced that NATO can do for Europe's East what it did for Europe's West: prevent a return to local rivalries, strengthen democracy against future threats, and create the conditions for prosperity to flourish. That's why the United States has taken the lead in a three part effort to build a new NATO for a new era. First, by adapting NATO with new capabilities for new missions. Second, by opening its doors to Europe's emerging democracies. Third, by building a strong and cooperative relationship between NATO and Russia.

To adapt NATO we have taken on missions beyond the territory of its members for the first time, and done so in cooperation with non member states, shifting our emphasis to smaller and more flexible forces prepared to provide for our defense, but also trained and equipped for peacekeeping. We're setting up mobile headquarters to run these new missions more effectively and efficiently. We're giving our European allies a larger role within the Alliance, while preserving NATO's vital core, which is an integrated command military structure.

The United States will continue to take the lead in NATO, especially in the southern region where the most immediate threats to peace exist. But we welcome our allies' willingness to shoulder a greater share of the burden and to assume greater leadership. Bosnia has been the first major test of the new NATO. At first, NATO could act jointly only with the United Nations. But once NATO took charge, once its lead, its air power, together with its diplomatic leadership, was available fully, it pushed the Bosnian Serbs from the battlefield to the bargaining table. The NATO led Implementation Force has restored security to Bosnia. It has given the Bosnian people a chance not a guarantee, but a chance to build a lasting peace.

But for NATO to fulfill its real promise of peace and democracy in Europe it will not be enough simply to take on new missions as the need arises. NATO must also take in new members, including those from among its former adversaries. It must reach out to all the new democracies in Central Europe, the Baltics and the New Independent States of the former Soviet Union. At the first NATO summit I attended in January of 1994, I proposed that NATO should enlarge steadily, deliberately, openly. And our allies agreed. First, together, we created the Partnership For Peace as a path to full NATO membership for some and a strong and lasting link to the alliance for all. I think it would be fair to say that the Partnership For Peace has exceeded what even its most optimistic supporters predicted for it in the beginning. There are more than two dozen members now.

The more than two dozen members and the astonishing amount of cooperation and joint training and partnership that has developed as results of this Partnership For Peace has made it something of significance I believe enduring significance beyond what we ever imagined when we started it. And the strategy is paying off. The prospect of membership in or partnership with NATO has given Europe's new democracies a strong incentive to continue to reform and to improve relations with their neighbors.

Through the Partnership For Peace, prospective new members are actually gaining the practical experience they need to join NATO. Thirteen partner nations are serving alongside NATO troops and helping to secure the peace in Bosnia. There are Polish and Czech combat battalions, Hungarian and Romanian engineering troops, soldiers from Ukraine and the Baltic states, forces from Sweden and Finland and a full Russian brigade.

Just seven years ago, these soldiers served on opposite sides of the Iron Curtain. Today, their teamwork with our troops and other European NATO allies is erasing the lines that once divided Europe while bringing an end to the bloodiest conflict in Europe since World War II.

We have kept NATO enlargement on track. Now it is time to take the next historic step forward. Last month, I called for a summit in the spring or early summer of next year to name to first group of future NATO members and to invite them to begin accession talks. Today, I want to state America's goal. By 1999, NATO's 50th anniversary and 10 years after the fall of the Berlin Wall, the first group of countries we invite to join should be full fledged members of NATO.

I also pledged for my part, and I believe for NATO's part as well, that's NATO's doors will not close behind its first new members. NATO should remain open to all of Europe's emerging democracies who are ready to shoulder the responsibilities of membership. No nation will be automatically excluded. No country outside NATO will have a veto. We will work to deepen our cooperation, meanwhile, with all the nations in the Partnership For Peace. A gray zone of insecurity must not reemerge in Europe.

Now, I want to say that as we go forward the American people should be aware that this plan is not free of costs. Peace and security are not available on the cheap. Enlargement will mean extending the most solemn security guarantee to our new allies. To be a NATO member means that all the other members make a commitment to treat an attack on one as an attack on all. But mark my words, if we fail to seize this historic opportunity to build a new NATO in a new Europe, if we allow the Iron Curtain to be replaced by a veil of indifference, we will pay a much higher price later on down the road. America will be stronger and safer if the democratic family continues to grow, if we bring to our ranks partners willing to share the risks and responsibilities of freedom.

By overwhelming majorities this summer, both Houses of Congress passed a NATO Enlargement Facilitation Act. I greatly appreciate this bipartisan support for our efforts to forge a broader alliance of prosperity, of security and, as the First Lady said in Prague on the last 4th of July, an alliance of values with Europe. I look forward to working with Congress to ratify the accession of new members, to provide the resources we need to meet this commitment, to secure the support of the American people. NATO enlargement is not directed against anyone. It will advance the security of everyone NATO's old members, new members and non members alike.

I know that some in Russia still look at NATO through a Cold War prism and, therefore, look at our proposals to expand it in a negative light. But I ask them to look again. We are building a new NATO, just as we support the Russian people in building a new Russia. By reducing rivalry and fear, by strengthening peace and cooperation, NATO will promote greater stability in Europe and Russia will be among the beneficiaries. Indeed, Russia has the best chance in history to help to build that peaceful and undivided Europe, and to be an equal and respected and successful partner in that sort of future.

The great opportunity the Russian people have is to define themselves in terms of the future, not the past; to forge a new relationship with NATO as enlargement moves forward. The United States has suggested that Russia and NATO work out a formal agreement on cooperation. We should set up a regular mechanism for NATO Russia meetings at all levels. We should consult on European security issues so that whenever possible NATO and Russia can act jointly to meet the challenges of the new era, just as we have acted jointly in Bosnia.

Just think about it. In Bosnia, Russia and NATO are already partners for peace. We should set our sights on becoming full partners and bringing all of Europe together. Together we can help to turn the main battleground for the bloodiest century in history into a continent whose people remain secure and prosperous, free and at peace. These past four years, it's been one of the greatest privileges of my life to represent America around the world, from the halls of Kremlin to the hillsides of Port au Prince; from the deserts of Jordan to the Tokyo Harbor; from the Charles Bridge in Prague and Riga's Freedom Square to the DMZ in Korea. I have heard the voices and shaken the hands of presidents and prime ministers, and just as important, citizens on the streets of distant lands. Wherever I go, whomever I talk with, the message to me is the same: We believe in America. We trust America. We want America to lead. And America must lead.

Questions

Why, according to Clinton, should the United States pursue NATO expansion?
Does Clinton's argument in any way differ from Senator Lugar's argument in 1993 (see Part I Document 8)?

Reference

https://1997-2001.state.gov/www/about_state/detroit.html

Document 13

Summit Meeting between President Bill Clinton and President Boris Yeltsin, Helsinki, Finland, 21 March 1997

During their 11th summit meeting, Clinton and Russian leader Boris Yeltsin put forward a common agenda that looked to pursue further arms reduction through a START III process (Strategic Arms Reduction Talks), and continue to promote economic reforms and inward investment in Russia, with the goal of seeking Russian membership of the World Trade Organisation (WTO). Nevertheless, the press conference also attempted to overcome deep divisions on the issues of NATO enlargement and missile defence. In 1994 the NATO summit in Brussels had launched the Partnership for Peace (PfP) initiative, designed to pursue greater cooperation and build trust with the former Soviet republics and in particular Russia. PfP sought to reduce antagonisms through regular military-to-military contacts, joint training exercises, disaster response initiatives, and professionalization. The Helsinki summit saw the signing of the NATO-Russia Agreement to facilitate continuing relations following the invitation of Poland, Hungary, and the Czech Republic to join NATO (which they did in 1999). The Agreement stated that NATO would not station "substantial combat forces" or nuclear weapons in the newly accepted member states, although this was dependent on "the current and foreseeable security environment." Yeltsin, under pressure from both communist and nationalist political forces in Russia, expressed his negative view of NATO expansion very clearly in this press conference, and the negotiations on the Agreement had not been smooth. While US-Russian relations were maintained through the positive camaraderie of the two leaders, the agreement to disagree on NATO expansion exposed a fault line that would start to reappear strongly a decade later, under the leadership of President Vladimir Putin.

[This is an excerpt from the full press conference]

President Clinton. Here in Helsinki we have addressed three fundamental challenges: first, building an undivided, democratic, and peaceful Europe for the first time in history; second, continuing to lead the world away from the nuclear threat; and third, forging new ties of trade and investment that will help Russia to complete its remarkable transformation to a market economy and will bring greater prosperity to both our peoples.

A Europe undivided and democratic must be a secure Europe. NATO is the bedrock of Europe's security and the tie that binds the United States to that security. That is why the United States has led the way in adapting NATO to new missions, in opening its doors to new members, in strengthening its ties to nonmembers through the Partnership For Peace, in seeking to forge a strong, practical partnership between NATO and Russia. We are building a new NATO, just as the Russian people are building a new Russia. I am determined that Russia will become a respected partner with NATO in making the future for all of Europe peaceful and secure.

DOI: 10.4324/9781003159551-15

I reaffirmed that NATO enlargement in the Madrid summit will proceed, and President Yeltsin made it clear that he thinks it's a mistake. But we also have an important and, I believe, overriding agreement: We agreed that the relationship between the United States and Russia and the benefits of cooperation between NATO and Russia are too important to be jeopardized.

We also reached agreement in our work to preserve the Anti-Ballistic Missile [ABM] Treaty, a cornerstone of our arms control efforts. Distinguishing between ballistic missile systems restricted by the ABM Treaty and theater missile defenses that are not restricted has been a very difficult issue to resolve. Today, after 3 years of negotiations, we agreed to preserve the ABM Treaty while giving each of us the ability to develop defenses against theater missiles...

Russia and NATO

Q: Boris Nikolayevich, our first impression is that there was no breakthrough on NATO here in Helsinki. Tell me, can there be some kind of movement forward before the Madrid summit?

PRESIDENT YELTSIN: I don't agree with you. It was today that we had progress, very principled progress, and they consist of the following—that, yes, indeed, we do maintain our positions. We believe that the eastward expansion of NATO is a mistake and a serious one at that. Nevertheless, in order to minimize the negative consequences for Russia, we decided to sign an agreement with NATO, a Russia-NATO agreement. And this is the principal question here. We've agreed on the parameters of this document with President Bill Clinton.

This is the non-proliferation of nuclear weapons, to those new members of NATO to not proliferate conventional weapons in these countries. We agreed on non-use of the military infrastructure which remained in place after the Warsaw Pact in these countries of Central and Eastern Europe. The decision of joint actions with Russia alone, this, too, will be included in the agreement with NATO.

And finally, we've come to an agreement that this document will be binding for all. For that reason, everyone will sign this, all heads of state of all 16 member nations of NATO. This is a very principled issue, and we came to agreement on this with President Bill Clinton. That is, all states, all nations—and this will take place before Madrid—all heads of state will sign this document we sign together with Bill Clinton. And then there will be a signature of the General Secretary of NATO. And we believe that this document indeed is binding for NATO, for Russia, for all states whose leaders signed this document. So this is a very principled progress...

NATO Expansion

Q: President Yeltsin, after all that you've been told about how the world has changed and that there will be no nuclear weapons in Eastern Europe, do you still regard NATO's enlargement as a danger to Russia?

And to President Clinton, this exclusion of nuclear weapons from Eastern Europe and the promise that there will be no big troop buildup in the new states, does that mean that NATO's new members will be second-class citizens, second-class members?

PRESIDENT YELTSIN: No, of course not, no one will think of these as being secondary states. No one is calling that. That's not what's involved here. However, I believe and Bill believes the same thing, Bill Clinton believes the same, that these decisions that can be taken, they will be taken by all leaders of these nations, which is extremely, extremely important. I already mentioned this.

PRESIDENT CLINTON: Let me say, Terry, in answer to the question you raised to me, emphatically no, this does not mean any new members would be second-class members. That's one of the things that we have committed ourselves to. There are no second-class members.

What are the two most important things that you get if you're a member? One is the security guarantee, the mutual security guarantee. The other is a place in the military command structure. These will be available to any new members taken in.

Now, we also want to make it clear that in addition to the security guarantee and participation in the military command structure, NATO is a different organization today than it was. We have a different mission. What is the most important thing NATO is doing today? Working in Bosnia. NATO has a major partnership with Russia in Bosnia. And a partnership, I might add, with a number of other nonmember nations who are in our Partnership For Peace, where we've done joint military exercises and other things.

Now, on the two questions you mentioned—on the nuclear question, the NATO military commanders reached an independent judgment that, based on the facts that exist in the world today, they have no reason, therefore, no intention and no plan to station any nuclear weapons on members' soil. Look, we just announced an agreement here that will reduce nuclear weapons, if we can implement it, within a decade by 80 percent below their cold war height, number one...

Anti-Ballistic Missile Treaty

Q: President Clinton, it is known that in your Congress there's some criticism frequently that you are a supporter of the ABM Treaty. Today's meeting, did that convince you to strengthen the ABM Treaty?

PRESIDENT CLINTON: Some people have criticized me in my Congress because I do support the ABM Treaty. Yes, that's accurate; they have. I do support the ABM Treaty. I think it's important. I believe in it. And we have, I believe, strengthened the chances that the ABM Treaty will survive by the agreement we have made today and the distinctions we have drawn between the missiles that are covered by the ABM Treaty and by theater defense missiles. I believe that very strongly.

There are those in the Congress of the United States, but they are not a majority— let me emphasize, they are not a majority—who would undermine the ABM Treaty because they don't believe it's in our interest. I believe they're wrong. I believe that the ABM Treaty has served us well and will continue to serve us well, especially in view of the questions that we have clarified today between us.

Questions

Why was Boris Yeltsin under pressure due to the expansion of NATO?
What was the significance of the ABM Treaty at this time?

Reference

https://www.presidency.ucsb.edu/Referencess/the-presidents-news-conference-with-president-boris-yeltsin-russia-helsinki

Document 14

Kyoto Protocol to the United Nations Framework Convention on Climate Change, 10 December 1997

In 1988 the UN Environmental Programme (UNEP) and the World Meteorological Organization established the Intergovernmental Panel on Climate Change (IPCC) to provide objective, scientifically verified information on human-induced climate change, the risks involved, and possible responses. The year before the Montreal Protocol on Substances that Deplete the Ozone Layer had proved that international cooperation could achieve major breakthroughs when it came to human-induced, life-threatening developments in the earth's atmosphere. The IPCC's reports have formed the basis for the UN Framework Convention on Climate Change (UNFCCC), an international regime that seeks to "stabilize greenhouse gas concentrations in the atmosphere at a level that would prevent dangerous anthropogenic (human-induced) interference with the climate system." The Kyoto Protocol, an addition to the 1992 UNFCCC, set out specific targets for 38 advanced industrial nations and the EC (Appendix I signatories from Europe and North America) to reduce their greenhouse gas emissions for the 2008–2012 period. In 2004 Russia and Canada ratified the Protocol, bringing it into effect the following year. Kyoto represented a major advance in dealing with the issue, in that it formally recognised different responsibilities among nations for climate change, placing the principal burden of change on those nations that had a longer record of industrial development. It also saw a divide opening up in terms of the respective approaches of Europe and the United States. Whereas the EU made Kyoto a central plank of its response to climate change, the US was reticent to commit itself to any formal agreements on reductions. President Clinton signed the Protocol knowing that it would not pass a Republican-dominated Senate for ratification. Following his election, President George W. Bush spoke out against Kyoto in February 2001 precisely because it placed the burden of adaptation on the developed world and would harm the US economy.

[This is an excerpt from the full document]

Article 2

1   Each Party included in Annex I in achieving its quantified emission limitation and reduction commitments under Article 3, in order to promote sustainable development, shall:

   a   Implement and/or further elaborate policies and measures in accordance with its national circumstances, such as:

   i   Enhancement of energy efficiency in relevant sectors of the national economy;
   ii   Protection and enhancement of sinks and reservoirs of greenhouse gases not controlled by the Montreal Protocol, taking into account its commitments under relevant international environmental agreements; promotion of sustainable forest management practices, afforestation and reforestation;
   iii Promotion of sustainable forms of agriculture in light of climate change considerations;

DOI: 10.4324/9781003159551-16

iv Promotion, research, development and increased use of new and renewable forms of energy, of carbon dioxide sequestration technologies and of advanced and innovative environmentally sound technologies;

v Progressive reduction or phasing out of market imperfections, fiscal incentives, tax and duty exemptions and subsidies in all greenhouse gas emitting sectors that run counter to the objective of the Convention and apply market instruments;

vi Encouragement of appropriate reforms in relevant sectors aimed at promoting policies and measures which limit or reduce emissions of greenhouse gases not controlled by the Montreal Protocol;

vii Measures to limit and/or reduce emissions of greenhouse gases not controlled by the Montreal Protocol in the transport sector;

viii Limitation and/or reduction of methane through recovery and use in waste management, as well as in the production, transport and distribution of energy;

b Cooperate with other such Parties to enhance the individual and combined effectiveness of their policies and measures adopted under this Article, pursuant to Article 4, paragraph 2(e)(i), of the Convention. To this end, these Parties shall take steps to share their experience and exchange information on such policies and measures, including developing ways of improving their comparability, transparency and effectiveness. The Conference of the Parties serving as the meeting of the Parties to this Protocol shall, at its first session or as soon as practicable thereafter, consider ways to facilitate such cooperation, taking into account all relevant information.

2 The Parties included in Annex I shall pursue limitation or reduction of emissions of greenhouse gases not controlled by the Montreal Protocol from aviation and marine bunker fuels, working through the International Civil Aviation Organization and the International Maritime Organization, respectively.

3 The Parties included in Annex I shall strive to implement policies and measures under this Article in such a way as to minimize adverse effects, including the adverse effects of climate change, effects on international trade, and social, environmental and economic impacts on other Parties, especially developing country Parties and in particular those identified in Article 4, paragraphs 8 and 9 of the Convention, taking into account Article 3 of the Convention. The Conference of the Parties serving as the meeting of the Parties to this Protocol may take further action, as appropriate, to promote the implementation of the provisions of this paragraph.

4 The Conference of the Parties serving as the meeting of the Parties to this Protocol, if it decides that it would be beneficial to coordinate any of the policies and measures in paragraph 1(a) above, taking into account different national circumstances and potential effects, shall consider ways and means to elaborate the coordination of such policies and measures.

Questions

Why was there such resistance in the United States to fixing targets for limiting greenhouse gas emissions?

How did this disagreement between the United States and the European Union undermine transatlantic leadership on this issue globally?

Reference

https://newsroom.unfccc.int/Referencess/2409

Document 15

The St. Malo Declaration, signed by Prime Minister Tony Blair and President Jacques Chirac, 4 December 1998

The 1990s had not been a good decade for efforts to improve European security cooperation. The election of Tony Blair at the head of a largely pro-European Labour government in 1997 heralded the possibility for a greater involvement of Britain in EU affairs. The subsequent St Malo Declaration heralded a new era of Franco-British military cooperation, potentially laying the foundation for the further development of European responsibilities and capabilities in that field. The effects of a failed EU response to the Bosnian war, the wish of Blair to profile his pro-European outlook while avoiding the problematic issue of monetary union, and French desires to develop a stronger European military capability able to act more autonomously from the United States all fed into this declaration. The worsening situation in Kosovo and the likelihood that this would spill over into neighbouring states such as Macedonia and Albania once again raised the issue of a potential intervention in the Balkans, just over two years after the signing of the Dayton agreement on Bosnia. The Declaration's stated goal was that European common defence must include the capability for "autonomous action backed up by credible military forces," and this led both to the formulation of a European Security and Defence Policy (ESDP) and a Headline Goal, presented at the EU's Helsinki summit in 1999, of a Rapid Reaction Force of up to 60,000 combat personnel by 2003. In many ways the Declaration was also a statement of intent of the two most well-equipped military powers in the EU that they expected a greater level of commitment from their European partners. Britain's involvement marked a potentially significant shift, since its "special relationship" stance towards the US was now being blended with a genuine effort to reach out to its EU neighbour in order to promote a greater level of European self-sufficiency in security affairs. However, the fallout caused by the Iraq invasion of 2003, which saw Europe divided along the lines of those who joined the US and those who opposed it (with some nations such as the Netherlands choosing for "political not military support"), greatly undermined the cohesion that St. Malo wanted to create. Stagnating defence budgets and the ongoing lack of clarity as to the EU-NATO relationship have continued to prevent the ambitions of St. Malo from being realised.

Joint Declaration on European Defence issued at the British-French Summit, St-Malo, 4 December 1998

The Heads of State and Government of France and the United Kingdom are agreed that:

1   The European Union needs to be in a position to play its full role on the international stage. This means making a reality of the Treaty of Amsterdam, which will provide the essential basis for action by the Union. It will be important to achieve full and rapid implementation of the Amsterdam provisions on CFSP. This includes the responsibility of the European Council to decide on the progressive framing of a common defence policy in the framework of CFSP. The Council must be able to take

DOI: 10.4324/9781003159551-17

decisions on an intergovernmental basis, covering the whole range of activity set out in Title V of the Treaty of European Union.

2   To this end, the Union must have the capacity for autonomous action, backed up by credible military forces, the means to decide to use them, and a readiness to do so, in order to respond to international crises.

In pursuing our objective, the collective defence commitments to which member states subscribe (set out in Article 5 of the Washington Treaty, Article V of the Brussels Treaty) must be maintained. In strengthening the solidarity between the member states of the European Union, in order that Europe can make its voice heard in world affairs, while acting in conformity with our respective obligations in NATO, we are contributing to the vitality of a modernised Atlantic Alliance which is the foundation of the collective defence of its members.

Europeans will operate within the institutional framework of the European Union (European Council, General Affairs Council, and meetings of Defence Ministers).

The reinforcement of European solidarity must take into account the various positions of European states. The different situations of countries in relation to NATO must be respected.

3   In order for the European Union to take decisions and approve military action where the Alliance as a whole is not engaged, the Union must be given appropriate structures and a capacity for analysis of situations, sources of intelligence, and a capability for relevant strategic planning, without unnecessary duplication, taking account of the existing assets of the WEU and the evolution of its relations with the EU. In this regard, the European Union will also need to have recourse to suitable military means (European capabilities pre-designated within NATO's European pillar or national or multinational European means outside the NATO framework).

4   Europe needs strengthened armed forces that can react rapidly to the new risks, and which are supported by a strong and competitive European defence industry and technology.

5   We are determined to unite in our efforts to enable the European Union to give concrete expression to these objectives.

Question

Why did a credible European security framework mainly depend on British-French cooperation?
Is the creation of a European Army a good idea?

References

© Her Majesty's Stationery Office (HMSO)
Permission: Open Government License (OGL)
Source: Centre for Contemporary and Digital History (C2DH), UNIVERSITÉ DU LUXEMBOURG

Document 16

Secretary of State Madeleine K. Albright, Statement to the North Atlantic Council, Brussels, Belgium, 8 December 1998

During the preparations for the 1999 Washington Summit and a new Strategic Concept, Albright delivered a key speech to NATO allies that set out the US position for the way ahead. In 1997 Albright had become the first female US Secretary of State, successfully lobbying for the position against the candidacy of Senator Sam Nunn. Famous for its reference to no de-linking, duplication, or discrimination between potentially rival European and transatlantic security apparatuses and agendas, Albright also used this speech to enthusiastically call for greater clarity on the role and meaning of a European Security and Defense Identity (ESDI) within NATO. Essentially picking up the 'enlargement' approach to democracy promotion and free market capitalism that had been put forward by National Security Advisor Anthony Lake, Albright used the speech to lay out a broad seven-point agenda that sought to confirm the continuing centrality of the transatlantic relationship. Delivered only four days after the St. Malo Declaration (see Document 15), the speech indicates clearly how the struggle to forge a post-Cold War transatlantic security architecture that would allow for more European autonomy but also preserve the decisive role of the United States was proving to be one of the major issues of the decade. Significantly, the focus on Weapons of Mass Destruction (WMD) as a threat to the region presaged how this issue would prove fundamentally divisive only four years later when the United States under President George W. Bush used this argument to gain support for an attack on Iraq.

[This is an excerpt from the full document]

I view NATO's future role in that broader partnership as the institution of choice when North America and Europe must act together militarily.

My vision of a new and better NATO can be summarized in one sentence: we want an Alliance strengthened by new members; capable of collective defense; committed to meeting a wide range of threats to our shared interests and values; and acting in partnership with others to ensure stability, freedom and peace in and for the entire trans-Atlantic area.

As we look to the Washington Summit, we may divide our work into seven essential tasks.

The first is to speak in clear and understandable terms to our public and parliaments about NATO's future role and purpose.

Our second task is to develop, for unveiling at the Washington Summit, an updated Strategic Concept.

The NATO of the twenty-first century will confront a very different strategic environment than in the past. During the Cold War, we had no trouble identifying an Article V threat to our territory and security. It stared at us from across the Fulda Gap.

DOI: 10.4324/9781003159551-18

But the threats we face today and tomorrow could come from a number of different sources, including from areas beyond NATO's immediate borders. I often remind people that a ballistic missile attack using a weapon of mass destruction from a rogue state is every bit as much an Article V threat to our borders now as a Warsaw Pact tank was two decades ago.

I know that there are those who try to suggest that by assuming these new missions, or by talking about common Euro-Atlantic interests beyond collective defense, we are somehow tinkering with the original intent of the North Atlantic Treaty. I've said it before; I will repeat it again today: this is hogwash.

The third task we face is to maintain our commitment to NATO enlargement. Our commitment to our Open Door strategy is central to our vision of a new and better NATO for the twenty-first century. Getting a robust and credible Open Door package is one of the key challenges we face for the Washington Summit.

As an Alliance strengthened by new members, our fourth task must be to reach agreement on a long-term program to adapt NATO's defense capabilities to carry out the full spectrum of missions in the new Strategic Concept. We need military forces that are designed, equipped, and prepared for twenty-first century missions.

Our fifth task is related closely to the previous ones. The Summit should address the threat posed to our populations, territory and to our military forces by weapons of mass destruction, or WMD.

We have proposed a comprehensive WMD initiative that builds on the successful work we inaugurated at the 1994 summit. The initiative is designed to ensure that we can effectively address the threat posed by the proliferation of such weapons and their means of delivery. Our plan is to increase information and intelligence-sharing in the Alliance, accelerate the development of capabilities to deter and protect against potential WMD use, and underscore our shared commitment to prevent proliferation.

Our sixth task is working together to develop a European Security and Defense Identity, or ESDI, within the Alliance, which the United States has strongly endorsed. We enthusiastically support any such measures that enhance European capabilities. The United States welcomes a more capable European partner, with modern, flexible military forces capable of putting out fires in Europe's own back yard and working with us through the Alliance to defend our common interests.

The key to a successful initiative is to focus on practical military capabilities. Any initiative must avoid preempting Alliance decision-making by de-linking ESDI from NATO, avoid duplicating existing efforts, and avoid discriminating against non-EU members.

Our seventh and final task is to further intensify and strengthen relations with our European partners. Indeed, in facing future security challenges, the Euro-Atlantic Partnership Council must also be seen as an instrument of choice. Specifically, the Alliance needs to define, in time for the Washington Summit, a framework for joint crisis response operations. We also welcome ideas on developing new mechanisms to improve Allied and Partner national and multinational forces' ability to act together.

Some decades ago, in the depth of Cold War tensions, Walter Lippmann wrote about the realities of his time in words that may serve as a warning to ours.

> With all the danger and worry it causes... [wrote Lippman] the Soviet challenge may yet prove ... a blessing. For ... if our influence ... were undisputed, we would, I feel sure, slowly deteriorate. Having ... lost our daring because everything was ... so comfortable. We would ... enter into the decline which has marked ... so many societies ... when they have come to think there is no great work to be done. For then the night has come and they doze off and they begin to die.

Lippman's fear is being put to the test in this decade. Certainly, there are some in each of our countries who now believe "there is no great work to be done," and that all we have to do to ensure our prosperity, security and freedom is hold on and stay put.

Today the responsibility is ours to rise above the barrier of complacency of which Walter Lippman wrote, and to build a new framework for freedom. In so doing, we will rely not only on this Alliance, but on all the great institutions of this continent and of our Community. We will keep our door open to new allies and partners, to new ideas and approaches. We will derive inspiration from the enduring principles that brought our predecessors together at this century's midpoint. And we will prepare together with vigor and determination for the challenges of the next.

Questions

How does Albright use this speech to argue for a different interpretation of Article V?
What is the meaning of the quote from Walter Lippmann, in the context of NATO and
   transatlantic relations?

Reference

https://1997-2001.state.gov/statements/1998/981208.html

Document 17

Prime Minister Tony Blair, "Doctrine of the International Community," Speech to the Economic Club, Chicago, 24 April 1999

Tony Blair had been elected British prime minister in 1997 with an agenda for change after 18 years of Conservative party rule. A professed pro-European who was keen to revitalize Britain's relationship with the EU, Blair would gradually move closer to the United States in an effort to maintain a US-European alignment on strategic thinking. The right to militarily intervene in other states on the basis of humanitarian principles was a major topic of debate in the post-Cold War 1990s, changing the dynamics of a state system that had up till then placed state sovereignty as the central element of international law. Given at the time of NATO's Operation Allied Force bombing of Serbian targets in Kosovo and other locations, an operation that had not received a UN mandate, Blair delivered an argument in favour of overruling non-interference in circumstances of humanitarian crisis. For this reason Blair described the Kosovo operation, strictly speaking, as illegal but not illegitimate: it lacked a UN mandate, but it was a legitimate response to an immediate human tragedy. Blair's speech in Chicago was a sweeping appraisal of global affairs, in particular arguing that global interdependence was requiring "new rules for international co-operation and new ways of organizing our international institutions … global financial markets, the global environment, global security and disarmament issues: none of these can be solved without intense international co-operation." Blair also took the opportunity to pitch the Third Way and unite his Labour party with the Democrats in the US around an agenda "that is neither old left nor 1980s right" (see Part I Document 19).

[This is an excerpt from the full document]

International Security

The principles of international community apply also to international security.

We now have a decade of experience since the end of the Cold War. It has certainly been a less easy time than many hoped in the euphoria that followed the collapse of the Berlin Wall. Our armed forces have been busier than ever – delivering humanitarian aid, deterring attacks on defenceless people, backing up UN resolutions and occasionally engaging in major wars as we did in the Gulf in 1991 and are currently doing in the Balkans.

Have the difficulties of the past decade simply been the aftershocks of the end of the Cold War? Will things soon settle down, or does it represent a pattern that will extend into the future?

Many of our problems have been caused by two dangerous and ruthless men – Saddam Hussein and Slobodan Milosevic. Both have been prepared to wage vicious campaigns against sections of their own community. As a result of these destructive policies both have brought calamity on their own peoples. Instead of enjoying its oil wealth Iraq has

DOI: 10.4324/9781003159551-19

been reduced to poverty, with political life stultified through fear. Milosevic took over a substantial, ethnically diverse state, well placed to take advantage of new economic opportunities. His drive for ethnic concentration has left him with something much smaller, a ruined economy and soon a totally ruined military machine.

One of the reasons why it is now so important to win the conflict is to ensure that others do not make the same mistake in the future. That in itself will be a major step to ensuring that the next decade and the next century will not be as difficult as the past. If NATO fails in Kosovo, the next dictator to be threatened with military force may well not believe our resolve to carry the threat through.

At the end of this century the US has emerged as by far the strongest state. It has no dreams of world conquest and is not seeking colonies. If anything Americans are too ready to see no need to get involved in affairs of the rest of the world. America's allies are always both relieved and gratified by its continuing readiness to shoulder burdens and responsibilities that come with its sole superpower status. We understand that this is something that we have no right to take for granted, and must match with our own efforts. That is the basis for the recent initiative I took with President Chirac of France to improve Europe's own defence capabilities.

As we address these problems at this weekend's NATO Summit we may be tempted to think back to the clarity and simplicity of the Cold War. But now we have to establish a new framework. No longer is our existence as states under threat. Now our actions are guided by a more subtle blend of mutual self interest and moral purpose in defending the values we cherish. In the end values and interests merge. If we can establish and spread the values of liberty, the rule of law, human rights and an open society then that is in our national interests too. The spread of our values makes us safer. As John Kennedy put it "Freedom is indivisible and when one man is enslaved who is free?"

The most pressing foreign policy problem we face is to identify the circumstances in which we should get actively involved in other people's conflicts. Non-interference has long been considered an important principle of international order. And it is not one we would want to jettison too readily. One state should not feel it has the right to change the political system of another or foment subversion or seize pieces of territory to which it feels it should have some claim. But the principle of non-interference must be qualified in important respects. Acts of genocide can never be a purely internal matter. When oppression produces massive flows of refugees which unsettle neighbouring countries then they can properly be described as "threats to international peace and security". When regimes are based on minority rule they lose legitimacy – look at South Africa.

Looking around the world there are many regimes that are undemocratic and engaged in barbarous acts. If we wanted to right every wrong that we see in the modern world then we would do little else than intervene in the affairs of other countries. We would not be able to cope. So how do we decide when and whether to intervene. I think we need to bear in mind five major considerations.

First, are we sure of our case? War is an imperfect instrument for righting humanitarian distress; but armed force is sometimes the only means of dealing with dictators. Second, have we exhausted all diplomatic options? We should always give peace every chance, as we have in the case of Kosovo. Third, on the basis of a practical assessment of the situation, are there military operations we can sensibly and prudently undertake? Fourth, are we prepared for the long term? In the past we talked too much of exit strategies. But having made a commitment we cannot simply walk away once the fight is over; better to stay with moderate numbers of troops than return for repeat performances with large numbers. And finally, do we have national interests involved? The mass expulsion of ethnic Albanians from Kosovo demanded the notice of the rest of the world. But it does make a difference that this is taking place in such a combustible part of Europe. I am not suggesting that these are absolute tests. But they are the kind of issues we need to think about in deciding in the future when and whether we will intervene.

Any new rules however will only work if we have reformed international institutions with which to apply them. If we want a world ruled by law and by international co-operation then we have to support the UN as its central pillar. But we need to find a new way to make the UN and its Security Council work if we are not to return to the deadlock that undermined the effectiveness of the Security Council during the Cold War. This should be a task for members of the Permanent Five to consider once the Kosovo conflict is complete.

Questions

What are the main threats to peace in the post-Cold War world, according to Blair?
Are Blair's five considerations for deciding on whether to militarily intervene in another country sufficient?

References

Source: http://www.britishpoliticalspeech.org/speech-archive.htm?speech=279
Permission: Open Government License (OGL)

Document 18

Presentation by Sirkka Hämäläinen, Member of the Executive Board of the European Central Bank, at the meeting of the Institut International d'Etudes Bancaires, Helsinki, 21 May 1999

Achieving economic and monetary union had been an ambition of the European integration process since the 1960s. The European Monetary System, established in 1979, was the first major step towards aligning the value of currencies of member states, and a decade later the president of the EU Commission, Jacques Delors, initiated the next step towards monetary union with the introduction of a single currency. This was then sanctioned in the Treaty on European Union (Maastricht Treaty) in 1992. The introduction of the Euro came in two stages. As of 1 January 1999, the currency could be traded as an accounting unit, and from 1 January 2002 it was introduced as a physical everyday currency. Originally adopted by eleven EU members, Greece joined as the twelfth on 1 January 2001 (as of 2020, 19 of the 27 member states have joined). Member states had to satisfy strict criteria on national debt levels (no more than 60% of GDP) and annual budget deficits (no more than 3%), but the need for a solid block of European states meant that Italy and Greece were granted access even though it was fairly apparent that their economies did not meet the targets. Hence, political interests ultimately outweighed economic calculations. The Euro marked a whole new level of structural integration for the EU, with participating nations losing control over monetary policy (the ability to set interest rates and currency exchange rates) to the European Central Bank (ECB). Critics at the time focused on the wide economic disparities between the Euro's members, which could lead to dysfunctional consequences due to the ECB setting the same interest rate for very different national economic systems. The Euro was also seen by some as a direct challenge to the US\$ as the world's number one reserve currency. This was combined with American fears of a protectionist "Fortress Europe" (prevalent in the 1980s) creating the impression of an EU bent on challenging US economic and financial power. However, as of 2020 the Euro had never gone above 25% in terms of its share of global foreign exchange reserves. Hämäläinen's speech reflects the guarded optimism of 1999, that the Euro would herald a new phase of market integration and prosperity across Europe.

[This is an excerpt from the full document]

It is a great pleasure and honour for me to have been invited here today to say a few words about the birth of the new European currency – the euro.

On 1 January 1999, eleven European countries took a historical step forwards by entering Stage Three of Economic and Monetary Union. Thereby, the national currencies of these eleven countries became denominations of a single currency. At the same time, the "Eurosystem" (which is composed of the European Central Bank (ECB) and the eleven national central banks of the participating Member States) assumed responsibility for the monetary policy of the euro area.

In hindsight, I think we can say that the technical change over to the euro was a tremendous success. Taking into account the monumental task of more or less simultaneously

DOI: 10.4324/9781003159551-20

implementing changes in thousands of computer programs and operational procedures throughout the financial markets, it is astonishing that we experienced only minor teething problems; and these problems seem to have been corrected in the meantime. The successful technical launch of the euro was made possible thanks to the careful preparations of the project. It also showed that all participants (i.e. the ECB, the national central banks, public authorities and, above all, banks and other financial institutions) were committed to the project and that they carried out their preparations in a professional manner.

However, the changeover to the euro has not yet been completed. The euro still exists only in non-tangible form, i.e. in the form of book entries in information systems. The absence of euro coins and banknotes may have implied that the introduction of the new currency was perceived by most people as a rather abstract event.

The national banknotes and coins will remain in circulation until the euro banknotes and coins are introduced in 2002. This "second" changeover will likewise require substantial preparations. Apart from the one-off large-scale printing of banknotes and minting of coins, it will also require important changes for the handling of cash in the retail sector, e.g. the adaptation of teller and vending machines. I am convinced that all the parties involved will execute this "second" changeover just as professionally as the "first" changeover at the beginning of this year.

Clearly, the launch of the euro was a truly historical event, not only in view of the complexity of the task and its careful preparations, but mainly in that it would have far-reaching economic and political consequences for the participating countries and for the international monetary system as a whole. Most of these consequences are of a gradual and long-term nature.

The euro will have important consequences at many different levels:

- first, we should not forget that the idea of introducing a single currency was originally motivated by the overall political arguments that an increased integration of the European countries would reduce the risk of war and crises on the continent. Through the establishment of common institutions, political conflicts could be avoided or, at least, resolved through discussion and compromise, rather than by resorting to force. Hence, at a general level, the introduction of a single currency in the euro area is an important symbol for political and social integration in Europe which should serve as a catalyst for further co-ordination and integration also in other policy areas;
- second, on a macroeconomic level, a single monetary policy in the euro area which is firmly geared towards price stability will enhance political and economic stability, not only in the euro area, but also in a global context;
- third, on a microeconomic level, the use of the same currency in the euro area will increase cross-border competition and market integration, thereby improving the efficiency of the markets for goods, services and capital in the participating countries. This should lead to reduced transactions costs, improved price transparency and lower price pressures.

Concluding remarks

I should like to conclude by underlining once more that, although it is too early to make a firm assessment of the long-term success of the euro and its role in the international monetary system, it is beyond any doubt that the euro will further strengthen its role as one of the world's leading currencies.

In addition to its economic impact, Economic and Monetary Union has and will continue to have an immense psychological and political impact at the global level. Europe may have been perceived – especially from outside – as excessively inward-looking throughout this period. But the construction of strong institutions for a common Europe has been and will continue to be necessary before Europe will be ready to assume its share of the responsibility for and play its role in the resolution of global problems.

The sheer size of the euro area in the world economy as well as the institutional set up of the Eurosystem, ensuring a firm commitment to price stability, are important factors determining the international role of the euro. However, the long-term success of the euro also depends crucially on the determination of governments to maintain fiscal discipline and undertake necessary structural reforms. It also depends on the ability of the private sector, and not least the financial services industry, to respond to the demands of the new environment by improving competitiveness and foster innovation. In this respect, the experience gained after the first five months of the new currency is very encouraging. The successful technical implementation of the euro, the rapid establishment of a fully integrated money market in the euro area and the on-going developments in the euro area capital markets seem to indicate a high degree of preparedness by the banking system to meet the challenges of the new environment.

Questions

Do you think it is essential for the EU, as a single economic unit, to have its own single currency?

Why did some in the United States argue against the Euro?

Reference

https://www.ecb.europa.eu/press/key/date/1999/html/sp990521.en.html

Document 19

Tony Blair and Gerhard Schroeder, Europe: The Third Way/Die Neue Mitte, 19 August 1999

In the late 1990s the turn to social democratic parties in Britain, Germany, the Netherlands, and the United States led to talk of a Third Way that could combine the principles of social justice and equality with an acceptance of the realities of economic and financial globaliza-tion. This turned away from established social democratic platforms, such as the use of state mechanisms to nationalize industries and redistribute wealth through progressive taxation, to instead embrace market forces as drivers of egalitarian growth. At the G7 meeting in Denver in June 1997, Dutch premier Wim Kok was asked by President Clinton to explain his imple-mentation of the Third Way in the Netherlands. Two years later, Labour's Tony Blair (Prime Minister 1997–2007) and the Sozialdemokratische Partei Deutschlands' (SDP) Gerhard Schroeder (Chancellor 1998–2005) produced a document that laid out their common vision for reforming their respective societies. Blair had led a campaign to reform the Labour party away from its socialist roots, winning a debate in 1997 to amend the clause in its constitution that committed the party to large-scale state ownership of major industries and services. For a while the pro-globalisation moderate left held the political high ground in the transatlantic region, but this unity of purpose would be broken up by first the effects of 9/11 and then, from 2008, the financial crisis.

[This is an excerpt from the full document]

Introduction

Social democrats are in government in almost all the countries of the Union. Social de-mocracy has found new acceptance – but only because, while retaining its traditional values, it has begun in a credible way to renew its ideas and modernise its programmes. It has also found new acceptance because it stands not only for social justice but also for economic dynamism and the unleashing of creativity and innovation.

The trademark of this approach is the New Centre in Germany and the Third Way in the United Kingdom. Other social democrats choose other terms that suit their own na-tional cultures. But though the language and the institutions may differ, the motivation is everywhere the same. Most people have long since abandoned the world view represented by the dogmas of left and right. Social democrats must be able to speak to those people.

Fairness and social justice, liberty and equality of opportunity, solidarity and responsi-bility to others – these values are timeless. Social democracy will never sacrifice them. To make these values relevant to today's world requires realistic and forward-looking policies capable of meeting the challenges of the 21st century. Modernisation is about adapting to conditions that have objectively changed, and not reacting to polls.

Similarly, we need to apply our politics within a new economic framework, modernised for today, where government does all it can to support enterprise but never believes it is

DOI: 10.4324/9781003159551-21

a substitute for enterprise. The essential function of markets must be complemented and improved by political action, not hampered by it. We support a market economy, not a market society.

We share a common destiny within the European Union. We face the same challenges – to promote employment and prosperity, to offer every individual the opportunity to fulfil their unique potential, to combat social exclusion and poverty, to reconcile material progress with environmental sustainability and our responsibility to future generations, to tackle common problems that threaten the cohesion of society such as crime and drugs, and to make Europe a more effective force for good in the world.

We need to strengthen our policies by benchmarking our experiences in Britain and Germany, but also with like-minded counterparts in Europe and the rest of the world. We must learn from each other and measure our own performance against best practice and experience in other countries. With this appeal, we invite other European social democratic governments who share our modernising aims to join us in this enterprise.

Adaptability and flexibility are at an increasing premium in the knowledge-based service economy of the future

Our economies are in transition – from industrial production to the knowledge-based service economy of the future. Social democrats must seize the opportunity of this radical economic change. It offers Europe a chance to catch up with the United States. It offers millions of our people the chance to find new jobs, learn new skills, pursue new careers, set up and expand new businesses – in summary, to realise their hopes of a better future.

But social democrats have to recognise that the basic requirements for economic success have changed. Services cannot be kept in stock: customers use them as and when they are needed – at many different times of day, outside what people think of as normal working hours. The rapid advance of the information age, especially the huge potential of electronic commerce, promises to change radically the way we shop, the way we learn, the way we communicate and the way we relax. Rigidity and over-regulation hamper our success in the knowledge-based service economy of the future. They will hold back the potential of innovation to generate new growth and more jobs. We need to become more flexible, not less.

Questions

Why was it necessary to revise and revive the political programme of the Left after the end of the Cold War?

Do you think it is possible for the Left to promote both 'social justice' and 'economic dynamism'?

References

https://library.fes.de/pdf-files/bueros/suedafrika/02828.pdf
Permission: Friedrich Ebert Stiftung South Africa

Document 20

Secretary of Defense William Cohen, Transcript of Press Conference, NATO Headquarters, 2 December 1999

By the late 1990s there were gaps opening up in conceptions of the transatlantic security relationship, in particular related to threat perception and the capabilities gap between the military apparatuses of the US and European NATO members. These concerns centred on two issues: the post-Maastricht development of a European Security and Defence Identity within NATO, and the US ambitions for National Missile Defence (NMD). The latter referred to US ambitions to construct a defence system that could withstand an incoming missile attack, something that would have major implications regarding the ability of the US to act internationally in the knowledge that it was not vulnerable to certain kinds of threat. NMD developed as a scaled-down version of the Strategic Defense Initiative (SDI) of the 1980s, which had foreseen using multiple space-based platforms to prevent a large-scale Intercontinental Ballistic Missile attack. In contrast, NMD represented reduced ambitions, being able to prevent only a limited missile attack. In this sense it was less relevant in terms of US relations with a nuclear power such as Russia or even China, but more relevant in terms of North Korea or, potentially, Iran. Nevertheless, NMD was seen as undermining the shared security interests of the US and Europe, possibly separating the "protected" from the "unprotected" within NATO and changing the context of the US "security umbrella" over Europe. In particular, the development of NMD placed existing US commitments to the Anti-Ballistic Missile (ABM) Treaty (1972) and the Strategic Arms Reduction Talks (START) in doubt, creating the impression that the US could increasingly act alone against adversaries because of its extra level of protection from attack. In this press conference, held in the wake of NATO's bombing campaign against Serbia earlier that year, Secretary of Defense Cohen still presents a picture of a trouble-free alliance, able to accommodate change, in the face of searching questions from journalists. Eight years later, in 2007, the decision of the George W. Bush administration to site missile defence bases in Poland and the Czech Republic met with severe criticism from Russia's Vladimir Putin, who claimed that this upset the basic agreements that had led to military de-escalation in Europe at the end of the Cold War. The decision was reversed by President Obama in 2009, who instead transferred missile defence systems to US Navy warships.

[This is an excerpt from the full press conference]

Secretary Cohen: This meeting is taking place at a very important time, as we review the lessons of Operation Allied Force. Allies on both sides of the Atlantic recognize that we need new capabilities for a new century.

In his first defense ministers' meeting as Secretary General, George Robertson stressed that all members of the Alliance must do more to improve NATO's strength. European Allies are recognizing this as they prepare for the European Council meeting in Helsinki.

At their recent summits, leaders of the U.K., France, and Germany agreed to work together to build forces that are more able to deploy more quickly and fight more effectively

DOI: 10.4324/9781003159551-22

for longer periods of time. The United States is taking similar action by making our forces more deployable and by purchasing new and better precision munitions. European leaders also agreed to avoid duplication as they work to improve their defenses and these are important commitments and it is important that everyone realizes that the need turn promises into performance.

A stronger Europe means a stronger Alliance, and a stronger Alliance is able to deter the threats and maintain peace and stability.

Let me entertain your questions.

Q: I realize that President Clinton has made no decision yet on ballistic missile defense. If the United States decides that it is in its national interest to do this, would you put the ABM treaty aside and put the START treaties at risk in order to build a missile defense?

SECRETARY COHEN: First, as you indicated, no decision has been made. Secondly, I should indicate that only one person could make the recommendation, and that is the President of the United States. Third, I would also indicate what George Robertson most recently stated here at this podium – that no decision will be made until next year. At that time, the President will consider many factors: the technological aspects of the NMD, questions about our relations with the Russians, questions about the importance of consulting with our allies and their opinions and taking it all into account, as well at the threat that has been emerging. So, those factors will all be taken into account by the President before he makes a decision. I did take the occasion today to lay out the architecture of what an NMD would look like, should the President decide to go forward. But I think it is very much premature to speculate what will happen next year.

Q: Secretary Cohen, given the European Allies questions about the U.S. plans for possible missile defense; given the discussion about creating a separate European crisis response force; do you see a trend in which increasingly the United States, Europe, and NATO are going their separate ways? Do you think any of these stress points weaken the Alliance in any way?

SECRETARY COHEN: As Secretary Robertson just indicated to all of you, the NATO Alliance has never been stronger. This was a very positive meeting today where we had a full range of discussions and we will have these discussions continue tomorrow. This is precisely what nineteen democracies should do. We should raise issues of mutual concern; we should discuss them, debate them if necessary and ultimately resolve them. That is the essence of a democratic system. That is precisely what we have here, nineteen democracies that treasure the ability to engage in this kind of free and open debate and discussion. I would say to the contrary, that the Alliance is strong today, and by virtue of the kind of openness that we have and under leadership of Secretary Robertson, that will only strengthen the future. So I see no cracks as such developing in the institution.

The issue has come up as far as ESDI, the European Security Defense Identity. For many years, members of Congress have been asking Europeans to assume a greater share of the burden. That is precisely what is involved with ESDI: to strengthen a European pillar of the NATO Alliance. We welcome this, and as long as it is understood – as Secretary General Robertson outlined to you – that this is done within the context of having a European capability that will strengthen NATO itself, there is no ground for this speculation that somehow, this is leading to a division between Europe and the United States.

Q: Have you been satisfied today that the Europeans indeed will see their European defense pillar as being squarely in the framework of the Alliance? Have the other Non-EU

NATO members been satisfied and do you have any expectations of what the Helsinki EU Summit should do on that next week?

SECRETARY COHEN: I think that all the members really are committed to the Defense Capability Initiative. The point that George Robertson and I have made separately and together is that the initiative undertaken pursuant to ESDI should and must be compatible with the objectives of the defense capability initiative: In other words mobility, flexibility, command control, communications that are secure, effective engagement and sustainability. Those are the key and core elements of the Defense Capabilities Initiative. They also should be the core elements of any ESDI, so that the two are compatible. You would not want to see the development of a separate capability, which is not compatibility [sic] with the NATO capability. So everyone, as far as the defense ministers are concerned, fully understands that proposition and endorses it. With respect to the non-EU members, I believe they are satisfied that their concerns and participation will be taken into account in any ESDI formulation. This is something that is very important to the non-EU members of NATO, and I believe that the formulation that was adopted today will satisfy their concerns.

Q: Concerning this NMD, has there been a positive reaction of the European Allies to this idea? Are they interested in being involved in this initiative?

SECRETARY COHEN: There were several members who spoke positively about the nature of the threat that is growing and about the need to have some limited capability, but it is by no means a consensus within the Alliance. I think that the more information that is shared, and it was very helpful today to have that information presented to the members, that they will evaluate their own needs. It would be my own recommendation that the European members of NATO look very closely at it so that they can make a judgment and evaluation as to whether the threat that is emerging places their own population at risk, which cannot be satisfied in terms of just having a deterrent capacity, but rather having some limited capability within the NATO Alliance itself. It is something that they will look at and we will discuss in the coming year or so, as this concept is being refined. I think it was helpful today. I think they appreciated having an explanation from me, in terms of the threat, and the type of response that we would propose.

Again, this is something that is of a very limited nature. It is designed to deal with rogue states. It is not directed against the Russians, or others, and it would not undercut the Russian strategic deterrent. This is something that we must make very clear. The Russians have many thousands of nuclear weapons, which they are trying to reduce in START II and, hopefully, going into START III. This would in no way undercut that strategic deterrent and capability they have. That is really the essence of what I tried to lay out for the members today.

Questions

Was Russia correct in protesting so strongly against the placement of NMD systems in Europe?

Why did missile defence threaten to open up major differences in threat perception between the United States and Europe?

Reference

https://www.nato.int/docu/speech/1999/s991202b.htm

Document 21
NATO Strategic Concept, April 1999

In 1999 NATO issued a new Strategic Concept, coinciding with the alliance's fiftieth anniversary. The document was produced at a crucial time for NATO. Operation Allied Force (or Noble Anvil in the United States), aimed at forcing the end of Serbian military operations in Kosovo, had been taking place from March through June, and it had not been sanctioned by a UN resolution. As a result, NATO had entered uncharted waters as a security organization, bypassing the likely veto of Russia and China in the UN Security Council in order to act against Serb military aggression. The Strategic Concept had been approved at the North Atlantic Council meeting in April, while the bombing was going on. More than its predecessor, this document recognized an expanded interpretation of security that took into account political, economic, social, and environmental factors. New threats emerging since the end of the Cold War included terrorism, ethnic conflict, human rights abuses, political instability and economic collapse, alongside more traditional threats. Crisis management was now one of the central tasks of the alliance, calling for multi-functional military forces that could be deployed in unconventional settings for the sake of enforcing peace. The Concept also addressed directly the developments in defence and security coordination at the EU level, and the forging of a European Security and Defence Identity within NATO, requiring close coordination with the EU's CFSP partner, the Western European Union (WEU). At the time the Concept seemed to herald a confident alliance that was adapting to changing circumstances and that, with the experience of Operation Allied Force behind it, was able to act decisively in the interests of humanitarian interests even when formal back-up from the UN was not present. However, by expanding the understanding of security and related threats, it also raised expectations as to NATO's capabilities, especially when there continued to be a major gap in military infrastructures between the US and most of its European allies. This was generating frustration on the American side that would emerge strongly soon after 9/11, leading to the forging of a "Coalition of the Willing" with selected NATO members to invade Iraq in 2003.

[This is an excerpt from the full document]

Part II – Strategic Perspectives

Security challenges and risks

Notwithstanding positive developments in the strategic environment and the fact that large-scale conventional aggression against the Alliance is highly unlikely, the possibility of such a threat emerging over the longer term exists. The security of the Alliance remains subject to a wide variety of military and non-military risks which are multi-directional and often difficult to predict. These risks include uncertainty and instability in and

DOI: 10.4324/9781003159551-23

around the Euro-Atlantic area and the possibility of regional crises at the periphery of the Alliance, which could evolve rapidly. Some countries in and around the Euro-Atlantic area face serious economic, social and political difficulties. Ethnic and religious rivalries, territorial disputes, inadequate or failed efforts at reform, the abuse of human rights, and the dissolution of states can lead to local and even regional instability. The resulting tensions could lead to crises affecting Euro-Atlantic stability, to human suffering, and to armed conflicts. Such conflicts could affect the security of the Alliance by spilling over into neighbouring countries, including NATO countries, or in other ways, and could also affect the security of other states.

The existence of powerful nuclear forces outside the Alliance also constitutes a significant factor which the Alliance has to take into account if security and stability in the Euro-Atlantic area are to be maintained.

The proliferation of NBC weapons [Nuclear, Biological, and Chemical] and their means of delivery remains a matter of serious concern. In spite of welcome progress in strengthening international non-proliferation regimes, major challenges with respect to proliferation remain. The Alliance recognises that proliferation can occur despite efforts to prevent it and can pose a direct military threat to the Allies' populations, territory, and forces. Some states, including on NATO's periphery and in other regions, sell or acquire or try to acquire NBC weapons and delivery means. Commodities and technology that could be used to build these weapons of mass destruction and their delivery means are becoming more common, while detection and prevention of illicit trade in these materials and know-how continues to be difficult. Non-state actors have shown the potential to create and use some of these weapons.

The global spread of technology that can be of use in the production of weapons may result in the greater availability of sophisticated military capabilities, permitting adversaries to acquire highly capable offensive and defensive air, land, and sea-borne systems, cruise missiles, and other advanced weaponry. In addition, state and non-state adversaries may try to exploit the Alliance's growing reliance on information systems through information operations designed to disrupt such systems. They may attempt to use strategies of this kind to counter NATO's superiority in traditional weaponry.

Any armed attack on the territory of the Allies, from whatever direction, would be covered by Articles 5 and 6 of the Washington Treaty. However, Alliance security must also take account of the global context. Alliance security interests can be affected by other risks of a wider nature, including acts of terrorism, sabotage and organised crime, and by the disruption of the flow of vital resources. The uncontrolled movement of large numbers of people, particularly as a consequence of armed conflicts, can also pose problems for security and stability affecting the Alliance. Arrangements exist within the Alliance for consultation among the Allies under Article 4 of the Washington Treaty and, where appropriate, co-ordination of their efforts including their responses to risks of this kind.

Part III – The Approach to Security in the 21st Century

The Alliance is committed to a broad approach to security, which recognises the importance of political, economic, social and environmental factors in addition to the indispensable defence dimension. This broad approach forms the basis for the Alliance to accomplish its fundamental security tasks effectively, and its increasing effort to develop effective cooperation with other European and Euro-Atlantic organisations as well as the United Nations. Our collective aim is to build a European security architecture in which the Alliance's contribution to the security and stability of the Euro-Atlantic area and the contribution of these other international organisations are complementary and mutually reinforcing, both in deepening relations among Euro-Atlantic countries and in managing crises. NATO remains the essential forum for consultation among the Allies and the forum for agreement on policies bearing on the security and defence commitments of its members under the Washington Treaty.

The Alliance seeks to preserve peace and to reinforce Euro-Atlantic security and stability by: the preservation of the transatlantic link; the maintenance of effective military capabilities sufficient for deterrence and defence and to fulfil the full range of its missions; the development of the European Security and Defence Identity within the Alliance; an overall capability to manage crises successfully; its continued openness to new members; and the continued pursuit of partnership, cooperation, and dialogue with other nations as part of its co-operative approach to Euro-Atlantic security, including in the field of arms control and disarmament.

The Transatlantic Link

NATO is committed to a strong and dynamic partnership between Europe and North America in support of the values and interests they share. The security of Europe and that of North America are indivisible. Thus the Alliance's commitment to the indispensable transatlantic link and the collective defence of its members is fundamental to its credibility and to the security and stability of the Euro-Atlantic area.

The European Security And Defence Identity

The Alliance, which is the foundation of the collective defence of its members and through which common security objectives will be pursued wherever possible, remains committed to a balanced and dynamic transatlantic partnership. The European Allies have taken decisions to enable them to assume greater responsibilities in the security and defence field in order to enhance the peace and stability of the Euro-Atlantic area and thus the security of all Allies. On the basis of decisions taken by the Alliance, in Berlin in 1996 and subsequently, the European Security and Defence Identity will continue to be developed within NATO. This process will require close cooperation between NATO, the WEU and, if and when appropriate, the European Union. It will enable all European Allies to make a more coherent and effective contribution to the missions and activities of the Alliance as an expression of our shared responsibilities; it will reinforce the transatlantic partnership; and it will assist the European Allies to act by themselves as required through the readiness of the Alliance, on a case-by-case basis and by consensus, to make its assets and capabilities available for operations in which the Alliance is not engaged militarily under the political control and strategic direction either of the WEU or as otherwise agreed, taking into account the full participation of all European Allies if they were so to choose.

Questions

Why is there so much emphasis on building up a "European security architecture"?
In what ways does this Strategic Concept indicate that NATO is aiming to become a "global security provider"?

Reference

https://www.nato.int/cps/en/natolive/official_texts_27433.htm

Part II
2000–2010: divergence?

Document 1

Statement by NATO Secretary General, Lord Robertson, 12 September 2001 (NATO Article 5 invoked)

Article 5 of the Washington Treaty (April 1949) was invoked for the first time in NATO's history on 12 September 2001 after the attacks on New York and Washington, DC on "9/11". Canada and the European allies insisted on offering assistance to the US, and the administration of President George W. Bush quickly welcomed the gesture. For the Europeans it was foremost an act of (political) solidarity. Few military capabilities were on offer (or accepted by the US for that matter). The most visible contribution consisted of five NATO AWACS surveillance aircraft for patrolling US airspace.

Two weeks after NATO invoked Article 5, the US announced its post-"9/11" doctrine that "the mission determines the coalition", devaluing the status of permanent alliances, NATO included. This communication annoyed the European allies and illustrated the Bush administration's scepticism towards multilateral institutions. The indifference of America's top officials contributed to a sense of political uncertainty within Europe. The ensuing "Global War on Terror" would have long-lasting consequences for NATO, including its largest ever military operation (ISAF) in Afghanistan under UN auspices (see Document 21).

Strictly speaking, there is no formal procedure at hand to revoke Article 5, which means the decision continues to stand.

[This is an excerpt from the full document, which was updated on 2 October 2001]

This morning, the United States briefed the North Atlantic Council on the results of the investigation into who was responsible for the horrific terrorist attacks which took place on 11 September. The briefing was given by Ambassador Frank Taylor, the United States Department of State Coordinator for Counter-terrorism.

This morning's briefing follows those offered by United States Deputy Secretary of State Richard Armitage and United States Deputy Secretary of Defense Paul Wolfowitz, and illustrates the commitment of the United States to maintain close cooperation with Allies. Today's was classified briefing and so I cannot give you all the details. Briefings are also being given directly by the United States to the Allies in their capitals. The briefing addressed the events of 11 September themselves, the results of the investigation so far, what is known about Osama bin Laden and the Al-Qaida organisation and their involvement in the attacks and in previous terrorist activity, and the links between Al-Qaida and the Taliban regime in Afghanistan. The facts are clear and compelling. The information presented points conclusively to an Al-Qaida role in the 11 September attacks.

We know that the individuals who carried out these attacks were part of the world-wide terrorist network of Al-Qaida, headed by Osama bin Laden and his key lieutenants and protected by the Taliban. On the basis of this briefing, it has now been determined that the attack against the United States on 11 September was directed from abroad and shall therefore be regarded as an action covered by Article 5 of the Washington Treaty, which

DOI: 10.4324/9781003159551-25

states that an armed attack on one or more of the Allies in Europe or North America shall be considered an attack against them all. I want to reiterate that the United States of America can rely on the full support of its 18 NATO Allies in the campaign against terrorism.

Questions

What does Article 5 of the Treaty of Washington (1949) actually say about collective defence?

Do you think NATO is the right organization to fight terrorism? Why or why not?

Reference

https://www.nato.int/Referencesu/speech/2001/s011002a.htm

Document 2

George W. Bush, State of the Union Address, 29 January 2002 ("Axis of Evil")

In his first State of the Union Address, four months after "9/11", President George W. Bush emphasized the vigilance and determination of the US to bring the terrorists behind the "9/11" attacks to justice. He called for close cooperation among all nations to fight terrorism and gave a warning to "regimes" threatening America and its allies. He specifically referred to Iraq, North Korea and Iran, which he accused of intending to produce weapons of mass destruction. He warned these three countries – the "axis of evil" – that the US would prevent them from attaining this goal, without being specific about how this would be done. Bush's speech also reflects strongly the influence of neoconservatism, a school of thought that preached not only unchallengeable US dominance in world affairs but also that this dominance was driven by a unique belief system based on freedom and justice. Key members of President Bush's administration followed the neoconservative line, such as Paul Wolfowitz, Elliott Abrams, and Richard Perle, and this speech reflects the general tone of this thinking. Powerful figures in Bush's cabinet such as Defense Secretary Donald Rumsfeld and Vice-President Dick Cheney were more "offensive realists" and less interested in the value-system being promoted, but they shared the neoconservative line that the United States should take hold of the post-9/11 situation and pursue outright dominance in the Middle East. This is one of the rare examples in which foreign policy dominated the subject matter of the annual State of the Union speech.

[This is an excerpt from the full document]

As we gather tonight, our nation is at war, our economy is in recession, and the civilized world faces unprecedented dangers. Yet the state of our Union has never been stronger. What we have found in Afghanistan confirms that, far from ending there, our war against terror is only beginning. Most of the 19 men who hijacked planes on September the 11th were trained in Afghanistan's camps, and so were tens of thousands of others. Thousands of dangerous killers, schooled in the methods of murder, often supported by outlaw regimes, are now spread throughout the world like ticking time bombs, set to go off without warning. My hope is that all nations will heed our call, and eliminate the terrorist parasites who threaten their countries and our own. Many nations are acting forcefully. But some governments will be timid in the face of terror. And make no mistake about it: If they do not act, America will.

Our second goal is to prevent regimes that sponsor terror from threatening America or our friends and allies with weapons of mass destruction. Some of these regimes have been pretty quiet since September the 11th. But we know their true nature. North Korea is a regime arming with missiles and weapons of mass destruction, while starving its citizens. Iran aggressively pursues these weapons and exports terror, while an unelected few repress the Iranian people's hope for freedom. Iraq continues to flaunt its hostility toward America and to support terror. The Iraqi regime has plotted to develop anthrax,

DOI: 10.4324/9781003159551-26

and nerve gas, and nuclear weapons for over a decade. States like these, and their terrorist allies, constitute an axis of evil, arming to threaten the peace of the world. By seeking weapons of mass destruction, these regimes pose a grave and growing danger. They could provide these arms to terrorists, giving them the means to match their hatred. They could attack our allies or attempt to blackmail the United States. In any of these cases, the price of indifference would be catastrophic. America will lead by defending liberty and justice, because they are right and true and unchanging for all people everywhere. No nation owns these aspirations, and no nation is exempt from them. We have no intention of imposing our culture, but America will always stand firm for the nonnegotiable demands of human dignity, the rule of law, limits on the power of the state, respect for women, private property, free speech, equal justice, and religious tolerance. We choose freedom and the dignity of every life. We have sown freedom's power. And in this great conflict, we will see freedom's victory.

Questions

Who do you think is the intended audience of this speech?
Do you think it is rational to pursue international relations based on "good vs. evil"?

Reference

https://georgewbush-whitehouse.archives.gov/news/releases/2002/01/20020129-11.html

Document 3

President George W. Bush, Graduation Speech at West Point, NY, 1 June 2002 ("Bush Doctrine")

The development of the Bush Doctrine cannot be separated from the influence of the neocon-servative school of thought among members of the Bush administration. Neoconservatism arose in the 1970s among intellectuals and politicians who were fiercely opposed to com-munism and detested the rise of liberal values in US society during the 1960s and 1970s. One of the tenets of this school held that the US was ideologically at war with enemy states, and that this required a resolute response, including the need for unilateral action should it be necessary. Connected to this was the belief that the US had the capability and the legitimate mission to promote democratic values worldwide, ideally ushering in a long-term post-Cold War world order under US tutelage (see Part I Document 7). Based on this approach, the Bush administration withdrew in 2001 from the Anti-Ballistic Missile Treaty (ABM), one of the foundations of détente between the US and the Soviet Union during the Cold War. Bush also withdrew from the Kyoto Protocol (1997), aimed at securing international agreement on reductions in greenhouse gas emissions (see Part I Document 14). Another element of the Bush Doctrine (actually coined by American political scientist Charles Krauthammer and not Bush himself) consisted of the declared right to make use of a military pre-emptive strike against enemy states or groups should they be considered imminent threats (see Part II Docu-ment 5). The "war of choice" in Afghanistan in the wake of "9/11" can be seen as an example of that doctrine. The invasion of Iraq was defended as an extension of this, with the ultimate goal being the end of 'evil dictatorships' and the spread of democracy around the world.

[This is an excerpt from the full document]

In your last year, America was attacked by a ruthless and resourceful enemy. You grad-uate from this Academy in a time of war, taking your place in an American military that is powerful and is honorable. Our war on terror is only begun, but in Afghanistan it was begun well.

The gravest danger to freedom lies at the perilous crossroads of radicalism and tech-nology. When the spread of chemical and biological and nuclear weapons, along with ballistic missile technology – when that occurs, even weak states and small groups could attain a catastrophic power to strike great nations. Our enemies have declared this very intention, and have been caught seeking these terrible weapons. They want the capability to blackmail us, or to harm us, or to harm our friends – and we will oppose them with all our power.

For much of the last century, America's defense relied on the Cold War doctrines of de-terrence and containment. In some cases, those strategies still apply. But new threats also require new thinking. Deterrence – the promise of massive retaliation against nations – means nothing against shadowy terrorist networks with no nation or citizens to defend.

DOI: 10.4324/9781003159551-27

Containment is not possible when unbalanced dictators with weapons of mass destruction can deliver those weapons on missiles or secretly provide them to terrorist allies.

Homeland defense and missile defense are part of stronger security, and they're essential priorities for America. Yet the war on terror will not be won on the defensive. We must take the battle to the enemy, disrupt his plans, and confront the worst threats before they emerge. In the world we have entered, the only path to safety is the path of action. And this nation will act.

Because the war on terror will require resolve and patience, it will also require firm moral purpose. In this way our struggle is similar to the Cold War. Now, as then, our enemies are totalitarians, holding a creed of power with no place for human dignity. Now, as then, they seek to impose a joyless conformity, to control every life and all of life.

America confronted imperial communism in many different ways – diplomatic, economic, and military. Yet moral clarity was essential to our victory in the Cold War. When leaders like John F. Kennedy and Ronald Reagan refused to gloss over the brutality of tyrants, they gave hope to prisoners and dissidents and exiles, and rallied free nations to a great cause.

Some worry that it is somehow undiplomatic or impolite to speak the language of right and wrong. I disagree. Different circumstances require different methods, but not different moralities. Moral truth is the same in every culture, in every time, and in every place. Targeting innocent civilians for murder is always and everywhere wrong. Brutality against women is always and everywhere wrong. There can be no neutrality between justice and cruelty, between the innocent and the guilty. We are in a conflict between good and evil, and America will call evil by its name. By confronting evil and lawless regimes, we do not create a problem, we reveal a problem. And we will lead the world in opposing it.

As we defend the peace, we also have an historic opportunity to preserve the peace. We have our best chance since the rise of the nation state in the 17th century to build a world where the great powers compete in peace instead of prepare for war. The history of the last century, in particular, was dominated by a series of destructive national rivalries that left battlefields and graveyards across the Earth. Germany fought France, the Axis fought the Allies, and then the East fought the West, in proxy wars and tense standoffs, against a backdrop of nuclear Armageddon.

Competition between great nations is inevitable, but armed conflict in our world is not. More and more, civilized nations find ourselves on the same side – united by common dangers of terrorist violence and chaos. America has, and intends to keep, military strengths beyond challenge – thereby, making the destabilizing arms races of other eras pointless, and limiting rivalries to trade and other pursuits of peace.

Today the great powers are also increasingly united by common values, instead of divided by conflicting ideologies. The United States, Japan and our Pacific friends, and now all of Europe, share a deep commitment to human freedom, embodied in strong alliances such as NATO. And the tide of liberty is rising in many other nations.

America stands for more than the absence of war. We have a great opportunity to extend a just peace, by replacing poverty, repression, and resentment around the world with hope of a better day. Through most of history, poverty was persistent, inescapable, and almost universal. In the last few decades, we've seen nations from Chile to South Korea build modern economies and freer societies, lifting millions of people out of despair and want. And there's no mystery to this achievement.

When it comes to the common rights and needs of men and women, there is no clash of civilizations. The requirements of freedom apply fully to Africa and Latin America and the entire Islamic world. The peoples of the Islamic nations want and deserve the same freedoms and opportunities as people in every nation. And their governments should listen to their hopes.

A truly strong nation will permit legal avenues of dissent for all groups that pursue their aspirations without violence. An advancing nation will pursue economic reform, to unleash the great entrepreneurial energy of its people. A thriving nation will respect the rights of women, because no society can prosper while denying opportunity to half its citizens. Mothers and fathers and children across the Islamic world, and all the world, share the same fears and aspirations. In poverty, they struggle. In tyranny, they suffer. And as we saw in Afghanistan, in liberation they celebrate.

On behalf of the nation, I congratulate each one of you for the commission you've earned and for the credit you bring to the United States of America. May God bless you all.

Questions

Which elements of this speech indicate it to be ideological in intent?
Explain what Bush meant with the "clash of civilizations".

Reference

https://georgewbush-whitehouse.archives.gov/news/releases/2002/06/20020601-3.html

Document 4

Rome Statute of the International Criminal Court, 1 July 2002

The establishment of the International Criminal Court (ICC) by the Rome Statute represented a milestone in the history of international law. A tribunal based in The Hague, The Netherlands, the ICC is the only permanent international court with a mandate to prosecute individuals for war crimes, genocide, and crimes against humanity. The ICC is only meant to act in cases where national legal systems are unwilling or unable to undertake prosecution, and it may only act in the case of crimes committed by nationals of signatory states, or crimes referred by the UN Security Council. Following the required 60 ratifications of the Statute on 1 July 2002, the ICC was formally established. By 31 December 2020, 123 states had ratified and so become members. Although first proposed after World War I, it was after World War II, the formation of the United Nations, and the holding of the Nuremburg and Tokyo war crimes trials, that momentum for a permanent court began to build. However, initial proposals in the early 1950s were shelved due to Cold War tensions and the proposal was only revived in the 1990s. On 17 July 1998 the Rome Statute was adopted by the UN General Assembly by a vote of 120–7, with those rejecting it being China, Iraq, Israel, Libya, Qatar, the United States, and Yemen. The arrival of the ICC opened up a major divide in the field of international law between the United States and Europe. The US has maintained its opposition to the idea of any form of international law above the state, and this stance was strengthened due to concerns about actions by US military personnel in the wars in Afghanistan and Iraq. In August 2002 President Bush signed into law the American Servicemembers Protection Act, which controversially authorised military force to free any citizen of the US or US-allied nation being held by the ICC, and which subsequently became dubbed the "Hague Invasion Act". Although President Obama expressed the wish to seek "positive engagement" with the court, the Trump administration threatened prosecutions, sanctions, and visa bans in response to any move by the ICC to address alleged crimes by the US military in Afghanistan.

[This is an excerpt from the full document]

Preamble

- The States Parties to this Statute,
- Conscious that all peoples are united by common bonds, their cultures pieced together in a shared heritage, and concerned that this delicate mosaic may be shattered at any time,
- Mindful that during this century millions of children, women and men have been victims of unimaginable atrocities that deeply shock the conscience of humanity,
- Recognizing that such grave crimes threaten the peace, security and well-being of the world,

DOI: 10.4324/9781003159551-28

- Affirming that the most serious crimes of concern to the international community as a whole must not go unpunished and that their effective prosecution must be ensured by taking measures at the national level and by enhancing international cooperation,
- Determined to put an end to impunity for the perpetrators of these crimes and thus to contribute to the prevention of such crimes,
- Recalling that it is the duty of every State to exercise its criminal jurisdiction over those responsible for international crimes,
- Reaffirming the Purposes and Principles of the Charter of the United Nations, and in particular that all States shall refrain from the threat or use of force against the territorial integrity or political independence of any State, or in any other manner inconsistent with the Purposes of the United Nations,
- Emphasizing in this connection that nothing in this Statute shall be taken as authorizing any State Party to intervene in an armed conflict or in the internal affairs of any State,
- Determined to these ends and for the sake of present and future generations, to establish an independent permanent International Criminal Court in relationship with the United Nations system, with jurisdiction over the most serious crimes of concern to the international community as a whole,
- Emphasizing that the International Criminal Court established under this Statute shall be complementary to national criminal jurisdictions,

Resolved to guarantee lasting respect for and the enforcement of international justice,
Have agreed as follows:
    Part 1: Establishment of the Court

Article 1: The Court

An International Criminal Court ("the Court") is hereby established. It shall be a permanent institution and shall have the power to exercise its jurisdiction over persons for the most serious crimes of international concern, as referred to in this Statute, and shall be complementary to national criminal jurisdictions. The jurisdiction and functioning of the Court shall be governed by the provisions of this Statute.

Article 2: Relationship of the Court with the United Nations

The Court shall be brought into relationship with the United Nations through an agreement to be approved by the Assembly of States Parties to this Statute and thereafter concluded by the President of the Court on its behalf.

Article 3: Seat of the Court

1   The seat of the Court shall be established at The Hague in the Netherlands ("the host State").
2   The Court shall enter into a headquarters agreement with the host State, to be approved by the Assembly of States Parties and thereafter concluded by the President of the Court on its behalf.
3   The Court may sit elsewhere, whenever it considers it desirable, as provided in this Statute.

Article 4: Legal status and powers of the Court

1   The Court shall have international legal personality. It shall also have such legal capacity as may be necessary for the exercise of its functions and the fulfilment of its purposes.
2   The Court may exercise its functions and powers, as provided in this Statute, on the territory of any State Party and, by special agreement, on the territory of any other State.

Questions

Do you think the US refusal to acknowledge the ICC represents a fundamental weakening of transatlantic relations?
Is the creation of a court like the ICC a positive development in international relations?

References

http://www.icc-cpi.int/nr/rdonlyres/ea9aeff7-5752-4f84-be94-0a655eb30e16/0/rome_statute_english.pdf
Permission: Public Affairs Unit, ICC

Document 5

The National Security Strategy of the United States of America, September 2002

The National Security Strategy (NSS) of 2002 emphasized prevention, preemption, defence, and other actions to mitigate the security risks in the new security environment after '9/11'. Prevention was needed to deny countries and terrorists access to the technologies of weapons of mass destruction, and preemption was a step further – the declared right to act with force should a threat be deemed imminent. While these features dominated how the NSS was received, it did also make reference to diplomacy, arms control and multilateral export controls as instruments of equal importance for shaping international relations.

The NSS also argued, in line with the prevailing neoconservative political mood, that exporting freedom, democracy, and free enterprise around the world was both a strategic and moral obligation. This mission placed further strain on the transatlantic relationship by indicating that the United States would act without (all of) its European allies, despite the stance that NATO remained central for US security. This became apparent in only six months with the US invasion of Iraq, an act that split Europe between those supporting the US and those opposing it (see Part II Documents 6 and 7). The US tried in vain to engage NATO allies to broaden the legitimacy of the invasion, but the UK, led by Tony Blair, was the only country that answered the request for military support on a large scale. In November 2002, during a NATO summit, Bush used the phrase "coalition of the willing" to describe the US aim to move forward with its Iraq strategy even if there remained serious divisions among its European allies. The phrase came to represent the US desire for a more flexible transatlantic relationship that did not rely on unanimity and did not rely on NATO as the only security option.

[This is an excerpt from the full document]

OVERVIEW OF AMERICA'S INTERNATIONAL STRATEGY

The United States possesses unprecedented— and unequaled—strength and influence in the world. Sustained by faith in the principles of liberty, and the value of a free society, this position comes with unparalleled responsibilities, obligations, and opportunity. The great strength of this nation must be used to promote a balance of power that favors freedom.

For most of the twentieth century, the world was divided by a great struggle over ideas: destructive totalitarian visions versus freedom and equality.

That great struggle is over. The militant visions of class, nation, and race which promised utopia and delivered misery have been defeated and discredited. America is now threatened less by conquering states than we are by failing ones.

We are menaced less by fleets and armies than by catastrophic technologies in the hands of the embittered few. We must defeat these threats to our Nation, allies, and friends.

DOI: 10.4324/9781003159551-29

This is also a time of opportunity for America. We will work to translate this moment of influence into decades of peace, prosperity, and liberty.

The U.S. national security strategy will be based on a distinctly American internationalism that reflects the union of our values and our national interests. The aim of this strategy is to help make the world not just safer but better. Our goals on the path to progress are clear: political and economic freedom, peaceful relations with other states, and respect for human dignity.

And this path is not America's alone. It is open to all. To achieve these goals, the United States will:

- champion aspirations for human dignity;
- strengthen alliances to defeat global terrorism and work to prevent attacks against us and our friends;
- work with others to defuse regional conflicts;
- prevent our enemies from threatening us, our allies, and our friends, with weapons of mass destruction;
- ignite a new era of global economic growth through free markets and free trade;
- transform America's national security institutions to meet the challenges and opportunities of the twenty-first century.
- expand the circle of development by opening societies and building the infrastructure of democracy;
- develop agendas for cooperative action with other main centers of global power; and
- transform America's national security institutions to meet the challenges and opportunities of the twenty-first century. [...]

STRENGTHEN ALLIANCES TO DEFEAT GLOBAL TERRORISM AND WORK TO PREVENT ATTACKS AGAINST US AND OUR FRIENDS

The United States of America is fighting a war against terrorists of global reach. The enemy is not a single political regime or person or religion or ideology. The enemy is terrorism—premeditated, politically motivated violence perpetrated against innocents.

In many regions, legitimate grievances prevent the emergence of a lasting peace. Such grievances deserve to be, and must be, addressed within a political process. But no cause justifies terror. The United States will make no concessions to terrorist demands and strike no deals with them. We make no distinction between terrorists and those who knowingly harbor or provide aid to them.

The struggle against global terrorism is different from any other war in our history. It will be fought on many fronts against a particularly elusive enemy over an extended period of time. Progress will come through the persistent accumulation of successes—some seen, some unseen.

Today our enemies have seen the results of what civilized nations can, and will, do against regimes that harbor, support, and use terrorism to achieve their political goals. Afghanistan has been liberated; coalition forces continue to hunt down the Taliban and al-Qaida. But it is not only this battlefield on which we will engage terrorists. Thousands of trained terrorists remain at large with cells in North America, South America, Europe, Africa, the Middle East, and across Asia.

Our priority will be first to disrupt and destroy terrorist organizations of global reach and attack their leadership; command, control, and communications; material support; and finances. This will have a disabling effect upon the terrorists' ability to plan and operate.

We will continue to encourage our regional partners to take up a coordinated effort that isolates the terrorists. Once the regional campaign localizes the threat to a particular state, we will help ensure the state has the military, law enforcement, political, and financial tools necessary to finish the task.

The United States will continue to work with our allies to disrupt the financing of terrorism. We will identify and block the sources of funding for terrorism, freeze the assets of terrorists and those who support them, deny terrorists access to the international financial system, protect legitimate charities from being abused by terrorists, and prevent the movement of terrorists' assets through alternative financial networks.

However, this campaign need not be sequential to be effective, the cumulative effect across all regions will help achieve the results we seek.

We will disrupt and destroy terrorist organizations by:

- direct and continuous action using all the elements of national and international power. Our immediate focus will be those terrorist organizations of global reach and any terrorist or state sponsor of terrorism which attempts to gain or use weapons of mass destruction (WMD) or their precursors;
- defending the United States, the American people, and our interests at home and abroad by identifying and destroying the threat before it reaches our borders. While the United States will constantly strive to enlist the support of the international community, we will not hesitate to act alone, if necessary, to exercise our right of self-defense by acting preemptively against such terrorists, to prevent them from doing harm against our people and our country; and
- denying further sponsorship, support, and sanctuary to terrorists by convincing or compelling states to accept their sovereign responsibilities.

We will also wage a war of ideas to win the battle against international terrorism. This includes:

- using the full influence of the United States, and working closely with allies and friends, to make clear that all acts of terrorism are illegitimate so that terrorism will be viewed in the same light as slavery, piracy, or genocide: behavior that no respectable government can condone or support and all must oppose;
- supporting moderate and modern government, especially in the Muslim world, to ensure that the conditions and ideologies that promote terrorism do not find fertile ground in any nation;
- diminishing the underlying conditions that spawn terrorism by enlisting the international community to focus its efforts and resources on areas most at risk; and
- using effective public diplomacy to promote the free flow of information and ideas to kindle the hopes and aspirations of freedom of those in societies ruled by the sponsors of global terrorism.

While we recognize that our best defense is a good offense, we are also strengthening America's homeland security to protect against and deter attack.

While our focus is protecting America, we know that to defeat terrorism in today's globalized world we need support from our allies and friends. Wherever possible, the United States will rely on regional organizations and state powers to meet their obligations to fight terrorism. Where governments find the fight against terrorism beyond their capacities, we will match their willpower and their resources with whatever help we and our allies can provide.

In the war against global terrorism, we will never forget that we are ultimately fighting for our democratic values and way of life. Freedom and fear are at war, and there will be no quick or easy end to this conflict. In leading the campaign against terrorism, we are forging new, productive international relationships and redefining existing ones in ways that meet the challenges of the twenty-first century.

PREVENT OUR ENEMIES FROM THREATENING US, OUR ALLIES, AND OUR FRIENDS WITH WEAPONS OF MASS DESTRUCTION

The nature of the Cold War threat required the United States—with our allies and friends—to emphasize deterrence of the enemy's use of force, producing a grim strategy of mutual assured destruction. With the collapse of the Soviet Union and the end of the Cold War, our security environment has undergone profound transformation.

Having moved from confrontation to cooperation as the hallmark of our relationship with Russia, the dividends are evident: an end to the balance of terror that divided us; an historic reduction in the nuclear arsenals on both sides; and cooperation in areas such as counterterrorism and missile defense that until recently were inconceivable. But new deadly challenges have emerged from rogue states and terrorists. None of these contemporary threats rival the sheer destructive power that was arrayed against us by the Soviet Union. However, the nature and motivations of these new adversaries, their determination to obtain destructive powers hitherto available only to the world's strongest states, and the greater likelihood that they will use weapons of mass destruction against us, make today's security environment more complex and dangerous.

At the time of the Gulf War, we acquired irrefutable proof that Iraq's designs were not limited to the chemical weapons it had used against Iran and its own people, but also extended to the acquisition of nuclear weapons and biological agents. In the past decade North Korea has become the world's principal purveyor of ballistic missiles, and has tested increasingly capable missiles while developing its own WMD arsenal. Other rogue regimes seek nuclear, biological, and chemical weapons as well. These states' pursuit of, and global trade in, such weapons has become a looming threat to all nations.

We must be prepared to stop rogue states and their terrorist clients before they are able to threaten or use weapons of mass destruction against the United States and our allies and friends. Our response must take full advantage of strengthened alliances, the establishment of new partnerships with former adversaries, innovation in the use of military forces, modern technologies, including the development of an effective missile defense system, and increased emphasis on intelligence collection and analysis.

Our comprehensive strategy to combat WMD includes:

- *Proactive counterproliferation efforts.* We must deter and defend against the threat before it is unleashed. We must ensure that key capabilities—detection, active and passive defenses, and counterforce capabilities—are integrated into our defense transformation and our homeland security systems.
- *Strengthened nonproliferation efforts to prevent rogue states and terrorists from acquiring the materials, technologies, and expertise necessary for weapons of mass destruction.* We will enhance diplomacy, arms control, multilateral export controls, and threat reduction assistance that impede states and terrorists seeking WMD, and when necessary, interdict enabling technologies and materials. We will continue to build coalitions to support these efforts, encouraging their increased political and financial

support for nonproliferation and threat reduction programs. The recent G-8 agreement to commit up to $20 billion to a global partnership against proliferation marks a major step forward.

- *Effective consequence management to respond to the effects of WMD use, whether by terrorists or hostile states.* Minimizing the effects of WMD use against our people will help deter those who possess such weapons and dissuade those who seek to acquire them by persuading enemies that they cannot attain their desired ends. The United States must also be prepared to respond to the effects of WMD use against our forces abroad, and to help friends and allies if they are attacked.

It has taken almost a decade for us to comprehend the true nature of this new threat. Given the goals of rogue states and terrorists, the United States can no longer solely rely on a reactive posture as we have in the past. The inability to deter a potential attacker, the immediacy of today's threats, and the magnitude of potential harm that could be caused by our adversaries' choice of weapons, do not permit that option. We cannot let our enemies strike first.

For centuries, international law recognized that nations need not suffer an attack before they can lawfully take action to defend themselves against forces that present an imminent danger of attack. Legal scholars and international jurists often conditioned the legitimacy of preemption on the existence of an imminent threat—most often a visible mobilization of armies, navies, and air forces preparing to attack.

We must adapt the concept of imminent threat to the capabilities and objectives of today's adversaries. Rogue states and terrorists do not seek to attack us using conventional means. They know such attacks would fail. Instead, they rely on acts of terror and, potentially, the use of weapons of mass destruction—weapons that can be easily concealed, delivered covertly, and used without warning.

The targets of these attacks are our military forces and our civilian population, in direct violation of one of the principal norms of the law of warfare. As was demonstrated by the losses on September 11, 2001, mass civilian casualties is the specific objective of terrorists and these losses would be exponentially more severe if terrorists acquired and used weapons of mass destruction.

The United States has long maintained the option of preemptive actions to counter a sufficient threat to our national security. The greater the threat, the greater is the risk of inaction—and the more compelling the case for taking anticipatory action to defend ourselves, even if uncertainty remains as to the time and place of the enemy's attack. To forestall or prevent such hostile acts by our adversaries, the United States will, if necessary, act preemptively.

The United States will not use force in all cases to preempt emerging threats, nor should nations use preemption as a pretext for aggression. Yet in an age where the enemies of civilization openly and actively seek the world's most destructive technologies, the United States cannot remain idle while dangers gather.

The purpose of our actions will always be to eliminate a specific threat to the United States or our allies and friends. The reasons for our actions will be clear, the force measured, and the cause just.

DEVELOP AGENDAS FOR COOPERATIVE ACTION WITH THE OTHER MAIN CENTERS OF GLOBAL POWER

America will implement its strategies by organizing coalitions—as broad as practicable—of states able and willing to promote a balance of power that favors freedom. Effective coalition leadership requires clear priorities, an appreciation of others' interests, and consistent consultations among partners with a spirit of humility.

There is little of lasting consequence that the United States can accomplish in the world without the sustained cooperation of its allies and friends in Canada and Europe. Europe is also the seat of two of the strongest and most able international institutions in the world: the North Atlantic Treaty Organization (NATO), which has, since its inception, been the fulcrum of transatlantic and inter-European security, and the European Union (EU), our partner in opening world trade.

The attacks of September 11 were also an attack on NATO, as NATO itself recognized when it invoked its Article V self-defense clause for the first time. NATO's core mission—collective defense of the transatlantic alliance of democracies—remains, but NATO must develop new structures and capabilities to carry out that mission under new circumstances. NATO must build a capability to field, at short notice, highly mobile, specially trained forces whenever they are needed to respond to a threat against any member of the alliance.

The alliance must be able to act wherever our interests are threatened, creating coalitions under NATO's own mandate, as well as contributing to mission-based coalitions. To achieve this, we must:

- expand NATO's membership to those democratic nations willing and able to share the burden of defending and advancing our common interests;
- ensure that the military forces of NATO nations have appropriate combat contributions to make in coalition warfare;
- develop planning processes to enable those contributions to become effective multinational fighting forces;
- take advantage of the technological opportunities and economies of scale in our defense spending to transform NATO military forces so that they dominate potential aggressors and diminish our vulnerabilities;
- streamline and increase the flexibility of command structures to meet new operational demands and the associated requirements of training, integrating, and experimenting with new force configurations; and
- maintain the ability to work and fight together as allies even as we take the necessary steps to transform and modernize our forces.

If NATO succeeds in enacting these changes, the rewards will be a partnership as central to the security and interests of its member states as was the case during the Cold War. We will sustain a common perspective on the threats to our societies and improve our ability to take common action in defense of our nations and their interests. At the same time, we welcome our European allies' efforts to forge a greater foreign policy and defense identity with the EU, and commit ourselves to close consultations to ensure that these developments work with NATO. We cannot afford to lose this opportunity to better prepare the family of transatlantic democracies for the challenges to come.

The events of September 11, 2001, fundamentally changed the context for relations between the United States and other main centers of global power, and opened vast, new opportunities. With our long-standing allies in Europe and Asia, and with leaders in Russia, India, and China, we must develop active agendas of cooperation lest these relationships become routine and unproductive.

Questions

"The NSS of 2002 was as much a threat to Western unity as it was a threat to those regimes that threatened the West". Discuss.

What "specific" transformation of NATO is called for?

Reference

https://georgewbush-whitehouse.archives.gov/nsc/nss/2002/

Document 6

Secretary of Defense Donald Rumsfeld, Press Briefing, 23 January 2003 ("Old and New Europe")

During a briefing at the Foreign Press Center the US Secretary of Defense Donald Rumsfeld answered a question from a Dutch journalist regarding the support from European allies for US aggression towards Saddam Hussein's Iraq. In his answer Rumsfeld famously referred to "old" and "new" Europe. In his view "Old Europe" – predominantly France and Germany – were unwilling to stand up to oppose Saddam Hussein's dictatorship, whereas "New Europe" – mainly the UK, Spain, and NATO's new Central European members – were prepared to join the US in the cause for freedom and justice against an evil and violent regime. Due to his support for democracy promotion across Central and Eastern Europe, President George W. Bush was in general more popular there than in Western Europe, and Rumsfeld argued that this was part of a gravitational shift away from old US allies towards those more in tune with changing US priorities. A strategic divide in Europe regarding Russia – between those who insisted on a "hard" policy that demanded conditions and those favouring a "soft" approach aiming for improved relations – continued through the 2010s onwards. Former satellite states of the Soviet Union tend to be less politically accommodating towards the Kremlin. Germany and France, however, given their clear economic interests and different historical ties to Moscow, hold a more nuanced position (see Part III Document 22).

[This is an excerpt from the full press conference]

Q: Sir, a question about the mood among European allies. You were talking about the Islamic world a second ago. But now the European allies. If you look at, for example, France, Germany, also a lot of people in my own country – I'm from Dutch public TV, by the way – it seems that a lot of Europeans rather give the benefit of the doubt to Saddam Hussein than President George Bush. These are U.S. allies. What do you make of that?

RUMSFELD: Well, it's – what do I make of it?

Q: They have no clerics. They have no Muslim clerics there.

RUMSFELD: Are you helping me? (Laughter.) Do you think I need help? (Laughter.)

What do I think about it? Well, there isn't anyone alive who wouldn't prefer unanimity. I mean, you just always would like everyone to stand up and say, Way to go! That's the right to do, United States.

Now, we rarely find unanimity in the world. I was ambassador to NATO, and I – when we would go in and make a proposal, there wouldn't be unanimity. There wouldn't even be understanding. And we'd have to be persuasive. We'd have to show reasons. We'd have to – have to give rationales. We'd have to show facts. And, by golly, I found that Europe on any major issue is given – if there's leadership and if you're right, and if your facts are persuasive, Europe responds. And they always have.

DOI: 10.4324/9781003159551-30

Now, you're thinking of Europe as Germany and France. I don't. I think that's old Europe. If you look at the entire NATO Europe today, the center of gravity is shifting to the east. And there are a lot of new members. And if you just take the list of all the members of NATO and all of those who have been invited in recently – what is it? Twenty-six, something like that? – you're right. Germany has been a problem, and France has been a problem.

Q: But opinion polls –

RUMSFELD: But – just a minute. Just a minute. But you look at vast numbers of other countries in Europe. They're not with France and Germany on this, they're with the United States.

Now, you cite public opinion polls. Fair enough. Political leaders have to interest themselves in where the public is, and talk to them, and think about that, and then – and provide leadership to them. And you're quite right. You can find polls –

I can remember a poll – I won't – it was back in 1964. I watched it over something like a three-month period. It went from zero in favor of a certain topic to 55 percent in favor of it, down to 13 percent, all in three months. Now, does that suggest that polls can be fickle and rise and fall, depending on facts, depending on circumstances? Of course they can.

And that's – that's what political leaders are supposed to do, is to lead. And they – they're responsible for engaging facts and making assessments and then going out before their people and telling them their honest conviction as to what their country ought to do. And if a country doesn't agree with us, heck, that's happened lots of times in history.

Questions

Explain what Rumsfeld wanted to achieve by distinguishing between Old and New Europe. Do you think "coalitions of the willing" were a direct threat to the idea and purpose of NATO?

Reference

http://www.defense.gov/transcripts/transcript.aspx?transcriptid=1330

Document 7

Statement by French Foreign Minister Galouzeau de Villepin on the situation between Iraq and Kuwait, UN Security Council, 14 February 2003

The US-led invasion of Iraq in March 2003 became one of the most serious political contro-versies between the US and two of its main European allies, France and Germany. The dip-lomatic fight that took place between them at the UN Security Council was unprecedented in the post-1945 era. In the end the Bush administration was not able to form a UN-sanctioned international coalition for invading Iraq, which it regarded as a threat to US and interna-tional security interests. In particular, Bush accused the Iraqi dictator Saddam Hussein of developing and possessing weapons of mass destruction (WMD), an allegation that was never substantially proven. The US and the UK declined the demands of France and Germany that further UN inspections were needed to give Saddam Hussein more time to verify Iraq's WMD situation.

Despite the fact that there was no sympathy in Europe for the Iraqi dictator, the invasion of Iraq by the US and the UK was arguably even more unpopular than in the US. Public opinion felt misled by the information provided by the US government regarding Iraq's WMD program. What was left of any sympathy for the invasion and the removal of the dictator soon disappeared in view of the mounting death toll for US military personnel and Iraqi civilians, with the rise of sectarian hatred and crimes committed by Sunni and Shiite militias turning post-invasion Iraq into an ungovernable chaos.

It would take years to repair the political damage of this diplomatic rift in transatlantic relations. Arguably, the transatlantic fall-out ultimately cemented Franco-German coopera-tion. The popularity in Germany of Bush's successor, Barack Obama, never seemed to fully compensate for the perceived lost ideals of international cooperation or a common transat-lantic goal for global governance.

[This is an excerpt from the full document]

Mr. Galouzeau de Villepin (France) (spoke in French): I would like to thank Mr. Blix and Mr. ElBaradei for the information they have just given us on the ongoing inspections in Iraq. I would like to reiterate to them France's confidence in and complete support for their work.

One knows the value France has placed on the unity of the Security Council from the outset of the Iraqi crisis. Today this unity is based on two fundamental elements.

Together we are pursuing the objective of effectively disarming Iraq, and therefore we are obligated to achieve results. We must not call into question our common commitment in this regard. Collectively we bear this onerous responsibility that must leave no room for ulterior motives or assumptions. Let us be clear: none of us feels the least indulgence towards Saddam Hussain and the Iraqi regime.

In unanimously adopting resolution 1441 (2002) we collectively expressed our agree-ment with the two-stage approach proposed by France: disarmament through inspections

DOI: 10.4324/9781003159551-31

and, if this strategy should fail, consideration by the Security Council of all the options, including resorting to force. Clearly, it was in the event that inspections failed, and only in that case, that a second resolution could be justified.

The question today is simple: do we believe in good conscience that disarmament via inspections missions is now a dead end, or do we believe that the possibilities regarding inspections made available in resolution 1441 (2002) have not yet been fully explored?

In response to this question, France believes two things. First, the option of inspections has not been exhausted, and it can provide an effective response to the imperative of disarming Iraq. Secondly, the use of force would have such heavy consequences for the people, the region and international stability that it should be envisaged only as a last resort.

What have we just learned from the reports by Mr. Blix and Mr. ElBaradei? We learned that the inspections are producing results. Of course, each of us would like more, and we will continue, together, to put pressure on Baghdad in order to obtain more. But the inspections are producing results.

In previous reports to the Security Council, on 27 January 2003, the Executive Chairman of the United Nations Monitoring, Verification and Inspection Commission (UNMOVIC) and the Director General of the International Atomic Energy Agency (IAEA) identified with precision the areas in which progress was expected. Significant gains have now been made on several of these fronts.

The Iraqis have provided the inspectors with new documents regarding chemical and biological weapons and also announced they are establishing commissions of inquiry led by former officials of weapons programmes, in accordance with the requests of Mr. Blix. In the ballistic area, the information provided by Iraq has also enabled the inspectors to make progress. We now know exactly the real capabilities of the Al Samoud 2 missile. Dismantling of unauthorized programmes must now begin, in accordance with Mr. Blix's conclusions. In the nuclear domain, useful information has been given to IAEA on the important points discussed by Mr. ElBaradei on 27 January: the acquisition of magnets that could be used to enrich uranium and the list of contacts between Iraq and the country that may have provided it with uranium.

We are now at the heart of the logic of resolution 1441 (2002), which must ensure effective inspections through precisely identifying banned programmes and then eliminating them. We are all well aware that the success of the inspections presupposes that we get full and complete cooperation from Iraq, something France has consistently demanded.

We are starting to see real progress. Iraq has agreed to aerial reconnaissance over its territory. It has allowed Iraqi scientists to be questioned by inspectors without witnesses. A draft legislative bill barring all activities linked to programmes for weapons of mass destruction is being adopted, in accordance with a long-standing request from the inspectors. Iraq is providing a detailed list of the experts who witnessed the destruction of military programmes in 1991.

Naturally France expects these commitments to be verified. Beyond that we must maintain strong pressure on Iraq so that it goes further along the path of cooperation.

Progress like this strengthens us in our conviction that the inspections can be effective, but we must not close our eyes to the amount of work that remains to be done. Questions remain to be clarified, verifications must be made, and installations or equipment undoubtedly remain to be destroyed.

In order to do this we must give the inspections every opportunity to succeed. On 5 February I made proposals to the Council. Since then we detailed those proposals in a working document addressed to Mr. Blix and Mr. ElBaradei and distributed to Council members. What is the spirit of those proposals? They are practical and concrete proposals that can be quickly implemented and are designed to enhance the efficiency of inspection operations. They fall within the framework of resolution 1441 (2002) and consequently do not require a new resolution by the Council. These proposals support the efforts of Mr. Blix and Mr. ElBaradei, who are the best to tell us which ones they wish to accept to ensure maximum effectiveness in their work.

Mr. Blix and Mr. ElBaradei have already made useful and operational comments in their reports. France has already announced it has additional resources to make available to Mr. Blix and Mr. ElBaradei, starting with our Mirage IV reconnaissance aircraft.

Yes, I hear the critics: there are those who think that, in principle, inspections cannot be at all effective. But I recall that they are the very foundation of resolution 1441 (2002) and that the inspections are producing results. One may judge them to be insufficient, but they are there. Then there are those who believe that continuing the inspection process would be a kind of delaying tactic aimed at preventing military intervention. That naturally raises the question of the time allotted to Iraq. Here, we are at the centre of the debate. What is at stake is our credibility and our sense of responsibility. Let us have the courage to see things plainly.

There are two options. The option of war might seem, on the face of it, to be the swifter. But let us not forget that, after the war is won, the peace must be built. And let us not delude ourselves: that will be long and difficult, because it will be necessary to preserve Iraq's unity and to restore stability in a lasting way in a country and a region harshly affected by the intrusion of force. In the light of that perspective, there is the alternative offered by inspections, which enable us to move forward, day by day, on the path of the effective and peaceful disarmament of Iraq. In the end, is that not the surer and the swifter choice?

No one can maintain today that the path of war will be shorter than the path of inspections; no one can maintain that it would lead to a safer, more just and more stable world. For war is always the outcome of failure. Could it be our sole recourse in the face of today's many challenges?

Therefore, let us give the United Nations inspectors the time that is necessary for their mission to succeed. But let us together be vigilant and ask Mr. Blix and Mr. ElBaradei to report regularly to the Council. France, for its part, proposes another meeting at ministerial level, on 14 March, to assess the situation. Thus we would be able to judge the progress made and what remains to be accomplished.

In that context, the use of force is not justified at this time. There is an alternative to war: disarming Iraq through inspections. Moreover, premature recourse to the military option would be fraught with risks. The authority of our action rests today on the unity of the international community. Premature military intervention would call that unity into question, and that would remove its legitimacy and, in the long run, its effectiveness. Such intervention could have incalculable consequences for the stability of a scarred and fragile region. It would compound the sense of injustice, would aggravate tensions and would risk paving the way for other conflicts.

We all share the same priority: fighting terrorism mercilessly. That fight requires total determination; since the tragedy of 11 September 2001, it has been one of the main responsibilities of our peoples. And France, which has been struck hard several times by that terrible scourge, is wholly mobilized in this struggle, which involves all of us and which we must pursue together. That was the sense of the Security Council meeting held on 20 January at France's initiative.

Ten days ago, the United States Secretary of State, Mr. Powell, cited alleged links between Al-Qaeda and the Baghdad regime. Given the present state of our research and information, gathered in liaison with our allies, nothing enables us to establish such links. Moreover, we must assess the impact that a disputed military action would have on that level.

Would not such an intervention be likely to deepen divisions among societies, among cultures, among peoples—divisions that nurture terrorism?

France has always said that we do not exclude the possibility that, one day, we might have to resort to force if the inspectors' reports concluded that it was impossible for inspections to continue. Then the Council would have to take a decision, and its members would have to shoulder all of their responsibilities. In such a scenario, I want to recall here the questions that I stressed at our last debate, on 5 February, to which we must respond. To what degree do the nature and the extent of the threat justify immediate recourse to force? How do we ensure that the considerable risks of such an intervention can actually be kept under control?

In any case, in such an eventuality it is the unity of the international community that would guarantee its effectiveness. Likewise, it is the United Nations that, whatever may happen, will remain tomorrow at the centre of the peace to be built. To those who ask with anguish when and how we will yield to war, I should like to say that nothing will be done in the Security Council, at any time, in haste, out of a lack of understanding, out of suspicion or out of fear. In this temple, the United Nations, we are the guardians of an ideal; we are the guardians of a conscience. The heavy responsibility and the immense honour that are ours must lead us to give priority to disarmament through peace.

It is an old country, France, of an old continent such as mine, Europe, that speaks before the Council today, that has known war, occupation, barbarity — a country that does not forget and that is aware of all it owes to the fighters for freedom who came from America and elsewhere. And yet France has always stood upright in the face of history and before mankind. Faithful to its values, it wants to act resolutely with all the other members of the international community. We believe in our ability to build a better world together.

Questions

On what issues does Villepin express agreement with the United States?

How does Villepin use the meaning of "old Europe" as a way of criticising the United States?

Reference

https://unReferencess.org/pdf?symbol=en/S/PV.4707

Document 8

Jacques Derrida and Jürgen Habermas, "February 15, or What Binds Europeans Together: A Plea for a Common Foreign Policy, Beginning in the Core of Europe," *Constellations* 10/3 (2003), pp. 291–297

Jacques Derrida and Jürgen Habermas, the one a leading French intellectual of post-structuralism and the other the German heir to the Frankfurt School's project for social emancipation, joined forces to express public opposition to the invasion of Iraq. The resulting document put forward both an analysis and an appeal. They regarded it as necessary and urgent to speak out in favour of the unity of Europe, which had come under heavy pressure as a consequence of the discord across the Atlantic on the Iraq issue. In response they argued for new European political responsibilities and a strengthening of the belief in a progressive European destiny, but without falling back into Eurocentrism. They also called for a renewed confirmation and effective transformation of international law and its institutions, in particular the UN. This document echoes the deeply felt concerns and frustrations of intellectuals in France and Germany over the severe intra-European rift on Iraq, on the one hand, and the divide on the issue between continental Europe and the US, on the other.

[This is an excerpt from the full document]

We should not forget two dates: not the day the newspapers reported to their astonished readers the Spanish prime minister's invitation to the other European nations willing to support the Iraq war to swear an oath of loyalty to George W. Bush, an invitation issued behind the back of the other countries of the European Union. But we should also remember February 15, 2003, as mass demonstrations in London and Rome, Madrid and Barcelona, Berlin and Paris reacted to this sneak attack. The simultaneity of these overwhelming demonstrations – the largest since the end of the Second World War – may well, in hindsight, go down in history as a sign of the birth of a European public sphere. During the leaden months prior to the outbreak of the war in Iraq, a morally obscene division of labor provoked strong emotions. The large-scale logistical operation of ceaseless military preparation and the frenetic activity of humanitarian aid organizations meshed together as precisely as the teeth of a gear. Moreover, the spectacle took place undisturbed before the eyes of the very population which – robbed of their own initiative – was to be its victim. The precautionary mustering of relief workers, relief services, and relief goods dressed itself in the rash rhetoric of alleviation of suffering yet to be inflicted; the planned reconstruction of cities and administrations yet to be ruined. Like searchlights, they picked out the civilized barbarism of coolly planned death (of how many victims?).

There is no doubt that the power of emotions has brought European citizens jointly to their feet. Yet at the same time, the war made Europeans conscious of the failure of their common foreign policy, a failure that has been a long time in the making. As in the rest of the world, the impetuous break with international law has ignited a debate over the future of the international order in Europe as well. But here, the divisive arguments have cut deeper, and have caused familiar fault lines to emerge even more sharply. Controversies

DOI: 10.4324/9781003159551-32

over the role of the American superpower, over a future world order, over the relevance of international law and the United Nations – all have caused latent contradictions to break into the open.

The gap between continental and Anglo-American countries on the one side, and "the old Europe" and the Central and East European candidates for entry into the European Union on the other side, has grown deeper. This contradiction can no longer be finessed. The future constitution will grant us a European foreign minister. But what good is a new political office if governments don't unify in a common policy? A Fischer with a changed job description would remain as powerless as Solana.

For the moment, only the core European nations are ready to endow the EU with certain qualities of a state. But what happens if these countries can only find agreement on the definition of "self-interest"? If Europe is not to fall apart, these countries will have to make use of the mechanisms for "strengthened cooperation" created in Nice as a way of taking a first step toward a common foreign policy, a common security policy, and a common defense policy. Only such a step will succeed in generating the momentum that other member states – initially in the Euro zone – will not be able to resist in the long run. In the framework of the future European constitution, there can and must be no separatism. Taking a leading role does not mean excluding. The avant-gardist core of Europe must not wall itself off into a new Small Europe. It must – as it has so often – be the locomotive.

It is from their own self-interest, to be sure, that the more closely-cooperating member states of the EU will hold the door open. And the probability that the invited states will pass through that door will increase the more capable the core of Europe becomes of effective action externally, and the sooner it can prove that in a complex global society, it is not just divisions that count, but also the soft power of negotiating agendas, relations, and economic advantages.

In this world, the reduction of politics to the stupid and costly alternative of war or peace simply doesn't pay. At the international level and in the framework of the UN, Europe has to throw its weight on the scale to counterbalance the hegemonic unilateralism of the United States. At global economic summits and in the institutions of the WTO, the World Bank, and the IMF, it should exert its influence in shaping the design for a coming global domestic policy.

Political projects that aim at the further development of the EU are now colliding with the limits of the medium of administrative steering. Until now, the functional imperatives for the construction of a common market and the Euro-zone have driven reforms. These driving forces are now exhausted. A transformative politics, which would demand that member states not just overcome obstacles for competitiveness but form a common will, must take recourse to the motives and the attitudes of the citizens themselves. Majority decisions on highly consequential foreign policies can only expect acceptance assuming the solidarity of outnumbered minorities. But this presupposes a feeling of common political belonging on both sides. The population must so to speak "build up" their national identities, and add to them a European dimension. What is already a fairly abstract form of civic solidarity, still largely confined to members of nation-states, must be extended to include the European citizens of other nations as well.

This raises the question of "European identity." Only the consciousness of a shared political fate, and the prospect of a common future, can halt outvoted minorities from the obstruction of a majority will. The citizens of one nation must regard the citizens of another nation as fundamentally "one of us." This desideratum leads to the question that so many skeptics have called attention to: are there historical experiences, traditions, and achievements offering European citizens the consciousness of a political fate that has been shared together, and that can be shaped together? An attractive, indeed an infectious "vision" for a future Europe will not emerge from thin air. At present it can arise only from the disquieting perception of perplexity. But it well can emerge from the difficulties of a situation into which we Europeans have been cast. And it must articulate itself from out of the wild cacophony of a multi-vocal public sphere. If this theme has so far not even gotten on to the agenda, it is we intellectuals who have failed.

Contemporary Europe has been shaped by the experience of the totalitarian regimes of the twentieth century and through the Holocaust – the persecution and the annihilation of European Jews in which the National Socialist regime made the societies of the conquered countries complicit as well. Self-critical controversies about this past remind us of the moral basis of politics. A heightened sensitivity to injuries to personal and bodily integrity is reflected, among other ways, in the fact that both Europarat [sic!] and EU made the ban on capital punishment a condition for entrance.

A bellicose past once entangled all European nations in bloody conflicts. They drew a conclusion from that military and spiritual mobilization against one another: the imperative of developing new, supranational forms of cooperation after the Second World War. The successful history of the European Union may have confirmed Europeans in their belief that the domestication of state power demands a mutual limitation of sovereignty, on the global as well as the national state level.

Each of the great European nations has experienced the bloom of its imperial power. And, what in our context is more important still, each has had to work through the experience of the loss of its empire. In many cases this experience of decline was associated with the loss of colonial territories. With the growing distance of imperial domination and the history of colonialism, the European powers also got the chance to assume a reflexive distance from themselves. They could learn from the perspective of the defeated to perceive themselves in the dubious role of victors who are called to account for the violence of a forcible and uprooting process of modernization. This could support the rejection of Eurocentrism, and inspire the Kantian hope for a global domestic policy.

Questions

What kind of positive future do these intellectuals foresee for Europe?
How does their conception of European identity contrast with that of the United States?

References

Permission: John Wiley & Sons, Publishers

Document 9

Justin Vaïsse, "God and Foreign Policy: The Religious Divide Between the U.S. and Europe," July 2003

Justin Vaïsse, in 2003 a professor at Sciences Po in Paris, went on to become the Director-General of the Paris Peace Forum and one of the leading transatlantic intellectuals on international affairs. As a visiting fellow at the Brookings Institution in Washington DC, he contributed this text to a conference organised by the Pew Research Institute. The occasion of the conference was a global poll on the influence of religion on foreign policy. The issue under discussion was why religion seems to play a far greater role in US politics than in Europe. Vaïsse outlined the special place of religion in American society. Religion in the US is easily identified with freedom, whereas in Europe religion plays almost the opposite role because of a totally different historical context. These different historical experiences contribute, according to Vaïsse, to a so-called "God gap" between the US and Europe.

[This is an excerpt from the full document]

[The] difference in religion accentuates, rather than creates, the main political gap between Europe and the U.S., but one should not underestimate the effect that it has in at least three domains. First, it affects the image, especially the negative image, of Europe here and of the U.S. in Europe. It affects the approach we could have to third regions of the world, especially the Middle East. This is not a new thing; this has existed for at least a couple of years.

Let me try to put that into context. Let's get back to this poll on the necessity to believe in God to be moral. I find it interesting because France and the U.S. are at the two opposite ends of this. I think 58 percent of Americans said yes and only 13 percent of French say so. I think one of the things that is at play here is the fact of a belief in God. Is it necessary to believe in God? When you hear that in France, you hear basically "Are you Catholic?" You don't hear it the same way you do here; that is to say, Do you believe that there is a superior being, a transcendence, et cetera, with a sort of greater relativity? So I think this changes the answers, but the bulk of the lesson remains.

I think what needs to be said to understand this is that the separation of church and state is conceived of completely differently historically, especially between France and the U.S. History is really the best clue here. Historically, the separation of church and state in France was not about shielding the churches from the state as it was here. Here, religious freedom was really at the foundation of the United States, and many Pilgrims came to freely practice their religion, et cetera. In France, it's exactly the reverse; that is to say, the separation of church and state is to shield the state from the one church that was dominant, especially socially dominant, the Catholic Church. This gave birth to militant secularism, which basically sees religion as a threat to democracy and to a republican virtue.

DOI: 10.4324/9781003159551-33

To try to illustrate and explain this fantastic poll that you gave us last month, I would like to quote Tocqueville, because I think he explained very well in 1835 what is going on here for religion and politics. He said, in a new translation by Harvey Mansfield, "In the U.S., from the beginning, politics and religion were in accord, and they have not ceased to be so since." And further, he wrote, "I do not know if all Americans hare [sic!] faith in their religions, for who can read to the bottom of hearts; but I am sure that they believe it necessary to the maintenance of republican institutions." And then what did he say about Europe? "The unbelievers of Europe honed Christians as political enemies rather than as religious adversaries. They hate faith as the opinion of a party much more than as an erroneous belief."

To summarize Tocqueville, in the U.S., it's politically correct to be religious, politically correct in the large sense; and in Europe, and in France in particular, it's politically correct to be secular. In other words, religion is conceived as inherently destabilizing and threatening and should be confined to the private sphere.

The way Europeans and the French in particular hear about religion is in their history. There is this thing referred to, which is the war of religion of the 16th and 17th centuries, which is sort of still present in some way in European consciousness. When they hear about religion today in the news, it's about the Middle East, it's about Ireland, it's about Kosovo, it's about Islamic bombings that began in Europe much before they began here, and it's about the sects. Religion does not have this politically positive connotation that it has here. So in order to be moral, to be virtuous in a republican sense, it is definitely not necessary to be more religious.

The view here is really of the Bob Dylan song "With God on Our Side." That is to say, this idea that there could be a sort of William Bennett moral clarity is really an addition to the negative stereotyping, and it's seen as dangerous for conducting affairs in international relations. It's true that this view of America as very religious is part of the anti-American stereotyping, and it has been so not for that long, but at least for a couple of decades.

I think Europe felt much better with Clinton's morality and foreign policy because it was less about God, but it was more transposition of political correctness, the rights of the minority, et cetera, and not portrayed as a religious crusade as sometimes it has seemed to be the case with the Bush administration.

I'll make just a couple of other concluding remarks. I think the misunderstandings are largely based on this different perception of secularism. The separation between church and state is actually very strong here, and it is actually very strong in France, too; except they are totally different, and so they feed different perceptions.

To give the final context, there's a strong evolution in France and in Europe in general of the landscape about religion. In Europe, it's about the debates over our bill of rights, the Charter of Fundamental Rights of the EU in 2000. And then, in 2003, there was the big debate about the EU constitution. We are really back in 1787 and 1789 in this respect. The question is whether we should put God in our bill of rights and God in our constitution, and there was a huge fight about this. I don't have time to describe that in more detail, but we can do that in the questions and answers.

Of course there is a gap, and I think it does accentuate the differences, the political spat between Europe and the U.S., but at the same time, I think in both countries and in both continents the landscape is changing rapidly and is being warped by external factors. It would be important to keep that in mind for any prediction that we could make.

Questions

What reasons does Vaïsse give for the "God Gap"?
Do you think the US and Europe have become closer or moved further apart on the issue
of religion and foreign policy since 2003?

References

https://www.pewforum.org/2003/07/10/god-and-foreign-policy-the-religious-divide-between-the-
us-and-europe/
Permission: PEW Research Center

Document 10

Hans van Mierlo, "The Vitality of the Nation-State and Europe in the 21st Century," *De Gids*, 166/5 (2003), pp. 329–341

Around the turn of the century a lively debate took place among European elites about the future of the EU after the enlargement and the deepening processes of the 1990s. The Euro had been launched, and there was a need to clarify the EU's governance structures and its relationship with European citizens. A series of so-called Intergovernmental Conferences (IGC), held under the auspices of the European Council to negotiate changes to the founding treaties of the EU, led to the drafting of the Constitutional Treaty in June 2004. Voters in France and the Netherlands rejected this treaty in subsequent referenda (see Part II Document 15).

Joschka Fischer, the German Minister of Foreign Affairs (1998–2005), was an important contributor to this debate. In May 2000 he delivered a speech at the Humboldt University in Berlin entitled "From Confederacy to Federation: Thoughts on the Finality of European Integration," in which he outlined his ideas on the objectives "European project". He proposed a "constituent treaty" which would lay the foundation for a federal structure for the EU, clearly dividing sovereignty and competences between the European nation-states and the European Union.

Someone with an alternative view was Dutch Foreign Minister Hans van Mierlo. Starting his career as a journalist, he became the founding father of Democrats66, a social-liberal party that sought to reform Dutch politics, and served several times as Minister of Foreign Affairs in the 1980s and 1990s. His article below focused on one of his main political topics, the "distance" between citizens and the European project, and how this was opening up a democratic deficit that was undermining the project's legitimacy. In addition, he argued for strong nation states as the basis for a robust and closer European Union. He saw the impotence of the national ruling classes to bring about any progress regarding European integration as being a major obstacle for future progress. Nation states therefore represented both the limitations to European integration, as well as the means for breaking the deadlock. Unlike Fischer, however, he offered no blueprint for a future, reorganized European political framework.

[This is an excerpt from the full document]

The course of the twenty-first century is even less predictable today than that of the last century was in the year 1903. Anyone who knows how that century developed after 1903 becomes very humble.

Leaving the enigmatic China aside for a moment, today's data does not get me beyond a hazy suspicion that the world stage will be ruled by Islam and the power of the United States.

The other power, which could be the countervailing power – and I am not primarily thinking of military power here – is the European one. But it does not exist and if

DOI: 10.4324/9781003159551-34

everything remains as it is, it will not come into being. The reason is that the nation states in Europe are hardly, if at all, able – or willing – to relinquish some of their sovereignty in order to achieve a greater, collective one in return. This lack of willingness – and I am thinking especially of middle-sized countries such as France and the United Kingdom – stems from an outdated assessment of the importance of full sovereignty on its own. The impotence – and this applies to countries small and large – stems from the fact that all nation states are confused. They are suffering because their democracies are functioning less and less effectively. That is why they emphasize the importance of their own sovereignty. But it is primarily sovereignty on paper.

If I were to attempt to offer an instant diagnosis, it would be something like this. The democracies of the nation states are dysfunctional. That is why the nation state is weak. That is why it is not capable of making Europe strong. As a result, Europe is virtually absent from the world stage, making both Europe and the nation state even weaker. Who will break the vicious circle? The answer lies in the hands of the nation states of Europe.

There has been an erosion of national democracy that is reinforced by the actions of the European courts. Within the process of European integration, judicial power has done the best at retaining its position as a separate power.

In principle, Montesquieu's doctrine of the tripartite separation of powers can be found in Europe, but to see it in practice in concrete terms is almost impossible. All the basic conditions for such a system are missing. In concrete terms, separation of powers can take place in a clearly delineated space, which is stable and uniform in nature: the nation state. However, the space of European integration is an expanding area, which is diverse and unstable. In fact there are three spaces: the supranational space, the intergovernmental space, and the space of the individual member states, all of which have proposed a different interpretation of the tripartite separation of powers.

All these spaces are connected in a complicated way. Within that ensemble, legislative, executive, and judicial functions must be established. In addition, power is not a constant, but an unstable capacity, which is only partly fixed and to a greater extent must always be seized from the member states. Is it any wonder that "le pouvoir arrête le pouvoir" (power sets limits to power) functions differently here?

But it is not the separation of powers that stands in the way of further integration, nor is it the national power of the member states, as many think, but in fact their national impotence. The greatest obstacle to the creation of a truly democratic space in Europe lies in the democratic impasses in the member states themselves. National governments increasingly lack the authority to demand from their citizens the concessions that must be made in order to achieve integration.

Government leaders are usually involved in a semi-permanent struggle for survival. Often they meet in Brussels with only one thought: what message can I just come home with?

The impasses in European integration are essentially the sum of the government impasses in national democracies.

The surprising conclusion is that it is not the strength and flourishing of the nation state that complicates the integration process, but rather its weakness and impotence. There is a lot of hypocrisy in the concealment of that truth. The overriding consideration is not the interests of the citizens, but the political fortunes of the minister, of his party, of the power position of a coalition.

In addition, the nation state in several member states has an uncertain future in a geographical and political sense. In at least five of the fifteen current member states there are signs of some disintegration of the classic unity that the states enjoyed a few decades ago: fragmentation looms in Belgium, Spain, Italy, Great Britain, and also in Germany, where the emergence of the Länder seriously undermines the authority of the federal government in the integration process

In European democracy, the distance between the citizens of the member states and the power in Brussels is so great that they are completely invisible to each other. The analysis of the democratic deficit that has been offered to date falls short. Politicians perceive the democratic deficit as insufficient control, especially by the European Parliament.

The real deficit lies in the lack among citizens of any knowledge and feeling about what is going on in Brussels. Politically it does not exist for them.

They vote according to national emotions, because there is no knowledge of and no feeling for that second democracy. It is of course very important that the Convention now seeks to make the Union and the Community more transparent, simpler and easier to access. But that will not be of much use if, on the receiving end, citizens of the member states are not taught about and given reasons to feel emotionally attached to that Europe. They need to understand that Europe is their own interest and their own business.

Regarding this point, the integration process has been poorly thought out. We have not foreseen what it means to ask the citizens of Europe to live and feel in two democracies at the same time, their national and their European democracies. That is also a very difficult task. With direct elections, we have embarked on a path of a second democracy for citizens.

The tension between the national state and the Union is most visible when dealing with the issue of European foreign policy. It is a downright disaster that a common foreign policy just can't seem to get off the ground. When it comes down to it, the United States does what it wants to do and imposes its will on others.

There is yet another aspect that is important. Due to the lack of a common European foreign policy that makes any impression, European values and interests are also insufficiently propagated and protected. After the collapse of communism, the world's only choice in economic systems is between European capitalism, which is in principle based on fundamental social rights, and American capitalism, which is unfettered and based on the right of every American to the pursuit of happiness.

Therefore we need to gradually replace the consensus rule for decision-making with majority decisions. That means relinquishing some sovereignty. This can be done successfully without jeopardizing the interests of the national state. But for this to happen, the larger countries in particular have to overcome a mainly psychological barrier.

There is one more consideration that underlies the urgency of this point. The absence of Europe from the world stage also harms the integration process in other areas. It has a strong and negative effect on citizens' confidence and belief in their own cause. Every day, television broadcasts into European living rooms the dramas of the world, dramas that often evoke strong emotions. In almost every situation, Europe's inability to act is manifest. If anything is being done, it is being done by Americans, who have the capacity to do so. But they do not always make use of it, or they do so from a position that is not shared in Europe. As an alternative or corrective or additional factor, Europe increasingly falls short structurally. The disappointment over this failure compounds the distance between the citizen and the European idea.

The decision to accept new member states into the European Union has indeed been a great moment for Europe. Sometimes history writes the agenda. Do what you have to do – many objections are raised, but there is no alternative. It is embarrassingly shortsighted to make the financial aspects of this development the first consideration.

The less pretentious the nation states are in their attitudes and behavior, the more likely they are to propose something. Cooperation and / or integration is a precondition for the vitality of the nation state.

It is still better at the moment to refrain from making a decision about the blueprint of the final destination. Not because the decision about that final destination, a federation or a confederation, would have to be made without the involvement of the citizens, but because the information needed for that decision is not yet available, the time for the decision has not come, and a premature decision will lead to enormous stagnation in the integration process itself, which is urgent and in my opinion should be conducted on the basis of the principle: cooperation where possible, integration where necessary, the principle of Monnet and Schumann.

Enlargement complicates the process of integration, but also makes it more necessary. And that also applies if Turkey were to accede, if and when it in fact meets the Copenhagen criteria. Perhaps a multi-speed Europe or flexibility should be built in, such as with the euro. If that is necessary to bring about a convincing common foreign policy, it must be seriously considered. It is a misleading notion that Europe can be a real power on the world stage only if it is a federation. We and the world cannot wait that long.

Questions

How should the EU attempt to strengthen its political legitimacy, according to Van Mierlo's "diagnosis"?
Do you think the "final destination" of the European project should be a federal union?

References

Permission: The Heirs of Hans van Mierlo

Document 11

Maastricht and the Future of Europe, Speech by Dr. Willem F. Duisenberg, President of the European Central Bank, at the German Ministry of Finance, 22 October 2003

The address below by the Dutch banker Wim Duisenberg, who succeeded the first President of the ECB, Jean-Claude Trichet, illustrated the political character of the introduction of a single currency, but avoided its deeper political context. The first plans for an Economic and Monetary Union (EMU) originated in the 1960s and were meant to coordinate economic, monetary, and fiscal policies among the member states of the EU (at the time still the European Community). A common currency as an integral part of the common market was also part of the plan. Under the ambitious European Commission president, Frenchman Jacques Delors (1985–1994), a three-step approach over the period 1990 to 1999 was taken to introduce first EMU and then the Euro. The Treaty of Maastricht (1992), signed soon after the unification of Germany, laid the foundation for this development. Three years after the official introduction of the Euro as a mere unit of account, Euro cash was introduced in January 2002 to replace twelve national currencies. From the outset it was clear that the Euro was a "political" currency, drawing the national economies and thus the member states into 'an ever closer union'.

This proved to be a milestone in the European unification process. Previously, the different monetary policy traditions in Europe had varied considerably. The northern countries, Germany in particular, held that low inflation and a "hard" currency would best stimulate economic growth. The southern countries, on the other hand, were less focused on low inflation rates and used a "soft" currency as a means to promote their exports. When necessary, they turned to the monetary instrument of depreciation to lower the value of their currencies and so make their exports cheaper abroad. Germany, with its strong, export-oriented economy, had played a central role in deciding the monetary conditions in Europe, and this role increased in the 1990s leading up to the Euro. Once the European Central Bank became responsible for Eurozone monetary policies, Germany lost – at least formally – its predominant position in monetary affairs.

The introduction of the single currency turned out to be even more politically controversial than initially thought, as was revealed on 30 September 2010 by the German national weekly Die Zeit. *On the basis of interviews and classified diplomatic documents, the publication revealed the existence of secret Franco-German discussions leading to a compromise. This had become necessary because of the astonishing speed of the German unification process, which threatened to overthrow existing political and economic power relations in Europe. Fears in Paris ran high concerning Germany's national currency and the dominant influence of German monetary policy on other national economies. The response was to manoeuvre Germany into giving up its strong national currency, the basis of its economic power, with the threat that should Germany choose not to, France would not hesitate to torpedo Helmut Kohl's plans for German unification. As a result, the long-held German policy position that a European political union should precede a monetary union had to be given up.*

DOI: 10.4324/9781003159551-35

This outcome strongly suggested that, in the words of former German Finance Minister Peer Steinbrück, the Deutsche Mark was given up in return for the Euro and French consent for German reunification.

[This is an excerpt from the full document]

It is a great honour for me to make one of my final public appearances as President of the European Central Bank on the occasion of the launch of a "Sonderpostwertzeichen" – a special stamp – to commemorate the Treaty on European Union, better known as the Maastricht Treaty.

It is not as a Dutchman that I consider this Treaty to be one of the most important milestones of the European integration process, but as a truly convinced European. Together with the Governing Council of the ECB, I have been responsible for managing the single monetary policy and the single currency of the euro area, and I will not deny that my job has been inextricably linked to the wider historical process of building an "ever closer union" of the peoples of Europe. In this respect, I consider that the Maastricht Treaty embodies the most decisive impulse in the deepening of the European Communities established in the 1950s and strengthened by the Treaty of Rome. The move to Economic and Monetary Union (EMU) was a profoundly political act – despite the fact that the underlying rationale was predominantly economic, namely that a single market requires a single currency.

Having been instrumental in laying the foundations for the euro, the principles of the Maastricht Treaty will remain vital for the successful functioning of EMU. The medium-term macroeconomic policy framework laid down in the Maastricht Treaty has contributed to a stable macroeconomic environment, and will continue to do so. In addition, the Treaty provides for a clear allocation of responsibilities between EU institutions and Member States, as well as clear mandates for all involved. The maintenance of price stability (the ECB's primary objective), the independence of the Eurosystem and the provisions safeguarding fiscal discipline, in particular as enshrined in the Stability and Growth Pact, are among the hallmarks of this framework. Furthermore, the path towards participation in the euro area mapped out in the Maastricht Treaty, focusing on sustainable economic convergence as a prerequisite for adoption of the euro, will also serve to guide prospective Member States. The name "Maastricht" will therefore always be connected with the euro and will forever have a prominent place in the history of Europe.

When the Maastricht Treaty was ratified ten years ago, many doubted whether EMU would ever amount to more than the solemn words of a Treaty or a laudable objective to be reached at some point in the distant future. However, during the 1990s, policy-makers, governments, central bankers and other political and economic agents showed great resolve and determination to ensure that the single currency would become a reality. Today, we can look back on a period of more than five years in which the ECB has successfully pursued a stability-oriented single monetary policy serving more than 300 million citizens. And we all have the tangible proof of Monetary Union in our pockets, following a highly successful cash changeover process, which represents another historic milestone in the process of European integration. With the euro, this network of interrelations and mutual dependencies in Europe has undoubtedly reached a new level.

When talking about the possible political implications of the euro, there are fundamental questions about the future of Europe to be answered, and I hope that my subsequent remarks will provide some interesting insights. Can Monetary Union function properly without some form of political union? Is a "currency without a state" a viable construct?

Indeed, the question of whether a single currency requires – or inevitably leads to – a single state is hotly debated.

I think that one of the reasons for this confused state of affairs is that "political union" is a rather abstract concept. It can mean different things to different people. On the one hand, political union can be broadly understood as a dense network of integrated policies, common rules and established procedures, as a union with strong and active supranational institutions, with common symbols and a common identity. The European Union already exhibits many of these features.

If, on the other hand, we understand political union as the establishment of an entity that resembles the traditional nation state, the European Union may still have some way to go, if indeed this is the direction that Europeans want to take. Today's Union is not a European Federation, for example, or a United States of Europe, with a constitution and a single executive.

The euro marks the achievement of full integration in the monetary field. In purely functional terms, it is therefore an end point, rather than an intermediate step. However, with the euro, we now form a "Schicksalsgemeinschaft", a community with a shared future. Our economies are linked, and so our policy decisions have become a matter of concern for all. We have a legitimate interest in developments and political actions in other euro area countries, since we are affected by them – for better or for worse. If I may use a "domestic" metaphor, the marriage in which the euro has joined our countries is about more than just living under the same roof, it is about sharing a common vision and about managing life together.

Questions

Does Duisenberg see a direct connection between the single currency and the "political union" of Europe?

Why would the United States have regarded the Euro as a threat?

Reference

https://www.ecb.europa.eu/press/key/date/2003/html/sp031022.en.html

Document 12

ACLU Testimony at a Hearing on "America after 9/11: Freedom Preserved or Freedom Lost?", Senate Judiciary Committee, submitted by Nadine Strossen, President, and Timothy H. Edgar, Legislative Counsel, 18 November 2003

One of the many questions raised in the fight against terrorism was to what extent the civil liberties of US citizens as well as those of "opposing forces" (terrorist groups) could be maintained and not abrogated by federal security policies. As evidence of malpractice emerged, it was increasingly felt that civil rights were under pressure or actually being violated. The American Civil Liberties Union (ACLU) supported President Bush in his fight against terrorism, but they strived for the protection of the American Constitution and Rule of Law alongside it. The Patriot Act (October 2001) that followed the "9/11" terrorist attacks became increasingly problematic for the ACLU and many Americans, since it allowed the federal government to detain individuals indefinitely, without due process. In particular, Muslim non-citizens, often captured in Afghanistan, suffered the consequences of post-"9/11" government actions and the Patriot Act. Many were held in custody indefinitely at Guantanamo Bay, the US military base on Cuba, referred to as an "off-shore prison" and deemed outside of regular US legal jurisdiction.

[This is an excerpt from the full document]

Chairman Hatch, Senator Leahy and Members of the Committee:

On behalf of the American Civil Liberties Union and its over 400,000 members, dedicated to defending the Bill of Rights and its promise of due process under law for all persons, I welcome this opportunity to present the ACLU's views at this hearing on the impact of federal anti-terrorism efforts on civil liberties since September 11, 2001.

America faces a crucial test. That test is whether we – the political descendents of Jefferson and Madison, and citizens of the world's oldest democracy – have the confidence, ingenuity and commitment to secure our safety without sacrificing our liberty.

For here we are at the beginning of the 21st century, in a battle with global terror. Terrorism is a new and different enemy. As a nation, we learned this on September 11, 2001 when a group of terrorists attacked us here at home, and within the space of minutes murdered nearly 3,000 of our fellow Americans and citizens of other nations, innocent civilians going about their everyday lives.

ACLU lawyers and activists can never forget that day. Our national offices in New York and near the Capitol in Washington were evacuated. John William Perry, a New York Police Department officer and Board Member of the New York Civil Liberties Union, volunteered to assist employees escaping the World Trade Center on September 11, 2001, and himself became a victim. We pledged on that day to support President Bush in the battle against terror, while standing strong against any efforts to use the attacks to abridge civil liberties or our system of checks and balances.

DOI: 10.4324/9781003159551-36

We must be ready to defend liberty, for liberty cannot defend itself. We as a nation have no trouble understanding the necessity of a military defense. But there is another equally powerful defense that is required, and that is the defense of our Constitution – the defense of our most cherished freedoms.

Put aside our popular culture which changes by the day, and our material success which is now vulnerable to the vicissitudes of the global economy – strip away all that is truly superficial. What is left that distinguishes us if not our constitutional values? These values – freedom, liberty, equality and tolerance – are the very source of our strength as a nation and the bulwark of our democracy. They are what have permitted us to grow abundantly, and to absorb wave after wave of immigrants to our shores, reaping the benefits of their industrious energy.

Now, we are in danger of allowing ourselves to be governed by our fears, rather than our values. How else can we explain the actions of our government over the last two years to invade the privacy of our personal lives and to curtail immigrants' rights, all in the name of increasing our security?

PATRIOTISM AND GRASSROOTS DISSENT

Mr. Chairman, when Attorney General Ashcroft appeared before this Committee shortly after September 11, he accused the ACLU and other defenders of civil liberties of aiding the terrorists and weakening America's resolve with our criticism of some government policies. It was a statement profoundly unworthy of the Office of Attorney General.

Since September 11, 2001, the ACLU has been privileged to be an important part of a remarkable grassroots movement to defend the Bill of Rights. Resolutions have been passed in 210 communities in 35 states, including three state-wide resolutions.

The resolutions have passed in towns from Maine to Alaska, from New York to Texas. They have attracted support in liberal strongholds, like Berkeley, California, and in small towns in Utah, Idaho, and Alaska – three of the most conservative states in the Union. The resolutions are the most visible symbol of a growing movement that is perhaps most notable for uniting allies across the political spectrum – from the ACLU and its liberal allies like People for the American Way and MoveOn.org, to some of the nation's most important member-based conservative organizations: the Free Congress Foundation, Americans for Tax Reform, and the Gun Owners of America. Our campaign has included closely working with former Congressman Bob Barr (R-GA), a Board Member of the National Rifle Association. I am pleased to share the witness table with Congressman Barr today.

The resolutions take issue with portions of the PATRIOT Act and many other government actions, including Executive Orders and regulations undermining the right to counsel, the right to a jury trial, and the rights of immigrants. Hundreds of thousands of Americans have written their elected representatives to express their views about these issues, and to urge Congress to take corrective actions.

Some have accused these engaged citizens, who are acting in the best tradition of Thomas Jefferson, of being naïve, misinformed, even ignorant. On the contrary, while the arcane details of these issues can flummox the finest legal minds, I have found our supporters to be remarkably well informed.

This is a movement based on knowledge, not ignorance.

LISTEN TO THE PEOPLE

Americans are concerned because the PATRIOT Act put in place statutory authority for the government to get a court order to come into your home without your knowledge and even take property without notifying you until weeks or months later. Americans are concerned because the PATRIOT Act allows the government to obtain many detailed, personal records – including library and bookstore records, financial and medical records, and Internet communications – without probable cause and without meaningful judicial review. For those records that may be obtained using "national security letters," there is no judicial review at all. Americans are concerned because the PATRIOT Act – as well as changes to immigration regulations since 9/11 and the President's claimed authority to detain "enemy combatants" – all sanction indefinite detention without criminal charge and without meaningful judicial review.

Some have dismissed concerns about immigrants' rights, including the selective finger-printing and registration of visitors from the Arab and Muslim world under the National Security Entry-Exit Registration System (NSEERS), also known as special registration. This program is seriously damaging the image of the United States abroad and, as a result, hindering international cooperation against terrorism.

AMERICAN FREEDOMS LOST AFTER SEPTEMBER 11

The specific freedoms that have been abridged – by the PATRIOT Act and by other government actions – often involve technical and complex changes to surveillance laws, detention regulations, and government guidelines. However, they share common themes. The government's new surveillance and detention powers have undermined important checks and balances, diminished personal privacy, increased government secrecy, and exacerbated inequality.

Checks and Balances. At bottom, the issue with respect to all these powers – PATRIOT Act and non-PATRIOT Act alike – is the removal of basic checks and balances on government power. The genius of our founding fathers was to design a system in which no one branch of government possessed all power, but instead the powers were divided among legislative, executive and judicial branches.

The government's actions since September 11 have undermined this system. Prior to September 11, the government had ample power to investigate, detain, convict and punish terrorists, with meaningful judicial review. The changes have made that review less meaningful.

It is a myth to say that prior to September 11, the government could wiretap organized crime suspects but not terrorist suspects. In fact, the government has always had far greater powers to wiretap foreign terrorist suspects, because it could use either its criminal or its intelligence powers to do so. The PATRIOT Act simply enlarged further the already loose standards for both kinds of wiretapping.

It is a myth to say that prior to September 11, the government was prevented by the Foreign Intelligence Surveillance Act from sharing information acquired in intelligence investigations with criminal prosecutors. In fact, it could do so, under procedures designed to ensure the intelligence powers were not being abused as a prosecutorial end-run around the Fourth Amendment. The PATRIOT Act did not authorize such information sharing – it was already legal. Rather, the Act reduced the judicial oversight designed to prevent abuses of information sharing.

It is a myth that the government lacked adequate power to detain terrorist suspects. In fact, the government could, and did, detain many terrorist suspects prior to September 11 using both immigration and criminal powers. Indeed, President Bush joined the ACLU in criticizing the use of secret evidence against some Arab and Muslim immigration detainees under the Clinton Administration. The PATRIOT Act, and government changes to detention regulations, did not authorize detention of terrorism suspects. Rather, it made immigration hearings and judicial review of those detentions far less meaningful.

It is a myth that the government could not effectively prosecute foreign terrorists without revealing classified information. The Classified Information Procedures Act has long been on the books to protect the government's secrets while ensuring a fair trial, and prosecutors of prior Al Qaeda plots have said the Act worked well to protect both the rights of the accused and the national security interests of the government. The President's military tribunals order was not needed to safeguard classified information. Rather, its effect was to substitute a commission subject to Defense Department control for an independent judge in running terrorism trials.

It is a myth that the government could not listen to the conversations of attorneys who betrayed their profession by abusing the attorney-client privilege to implicate themselves in their clients' ongoing criminal acts. The government could always obtain a court order, based on probable cause, to listen in to conversations that lacked the protection of the attorney-client privilege. The monitoring regulation was drafted to evade that requirement of judicial oversight.

Understanding how these actions undermine checks and balances illustrates the sophistry of one of the government's main defenses of its post 9-11 actions. Government officials point out that courts have not struck down many of their actions – but their actions are a threat to liberty precisely because they are calculated to undermine the role of the courts, diminishing their oversight of government action.

Personal Privacy. The right of privacy, Justice Brandeis said, is that most simple and most important of freedoms – the right to be left alone. The PATRIOT Act and other legislation, coupled with new investigative guidelines, have eroded this right alarmingly.

Under section 215 of the PATRIOT Act, the government may now obtain any and all records, no matter how sensitive or personal, with a "business records" order from the Foreign Intelligence Surveillance Court, which sits in secret and has denied or modified a grand total of six out of more than 15,000 surveillance orders sought in a quarter century. Under section 505 of the PATRIOT Act, the FBI now has broader power to use what are called "national security letters" to obtain some records – including records of financial institutions, credit reports, and billing records of telephone and Internet service providers – on its own authority, without any court order at all.

National security letters and records demands under section 215 are not made in the course of ordinary criminal investigations, which involve grand jury subpoenas, search warrants, and other longstanding government powers; rather, they are intelligence powers that do not require any criminal wrongdoing on the part of those being investigated.

Section 213 of the PATRIOT Act substantially lowered the standard for government agents to come into your house, look around, and even take property. These "sneak and peek" warrants no longer require, as they did in some circuits, that notice be given within seven days – an indefinite "reasonable time" is the new standard. Nor do they require the government to show specific harms from notice, instead also permitting the government to get a delay under a catch-all provision that applies whenever harm to the prosecution may result.

As a result of this provision, the government has acknowledged using these warrants to invade dozens of homes and businesses without providing notice for as long as three months. The government has sought to delay notice in these cases over 200 times.

Government Secrecy. The American tradition of open government has suffered a severe blow as a result of the government's post 9-11 actions.

The Justice Department's guidance to federal agencies on implementation of the Freedom of Information Act (FOIA) prior to September 11 included a basic affirmation of the policy of open government the Act embodies, urging agencies to comply with FOIA requests absent a good reason. Shortly after September 11, the Attorney General issued a memorandum to all federal agencies reversing that presumption of openness and pledging the Justice Department's support for denial of FOIA requests.

Perhaps the most dramatic example of unwarranted secrecy has been the government's secret arrest and deportation of hundreds of Muslim and Arab immigrants after

September 11. The Justice Department refused to identify the detainees, arguing that to do so might jeopardize national security and tip its hand to terrorists. The secrecy was alarming and, after our repeated requests for basic information about the detainees were denied, the ACLU filed a federal lawsuit seeking names under the Freedom of Information Act.

Then, in a further effort to deny information to the public and press, the Justice Department closed all immigration hearings involving the September 11 detainees. Twice more, the ACLU went to court – with lawsuits arguing that transparency and accountability are essential to the workings of democracy. In an eloquent decision, a three-judge panel of the United States Court of Appeals in Cincinnati unanimously declared that secret deportation hearings were unlawful. "A government operating in the shadow of secrecy stands in complete opposition to the society envisioned by the framers of our Constitution," Judge Damon Keith wrote. He further noted that "democracy dies behind closed doors."

That was a clear victory for civil liberties and stands today, as the government chose not to seek Supreme Court review in that case. However, in the second lawsuit, the federal appeals court in Philadelphia sided with the government's position in a 2-1 ruling. The Supreme Court has declined to hear that case.

Increasing Inequality. "Equal Justice Under Law" is the motto inscribed above the Supreme Court building, but the legal system's treatment of the Arab and Muslim community in this country since September 11 has been separate, unequal and wrong.

Military detention of both citizen and non-citizen Arab and Muslim terrorism suspects stands in stark contrast to the treatment of homegrown terrorists like Timothy McVeigh. Arab and Muslim non-citizens – who enjoy the protection of the Bill of Rights no less than citizens – are facing what amounts to an entirely new legal system, with basic due process suspended. Not only do they face potential trial before special military tribunals – with access to counsel and information limited severely, unlike ordinary military courts – they can be whisked away without a hearing to face injustice in the legal netherworld of Guantanamo Bay, Cuba, or to detention and interrogation by governments with some of the worst human rights records in the world.

Recent reports indicate profoundly disturbing, and possibly criminal, United States collusion with regimes that practice torture, including Syria and Saudi Arabia. Maher Arar, a Canadian citizen, was detained by United States authorities in a New York airport while en route to his home in Canada, then sent to Syria, where he was held and, he alleges, tortured by the Syrian secret police. These allegations of torture, with the consent and possible encouragement of the United States, must be thoroughly investigated.

Many more Arab and Muslim non-citizens who have not faced the harrowing ordeal of detention without due process have had to undergo a demeaning registration process that is doing more to tarnish America's image abroad, and inhibit international cooperation, than any amount of money spent on public diplomacy could wash away.

Questions

Are strict security measures per definition incompatible with civil liberties?
How does this document indicate that US government actions following 9/11 undermined the protection of human rights in the transatlantic region?

References

https://www.aclu.org/other/aclu-testimony-hearing-america-after-911-freedom-preserved-or-freedom-lost-senate-judiciary
Permission: ACLU

Document 13

A Secure Europe in a Better World ("First European Security Strategy"), December 2003

After "9/11" and the Iraq invasion, the call for a separate European security strategy became louder. The EU High Representative for Common and Security Policy Javier Solana seemed, as a former Secretary General of NATO, to be the right person at the right time to draft the EU's first security strategy. He used it to outline the main priorities of and security threats to the EU. Despite emphasizing the need for multilateralism to deal with global challenges, a remarkable section in the document concerned the use of a pre-emptive strike. Surprisingly, the US concept of a pre-emptive strike was copied into the first European strategy paper, using more or less the same wording as the National Security Strategy (NSS) of the US published a year earlier. The 2002 NSS had been heavily criticized in Europe for several reasons, not least the statement that if necessary the UN Security Council would be circumvented in major questions of peace and war.

Nevertheless, Solana's strategy paper was clearly different in scope and starting point. The paper gives much more weight to multilateral cooperation in international affairs. Enlargement of the EU will clearly benefit Europe's stability as a whole, since, it was argued, it would work as a general process of pacification (this argument was also used in the 1990s with the enlargement of NATO). Nevertheless, the document re-emphasised that the US remained indispensable for transatlantic security, and hence the strategy was used to try and repair some of the damage caused by the US-led invasion of Iraq in March 2003.

[This is an excerpt from the full document]

Europe has never been so prosperous, so secure nor so free. The violence of the first half of the 20th Century has given way to a period of peace and stability unprecedented in European history.

The creation of the European Union has been central to this development. It has transformed the relations between our states, and the lives of our citizens. European countries are committed to dealing peacefully with disputes and to co-operating through common institutions. Over this period, the progressive spread of the rule of law and democracy has seen authoritarian regimes change into secure, stable and dynamic democracies. Successive enlargements are making a reality of the vision of a united and peaceful continent.

The United States has played a critical role in European integration and European security, in particular through NATO. The end of the Cold War has left the United States in a dominant position as a military actor. However, no single country is able to tackle today's complex problems on its own.

As a union of 25 states with over 450 million people producing a quarter of the world's Gross National Product (GNP), and with a wide range of instruments at its disposal, the European Union is inevitably a global player. In the last decade European forces have been deployed abroad to places as distant as Afghanistan, East Timor and the DRC

DOI: 10.4324/9781003159551-37

[Democratic Republic of the Congo]. The increasing convergence of European interests and the strengthening of mutual solidarity of the EU makes us a more credible and effective actor. Europe should be ready to share in the responsibility for global security and in building a better world.

No single country is able to tackle today's complex problems on its own. As a union of 25 states with over 450 million people producing a quarter of the world's Gross National Product (GNP), the European Union is inevitably a global player player. [I]t should be ready to share in the responsibility for global security and in building a better world.

The Security Environment: Global Challenges and Key Threats

Global Challenges

The post Cold War environment is one of increasingly open borders in which the internal and external aspects of security are indissolubly linked. Flows of trade and investment, the development of technology and the spread of democracy have brought freedom and prosperity to many people. Others have perceived globalisation as a cause of frustration and injustice. These developments have also increased the scope for non-state groups to play a part in international affairs. And they have increased European dependence – and so vulnerability – on an interconnected infrastructure in transport, energy, information and other fields.

Since 1990, almost 4 million people have died in wars, 90% of them civilians. Over 18 million people world-wide have left their homes as a result of conflict.

In much of the developing world, poverty and disease cause untold suffering and give rise to pressing security concerns. Almost 3 billion people, half the world's population, live on less than 2 Euros a day. 45 million die every year of hunger and malnutrition. AIDS is now one of the most devastating pandemics in human history and contributes to the breakdown of societies. New diseases can spread rapidly and become global threats. Sub-Saharan Africa is poorer now than it was 10 years ago. In many cases, economic failure is linked to political problems and violent conflict.

Security is a precondition of development. Conflict not only destroys infrastructure, including social infrastructure; it also encourages criminality, deters investment and makes normal economic activity impossible. A number of countries and regions are caught in a cycle of conflict, insecurity and poverty.

45 million people die every year of hunger and malnutrition. Aids contributes to the breakdown of societies ... Security is a precondition of development.

Competition for natural resources – notably water – which will be aggravated by global warming over the next decades, is likely to create further turbulence and migratory movements in various regions.

Energy dependence is a special concern for Europe. Europe is the world's largest importer of oil and gas. Imports account for about 50% of energy consumption today. This will rise to 70% in 2030. Most energy imports come from the Gulf, Russia and North Africa.

Key Threats

Large-scale aggression against any Member State is now improbable. Instead, Europe faces new threats which are more diverse, less visible and less predictable.

Terrorism: Terrorism puts lives at risk; it imposes large costs; it seeks to undermine the openness and tolerance of our societies, and it poses a growing strategic threat to the whole of Europe. Increasingly, terrorist movements are well-resourced, connected by electronic networks, and are willing to use unlimited violence to cause massive casualties.

The most recent wave of terrorism is global in its scope and is linked to violent religious extremism. It arises out of complex causes. These include the pressures of modernisation, cultural, social and political crises, and the alienation of young people living in foreign societies. This phenomenon is also a part of our own society.

Europe is both a target and a base for such terrorism: European countries are targets and have been attacked. Logistical bases for Al Qaeda cells have been uncovered in the UK, Italy, Germany, Spain and Belgium. Concerted European action is indispensable.

The last use of WMD was by the Aum terrorist sect in the Tokyo underground in 1995, using sarin gas. 12 people were killed and several thousand injured. Two years earlier, Aum had sprayed anthrax spores on a Tokyo street.

Proliferation of Weapons of Mass Destruction is potentially the greatest threat to our security. The international treaty regimes and export control arrangements have slowed the spread of WMD and delivery systems. We are now, however, entering a new and dangerous period that raises the possibility of a WMD arms race, especially in the Middle East. Advances in the biological sciences may increase the potency of biological weapons in the coming years; attacks with chemical and radiological materials are also a serious possibility. The spread of missile technology adds a further element of instability and could put Europe at increasing risk.

The most frightening scenario is one in which terrorist groups acquire weapons of mass destruction. In this event, a small group would be able to inflict damage on a scale previously possible only for States and armies.

Regional Conflicts: Problems such as those in Kashmir, the Great Lakes Region and the Korean Peninsula impact on European interests directly and indirectly, as do conflicts nearer to home, above all in the Middle East. Violent or frozen conflicts, which also persist on our borders, threaten regional stability. They destroy human lives and social and physical infrastructures; they threaten minorities, fundamental freedoms and human rights. Conflict can lead to extremism, terrorism and state failure; it provides opportunities for organised crime. Regional insecurity can fuel the demand for WMD. The most practical way to tackle the often elusive new threats will sometimes be to deal with the older problems of regional conflict.

State Failure: Bad governance – corruption, abuse of power, weak institutions and lack of accountability – and civil conflict corrode States from within. In some cases, this has brought about the collapse of State institutions. Somalia, Liberia and Afghanistan under the Taliban are the best known recent examples. Collapse of the State can be associated with obvious threats, such as organised crime or terrorism. State failure is an alarming phenomenon, that undermines global governance, and adds to regional instability.

Organised Crime: Europe is a prime target for organised crime. This internal threat to our security has an important external dimension: cross-border trafficking in drugs, women, illegal migrants and weapons accounts for a large part of the activities of criminal gangs. It can have links with terrorism.

Such criminal activities are often associated with weak or failing states. Revenues from drugs have fuelled the weakening of state structures in several drug-producing countries. Revenues from trade in gemstones, timber and small arms, fuel conflict in other parts of the world. All these activities undermine both the rule of law and social order itself. In extreme cases, organised crime can come to dominate the state. 90% of the heroin in Europe comes from poppies grown in Afghanistan – where the drugs trade pays for private armies. Most of it is distributed through Balkan criminal networks which are also responsible for some 200,000 of the 700,000 women victims of the sex trade world wide. A new dimension to organised crime which will merit further attention is the growth in maritime piracy.

Taking these different elements together – terrorism committed to maximum violence, the availability of weapons of mass destruction, organised crime, the weakening of the state system and the privatisation of force – we could be confronted with a very radical threat indeed.

Strategic Objectives

We live in a world that holds brighter prospects but also greater threats than we have known. The future will depend partly on our actions. We need both to think globally and to act locally.

In an era of globalisation, distant threats may be as much a concern as those that are near at hand. The first line of defence will be often be abroad. The new threats are dynamic.

Our traditional concept of self-defence – up to and including the Cold War – was based on the threat of invasion. With the new threats, the first line of defence will often be abroad. The new threats are dynamic. The risks of proliferation grow over time; left alone, terrorist networks will become ever more dangerous. State failure and organised crime spread if they are neglected – as we have seen in West Africa. This implies that we should be ready to act before a crisis occurs. Conflict prevention and threat prevention cannot start too early.

In contrast to the massive visible threat in the Cold War, none of the new threats is purely military; nor can any be tackled by purely military means. Each requires a mixture of instruments. Proliferation may be contained through export controls and attacked through political, economic and other pressures while the underlying political causes are also tackled. Dealing with terrorism may require a mixture of intelligence, police, judicial, military and other means. In failed states, military instruments may be needed to restore order, humanitarian means to tackle the immediate crisis. Regional conflicts need political solutions but military assets and effective policing may be needed in the post conflict phase. Economic instruments serve reconstruction, and civilian crisis management helps restore civil government. The European Union is particularly well equipped to respond to such multi-faceted situations.

Building Security in our Neighbourhood

Even in an era of globalisation, geography is still important. It is in the European interest that countries on our borders are well-governed. Neighbours who are engaged in violent conflict, weak states where organised crime flourishes, dysfunctional societies or exploding population growth on its borders all pose problems for enlargement should not create new dividing lines in Europe.

The integration of acceding states increases our security but also brings the EU closer to troubled areas. Our task is to promote a ring of well governed countries to the East of the European Union and on the borders of the Mediterranean with whom we can enjoy close and cooperative relations.

The importance of this is best illustrated in the Balkans. Through our concerted efforts with the US, Russia, NATO and other international partners, the stability of the region is no longer threatened by the outbreak of major conflict. The credibility of our foreign policy depends on the consolidation of our achievements there. The European perspective offers both a strategic objective and an incentive for reform.

It is not in our interest that enlargement should create new dividing lines in Europe. We need to extend the benefits of economic and political cooperation to our neighbours in the East while tackling political problems there. We should now take a stronger and more active interest in the problems of the Southern Caucasus, which will in due course also be a neighbouring region.

Resolution of the Arab/Israeli conflict is a strategic priority for Europe. Without this, there will be little chance of dealing with other problems in the Middle East. The European Union must remain engaged and ready to commit resources to the problem until it is solved. The two state solution – which Europe has long supported – is now widely accepted. Implementing it will require a united and cooperative effort by the European Union, the United States, the United Nations and Russia, and the countries of the region, but above all by the Israelis and the Palestinians themselves.

The Mediterranean area generally continues to undergo serious problems of economic stagnation, social unrest and unresolved conflicts. The European Union's interests require a continued engagement with Mediterranean partners, through more effective economic, security and cultural cooperation in the framework of the Barcelona Process. A broader engagement with the Arab World should also be considered.

An International Order Based on Effective Multilateralism

In a world of global threats, global markets, and global media, our security and prosperity increasingly depend on an effective multilateral system. The development of a stronger international society, well functioning international institutions and a rule-based international order is our objective.

We are committed to upholding and developing International Law. The fundamental framework for international relations is the United Nations Charter. The United Nations Security Council has the primary responsibility for the maintenance of international peace and security. Strengthening the United Nations, equipping it to fulfil its responsibilities and to act effectively, is a European priority.

We want international organisations, regimes and treaties to be effective in confronting threats to international peace and security, and must therefore be ready to act when their rules are broken.

Key institutions in the international system, such as the World Trade Organisation (WTO) and the International Financial Institutions, have extended their membership. China has joined the WTO and Russia is negotiating its entry. It should be an objective for us to widen the membership of such bodies while maintaining their high standards.

One of the core elements of the international system is the transatlantic relationship. This is not only in our bilateral interest but strengthens the international community as a whole. NATO is an important expression of this relationship.

Regional organisations also strengthen global governance. For the European Union, the strength and effectiveness of the OSCE and the Council of Europe has a particular significance. Other regional organisations such as ASEAN [Association of South-East Asian Nations], MERCOSUR [Mercado Común del Sur, or Southern Common Market] and the African Union make an important contribution to a more orderly world.

Our security and prosperity increasingly depend on an effective multilateral system. We are committed to upholding and developing International Law.

The fundamental framework for international relations is the United Nations Charter.

It is a condition of a rule-based international order that law evolves in response to developments such as proliferation, terrorism and global warming. We have an interest in further developing existing institutions such as the World Trade Organisation and in supporting new ones such as the International Criminal Court. Our own experience in Europe demonstrates that security can be increased through confidence building and arms control regimes. Such instruments can also make an important contribution to security and stability in our neighbourhood and beyond.

The quality of international society depends on the quality of the governments that are its foundation. The best protection for our security is a world of well-governed democratic states. Spreading good governance, supporting social and political reform, dealing with corruption and abuse of power, establishing the rule of law and protecting human rights are the best means of strengthening the international order.

Trade and development policies can be powerful tools for promoting reform. As the world's largest provider of official assistance and its largest trading entity, the European Union and its Member States are well placed to pursue these goals.

Contributing to better governance through assistance programmes, conditionality and targeted trade measures remains an important feature in our policy that we should further reinforce. A world seen as offering justice and opportunity for everyone will be more secure for the European Union and its citizens.

A number of countries have placed themselves outside the bounds of international society. Some have sought isolation; others persistently violate international norms. It is desirable that such countries should rejoin the international community, and the EU should be ready to provide assistance. Those who are unwilling to do so should understand that there is a price to be paid, including in their relationship with the European Union.

Policy Implications for Europe

The European Union has made progress towards a coherent foreign policy and effective crisis management. We have instruments in place that can be used effectively, as we have demonstrated in the Balkans and beyond. But if we are to make a contribution that matches our potential, we need to be more active, more coherent and more capable. And we need to work with others.

More active in pursuing our strategic objectives. This applies to the full spectrum of instruments for crisis management and conflict prevention at our disposal, including political, diplomatic, military and civilian, trade and development activities. Active policies are needed to counter the new dynamic threats. We need to develop a strategic culture that fosters early, rapid, and when necessary, robust intervention.

As a Union of 25 members, spending more than 160 billion Euros on defence, we should be able to sustain several operations simultaneously. We could add particular value by developing operations involving both military and civilian capabilities.

The EU should support the United Nations as it responds to threats to international peace and security. The EU is committed to reinforcing its cooperation with the UN to assist countries emerging from conflicts, and to enhancing its support for the UN in short-term crisis management situations.

We need to be able to act before countries around us deteriorate, when signs of proliferation are detected, and before humanitarian emergencies arise. Preventive engagement can avoid more serious problems in the future. A European Union which takes greater responsibility and which is more active will be one which carries greater political weight.

We need to develop a strategic culture that fosters early, rapid and when necessary, robust intervention.

More Capable. A more capable Europe is within our grasp, though it will take time to realise our full potential. Actions underway – notably the establishment of a defence agency – take us in the right direction.

To transform our militaries into more flexible, mobile forces, and to enable them to address the new threats, more resources for defence and more effective use of resources are necessary. The EU-NATO permanent arrangements, in particular Berlin Plus, enhance the operational capability of the EU and provide the framework for the strategic partnership between the two organisations in crisis management. This reflects our common determination to tackle the challenges of the new century.

More Coherent. The point of the Common Foreign and Security Policy and European Security and Defence Policy is that we are stronger when we act together. Over recent years we have created a number of different instruments, each of which has its own structure and rationale.

The challenge now is to bring together the different instruments and capabilities: European assistance programmes and the European Development Fund, military and civilian capabilities from Member States and other instruments. All of these can have an impact on our security and on that of third countries. Security is the first condition for development.

Diplomatic efforts, development, trade and environmental policies, should follow the same agenda. In a crisis there is no substitute for unity of command.

Working with partners. There are few if any problems we can deal with on our own. The threats described above are common threats, shared with all our closest partners. International cooperation is a necessity. We need to pursue our objectives both through multilateral cooperation in international organisations and through partnerships with key actors.

The transatlantic relationship is irreplaceable. Acting together, the European Union and the United States can be a formidable force for good in the world. Our aim should be an effective and balanced partnership with the USA. This is an additional reason for the EU to build up further its capabilities and increase its coherence.

Questions

How "European" is the (first) European Security Strategy?
In what ways does this Strategy aim to solidify transatlantic consensus on security threats?

Reference

https://data.consilium.europa.eu/References/Referencesument/ST-15895-2003-INIT/en/pdf

Document 14

"Technology and its Impact on Globalization," World Youth Report, United Nations Department of Economic and Social Affairs, October 2005

The 2000s saw a rapid evolution of relatively new technologies and their introduction into mainstream society. In 2006 Thomas Friedman would coin the expression "the world is flat," pointing out that due to forces of globalization, industrial production and commerce were no longer hindered by borders or any other obstacles. Geography seemed to have become irrelevant: the world had become one "flat" competitive market. Technological developments in the field of finance, such as the integration of financial markets, high-frequency trading and Fin-tech companies, made this possible. Most striking were consumer-related products under the overarching name of social media.

American companies led the way in this social media revolution. At the beginning of the century Steve Jobs, founder and owner of Apple, introduced the first iPhone and conquered the world with trending and innovative consumer products. Mark Zuckerberg founded Facebook and acquired other social media platforms, such as Instagram and WhatsApp. Twitter expanded quickly after 2006, introducing a new channel for rapid, compact communication. Android introduced a new operating system that soon would became a global standard. The early consolidation of social media platforms with global reach in mainly American hands – led by Facebook and Twitter – was a remarkable phenomenon. Another tech giant, Google, also grew exponentially into one of the biggest information-media service companies. This also led to increasing concerns about the power of these private companies, the amount of information on individuals that they held, and their political influence. While social media became ever-present in political campaigning during the 2010s, it was President Trump who used Twitter as a powerful tool of one-way communication with his supporters and also in direct communication with other world leaders. Having been based on freedom of information for all, social media corporations became increasingly under pressure to monitor their content due to rising concerns about "fake news" and the ability of foreign powers to manipulate public opinion (with special reference to the Russian efforts to influence the 2016 US presidential election). Additionally, the leaks by National Security Agency contractor Edward Snowden from 2013 onwards indicated clearly how these tech companies were deeply implicated in the surveillance strategies of the US security establishment (see Part III Document 4).

There were plenty of downsides to this increasing global connectivity, not least the new level of inequality that was emerging between those increasingly connected and those being fast left behind. This UN report highlighted the consequences of the social media revolution for large sections of the world's youth.

[This is an excerpt from the full document]

Globalization

1   Globalization, roughly defined as the global integration of economies and societies, affects many aspects of young peoples' lives. Youth have an ambiguous relationship

DOI: 10.4324/9781003159551-38

with the globalizing world, both economically and culturally. On the one hand, they are most flexible and perhaps best able to adapt to and make use of new opportunities offered. They are the best educated generation on new information technologies; they benefit from economic growth; many travel around the world for work, studies, exchange projects and vacation; and telephone and the Internet enable them to stay in touch with friends and relatives abroad. On the other hand, many youth, especially in developing countries, have been left out of the digitalization and modernization process and lack the economic power to benefit from the opportunities globalization offers.

2   Globalization can be a powerful force for poverty reduction. Many countries have seen improvements in their welfare and educational systems as a consequence of globalization. Unfortunately, about 2 billion people live in countries that do not benefit from globalization, mainly in parts of sub-Saharan Africa, Western Asia and the former Soviet Union. These countries have seen a declining economic growth rate, loss of jobs, low incomes, and poor education and health provision. The income gap is widening not only between, but also within countries.

3   Globalization has substantially changed the job market, to which young people, as newcomers, are "most vulnerable". New technologies have replaced manual labour, mainly affecting low skilled jobs in the service sector. Trade liberalization forces companies to become more flexible and competitive. Many have become increasingly dependent on low-cost, flexible labour, often employed on an irregular basis. The outsourcing of sophisticated programming assignments and semi-skilled jobs in call centres to low-wage countries is perhaps the best known example of the global shift of employment opportunities for young people.

4   Migration, both within and between countries, is another aspect of globalization. Young people have always been a significant group among migrants. As foreign investment often creates job opportunities in the cities of host countries, rural workers move to the cities. In 2003, 48 per cent of the world's population lived in urban areas, and it is projected that over 50 per cent will do so by 2007.

5   Globalization has numerous consequences for youth cultures. The increase in media streams has resulted in global consumerism. American and European-produced content is increasingly dominating entertainment around the world. Young people tend to adopt and interpret global products in terms of their own local cultures and experiences, thereby creating new hybrid cultural forms whose meanings vary with local and national circumstances.

6   Young people around the world show concern about the negative consequences of globalization, such as unequal distribution of wealth and environmental degradation. The anti-globalization movement has expanded all over the world and comprises a heterogeneous group of non-governmental organizations, student groups, political organizations and civil rights activists. The movement fights for various issues such as global justice, fair trade, debt relief, and sustainable development.

Questions

How has social media both enhanced and undermined transatlantic relations?

If the transatlantic region was leading the forces of globalization, how does this report indicate the positives and negatives of these processes?

Reference

https://www.un.org/development/desa/youth/globalization-wpay.html

Document 15

René Cuperus, "Why the Dutch Voted No: Anatomy of the New Euroscepticism in 'Old Europe'," *Progressive Politics*, 4/2 (Summer 2005), pp. 92–101

The rejection of the EU constitution (formally the European Constitutional Treaty) by French and Dutch voters in referenda came as a shock to European leaders. It showed that the assumptions of the pro-European political elites as to the level of popular support for major European initiatives were mistaken, and that more effort would have to be made to overcome a growing Euro-scepticism. In this article René Cuperus, at the time working at a Labour-affiliated think tank, assessed the reasons for the referenda outcomes and urged EU leaders to give time and space for reflection about the way Europe was developing. Only in this way could citizens be convinced of the value of the "European project". The term is derived from the French term "projet européene" and was used in place of the pejorative phrase "European integration". The final referendum results of the Dutch vote were: No 61,6%, Yes 38,4%. The turnout was 62,8%. In France the results were slightly better at No 54,7%, Yes 45,3%. The turnout was 69%. It would take the European leaders another four years before a similar, less triumphant but nevertheless far-reaching agreement – the Lisbon treaty in 2009 – could be signed (see Part II Document 19).

[This is an excerpt from the full document]

It was always thought that the Netherlands, being one of the Founding Fathers of the European Community, was a stable pro-European force. Now it seems to be the case, that the elitist character of the Dutch political party system for long covered up an undercurrent of Euro-scepticism. Ambivalent European sentiments have been increased considerably by the radical acceleration of the European Project in the last decade (enlargement, EMU & the euro, liberalisation). The referendum gave, for the first time, an opening for the Euro-sceptics and those who are ambivalent towards the actual speed and direction of European integration.

This can only be characterised as an 'anti-establishment landslide', because all mainstream political parties (from conservative-liberals to the Greens) and the majority of Dutch civil society (trade unions, the media, conservation and ecology movement) were supporting the yes-campaign for the Constitution.

Who were the no-voters?

Employees earning average incomes with relatively lower education; Protestant Christian fundamentalists; right wing populists; left wing populists (Socialist Party); half of the constituency of the social-democratic PvdA [Labour party]; half of the Greens constituency; half of social-liberal constituency (middle income groups; lower and middle class).

DOI: 10.4324/9781003159551-39

Which motives for the no-vote

The Netherlands is paying too much to the EU (the problem of being the highest net contributor); The Netherlands is no longer boss in it's own country; The Netherlands has too little influence in Europe compared to other countries; Netherlands is losing its identity; Netherlands is becoming too dependent of the EU; Because of Brussels bureaucracy; Because of the bad influence of the Euro; Because the Dutch lose jobs to foreigners.

A more fundamental analysis of the Dutch no-vote in the referendum on the European Constitution is a story with two faces:

It's a story about the political identity crisis of the Netherlands; and a story about the 'imperial overstretch' of the European Project.

The story of the Netherlands

One could say that an overall distrust in politics, politicians and political institutions is one of the key-ingredients of the new eurosceptical mood in the Netherlands. The yes-campaign unintentionally fuelled this fire of negative doubt. Not only, like in France, this campaign was led by a ruling government which is extremely unpopular (welfare state reform without any inspirational mobilization and weak political leadership), but also the campaign suffered from still a strong populist anti-establishment current in the Netherlands; the post-Pim Fortuyn era, which represents a deep distrust between political elites and citizens.

My country still faces a crisis of trust, a crisis of identity, a crisis of self-confidence. All to do with the political climate: distrust between political elite and the people, crisis of representation. [It] Came to the surface with the populist revolt of the citizens, of the Pim Fortuyn movement, growing worse with the murder of this Pim Fortuyn by a radical environmental activist. And later [the] killing [of] the filmmaker Theo van Gogh by a fundamentalist Muslim, shocked our relatively quiet and peaceful country again.

These grave incidents added to a more general feeling of discontent and fear. Western Europe is in the grip of a political identity crisis. The disrupting effects of globalisation and the permanent retrenchment of the welfare states are accompanied by fundamental changes in the political party system: the triumph of the floating voter, i.e. the unprecedented rise of electoral volatility, and the spectacular jump in the political arena of neo-populist movements.

The traditional mass parties that have ruled the region at least since the end of the Second World War have lost members, voters, élan, and a monopoly on ideas. Because they are the pillars of both the party-oriented parliamentary system and the welfare state, their slow but steady decline affects European societies as a whole. Due to changes in labour, family and cultural life styles, the Christian Democratic and Social Democratic pillars of civil society are eroding away, leaving behind "people's parties" with shrinking numbers of people. This erosion of political representation eats away at the foundations of the European welfare states and European party democracies.

The second ingredient of the European crisis is what might be called the paradox of the Holocaust trauma. Europeans seem unable to cope with the question of ethnic diversity. Intellectual discourse was long characterized by a species of political correctness which praised multiculturalism and 'The Foreigner' as enriching society while turning a blind eye to the *de facto* segregation of many new immigrants and the stress they placed on the welfare system in many nations. These problems did much to provoke a populist-xenophobic reaction. In this respect, Europe is facing two dilemmas: 1. how to maintain its 'communitarian' welfare states under conditions of permanent immigration?; 2. to what extent the integration patterns in Europe will be determined by multiculturalism or assimilationism?

A third ingredient of the crisis is widespread unease over the process of European integration. What should be a proud achievement of cosmopolitan cooperation between nations has become, instead, a cause of increasing insecurity and national alienation. This discontent with the European Union propelled considerably by the uncertain, unintended effects of the so-called European enlargement: the arrival of a series of 10 new East-Central European member states to the EU.

The fourth component is the fact that all this discontent is channeled through the rise of right wing populist movements and in Europe, totally unlike the American tradition, populism is more or less associated with fascism. This in itself adds up to the sense of crisis.

It was this potentially explosive mix that was first skilfully tapped by Pim Fortuyn, the flamboyant publicist-turned-politician slain in May 2002; it is this same mix that produces so much volatility in voting behaviour on the European constitution in one of the founding nations of the European Union.

There was no connection made whatsoever with people with doubts (Europe-agnosticists), people who are in favour of European integration and cooperation to a certain extent, but who fear the idea of a Super state Constitution or are worried about new steps towards an 'ever closer union'.

For the first time in say fifty years the people now have been asked about their opinions on the European integration. Before is [sic] was a plaything of the elites, Europe is meta-politics, *Politikerpolitik*, as the Germans call it: politics for politicians, not for ordinary citizens. With this referendum, and it was engineered for that purpose, it was the idea to close the gap between European Project and the people.

[The] story [is] also about Europe itself. The referendum asked a mandate of trust for a rapidly changing Europe, for a Europe in transformation. The Eurocrats act as if there is a natural, straight development line from the Europe of Schumann and Monnet to nowadays Europe, all to be defended by the old mantra of 'never war again', but in the meantime a silent metamorphosis took place. The acceleration of the European process (the seemingly endless enlargement, EMU, euro, geopolitical entity) made the European Project not stable, non-transparent, unpredictable and a easy prey for nationalist and right wing populist counter mobilization.

What are the main problems of Europe, as perceived by the Dutch?

Europe is perceived/felt by people as a transmitter or even accelerator of the globalisation process. Instead of being the shield or the filter against disrupting and dislocating globalisation and liberalisation, the EU (with its internal market dynamics and the social en cultural 'collateral damage') acts as a agent of Anglosaxon globalisation (with polarising and divergent consequences for different groups and sectors in society and economy).

There is no trust that the European Union will defend the 'European Social Model'.

The European Union seems not to be the umbrella under which the rich European diversity is flourishing, but instead acting as a razor blade making member states, national cultures and traditions and societies uniform, having not much respect for multicoloured diversity and differences (a Europe against Spanish bull-fighting, Buttiglione, Haider). This is the sentiment of Brussels, becoming a new Leviathan, a new centralised Super State, with its directories.

The lack of prudence, of modesty of the European regulation machinery, which sometimes have deep consequences for national, regional and local practices. It's about the penetration and intervention of European regulation (directories).

Although there is lot of rhetorical talk about the principle of subsidiarity and the lie that Europe restricts itself only to border crossing issues and problems, the day-to-day real world of Brussels points in another direction: jurisdiction of the European Court had deep technocratic uniforming and penetrating effects, so does the logic of the level playing field of the internal market.

The basic problem is that the Eurocratic establishment does not give any time and space for reflection, second thoughts and criticism about the way Europe is developing. This in itself is what makes the European Project very un-European, birthplace of intellectual self-criticism and reflection.

Questions

Do you think that the Dutch concerns and complaints about the European project are unique, or broadly shared by other European publics?
Is there a "transatlantic project", of which the "European project" is a part?

References

Permission: René Cuperus

Document 16
North Atlantic Council, Bucharest Summit Declaration, 3 April 2008

The NATO summit in Bucharest was the last one attended by the American President George W. Bush. His administration definitely wanted to leave behind a robust legacy, and this became clear in the intense discussions concerning possible NATO membership for Ukraine and Georgia. Both countries had recently experienced popular revolts against corruption and election fraud. The peaceful "Rose Revolution" in Georgia in November 2003 brought down the remains of the Soviet-influenced political system, with Eduard Shevardnadze (formerly Gorbachev's foreign minister) replaced by the pro-Western Mikheil Saakashvili. From November 2004 to January 2005 the "Orange Revolution" in Ukraine took place, with protestors contesting the fraudulent election victory of the pro-Russian Viktor Yanukovych and eventually ousting him in favour of the pro-Western Viktor Yushchenko. Both countries subsequently declared interest in membership of both NATO and the EU as a way of loosening the influence of Moscow. Russia looked upon these developments with suspicion, fearing it would lose control over its immediate neighbourhood.

From the start NATO allies had held differing views on the pace and scope of enlargement, in particular regarding countries directly bordering Russia. Germany and France above all warned about repercussions from Moscow. During the Bucharest summit some heated debates took place between the US, French and German delegations. Pressured by time constraints, the political leaders by-passed their diplomats and themselves personally edited the text covering NATO's future relationship with Ukraine and Georgia. The result (see Article 23 below) caused a stir in international diplomatic circles, because it ignored the accepted sequence for enlargement – an applicant state should first fulfil NATO's Membership Action Plan (MAP), and only then should an invitation to join the alliance be issued. The outcome, which demonstrated the pressure that the Bush administration had brought to bear on its NATO allies, set off alarm bells in Moscow. Georgia would be the first to experience Moscow's retaliation in the war of August 2008, with Ukraine following soon after (see Part III Document 5).

[This is an excerpt from the full document. The original numbers of the communiqué's articles have been kept]

1 We, the Heads of State and Government of the member countries of the North Atlantic Alliance, met today to enlarge our Alliance and further strengthen our ability to confront the existing and emerging 21st century security threats. We reviewed the significant progress we have made in recent years to transform NATO, agreeing that this is a process that must continue. Recognising the enduring value of the transatlantic link and of NATO as the essential forum for security consultations between Europe and North America, we reaffirmed our solidarity and cohesion and our commitment to the common vision and shared democratic values embodied in the Washington

DOI: 10.4324/9781003159551-40

Treaty. The principle of the indivisibility of Allied security is fundamental. A strong collective defence of our populations, territory and forces is the core purpose of our Alliance and remains our most important security task. We reiterate our faith in the purposes and principles of the United Nations Charter.

2   Today, we have decided to invite Albania and Croatia to begin accession talks to join our Alliance. We congratulate these countries on this historic achievement, earned through years of hard work and a demonstrated commitment to our common security and NATO's shared values. The accession of these new members will strengthen security for all in the Euro-Atlantic area, and bring us closer to our goal of a Europe that is whole, free, and at peace.

3   We look forward to the 60th Anniversary Summit in 2009, which will underscore the enduring importance of the transatlantic link. We continue to transform our Alliance with new members; better responses to security challenges, taking into account lessons learned; more deployable capabilities; and new relationships with our partners. The Summit will provide an opportunity to further articulate and strengthen the Alliance's vision of its role in meeting the evolving challenges of the 21st century and maintaining the ability to perform the full range of its missions, collectively defending our security at home and contributing to stability abroad. Accordingly, we request the Council in Permanent Session to prepare a Declaration on Alliance Security for adoption at the Summit to further set the scene for this important task.

18   NATO's ongoing enlargement process has been an historic success in advancing stability and cooperation and bringing us closer to our common goal of a Europe whole and free, united in peace, democracy and common values. NATO's door will remain open to European democracies willing and able to assume the responsibilities and obligations of membership, in accordance with Article 10 of the Washington Treaty. We reiterate that decisions on enlargement are for NATO itself to make.

23   NATO welcomes Ukraine's and Georgia's Euro-Atlantic aspirations for membership in NATO. We agreed today that these countries will become members of NATO. Both nations have made valuable contributions to Alliance operations. We welcome the democratic reforms in Ukraine and Georgia and look forward to free and fair parliamentary elections in Georgia in May. MAP is the next step for Ukraine and Georgia on their direct way to membership. Today we make clear that we support these countries' applications for MAP. Therefore we will now begin a period of intensive engagement with both at a high political level to address the questions still outstanding pertaining to their MAP applications. We have asked Foreign Ministers to make a first assessment of progress at their December 2008 meeting. Foreign Ministers have the authority to decide on the MAP applications of Ukraine and Georgia.

Questions

Why would NATO membership for Georgia and Ukraine be considered so problematic for Russia?

Does an organization like NATO always have to expand, or can its membership be static, or even contract?

Reference

https://www.nato.int/cps/en/natolive/official_texts_8443.htm

Document 17

Richard Fuld, Testimony to Congress on Lehman Brothers Bankruptcy, House Oversight and Reform Committee, Washington, DC, 6 October 2008

On 6 October 2008 the CEO of Lehman Brothers, Richard Fuld, testified before the House Oversight and Reform Committee about the bank's bankruptcy announced on 15 September 2008. It was the largest bankruptcy filing in American history, yet neither he nor anybody else at Lehman Brothers seemed to have anticipated it. The run on the bank and the consequent problems caused by "false information and rumours" circulated by the media were totally unforeseen. The bankruptcy triggered a crisis of confidence in the US banking system, starting with the mortgage markets and quickly spreading to the entire financial system of the United States and beyond.

In hindsight it was already clear that by 2007 the global financial markets were showing signs of an approaching financial crisis. A period of ultra-low interest rates, deliberately applied to stimulate economic growth following the shock of "9/11", had brought about a housing bubble and extensive markets for complicated, risky financial products (such as collateralized debt obligations) that were understood by only a few financial specialists, often not even by the bankers themselves. Once interest rates started to rise in 2004–2005, the financial pressure on the mortgage market and home owners became unsupportable, and widespread mortgage defaults were the result.

Public opinion was shocked by the Lehman Brothers bankruptcy, but anger was really directed at the practices of self-enrichment of the bank's management. The crisis would cost millions of people their jobs and homes, and would contribute to the rise of political populism on both sides of the Atlantic (see Part II Document 22, and Part III Document 8).

[This is an excerpt from the full document]

MR. FULD: Chairman Waxman, Ranking Member Davis, and Members of this distinguished committee:

Today there is unprecedented turmoil in our capital markets. Nobody, including me, anticipated how the problems that started in the mortgage markets would spread to our credit markets, and our banking system, and now threaten our entire financial system and our country.

Like many other financial institutions, Lehman Brothers got caught in this financial tsunami. But I want to be very clear. I take full responsibility for the decisions that I made and for the actions that I took. Based on the information that we had at the time, I believed that these decisions and actions were both prudent and appropriate.

None of us ever gets the opportunity to turn back the clock. But with the benefit of hindsight, would I have done things differently? Yes, I would have. As painful as this is for all of the people affected by the bankruptcy of Lehman Brothers, this is not just about Lehman Brothers. These problems are not limited to Wall Street, or even Main Street. This is a crisis for the global economy.

DOI: 10.4324/9781003159551-41

We live in a world where large investment – large independent U.S. investment banks are now extinct, where AIG and Fannie Mae and Freddie Mac are under government control, and where major institutions are being rescued, and where regulators are engaged in a daily struggle to stabilize the financial system. In this environment, it's not surprising that the media coverage of Lehman's demise has been rife with rumors and inaccuracies. I appreciate the opportunity to set the record straight for this committee, and to be as helpful as possible in explaining why we ultimately could not prevent a bankruptcy filing. And then I want to respond to your questions.

I'm a Lehman lifer. I joined as an intern in 1966, and got a full-time job as a commercial paper trader while earning my business degree at night. In 1994, when Lehman Brothers was spun out of American Express as a separate company and I became the CEO, we were a small domestic bond firm. By 2007, we had built Lehman into a diversified global firm with 28,000 employees. I feel a deep personal connection to those 28,000 great people, many of whom have dedicated their entire careers to Lehman Brothers. I feel horrible about what has happened to the company and its effects on so many – my colleagues, my shareholders, my creditors, and my clients.

As CEO, I was a significant shareholder, and my long-term financial interests were completely aligned with those of all the other shareholders. No one had more incentive to see Lehman Brothers succeed. And because I believed so deeply in the company, I never sold the vast majority of my Lehman Brothers stock, and still owned 10 million shares when we filed for bankruptcy.

As I said, following the spin-off of Lehman Brothers from American Express, our business was almost exclusively at a fixed income. We recognized the need for diversification, and over the subsequent 14 years we built and acquired significant equity and asset management businesses. We established a presence in 28 countries. We also continually strengthened our risk management infrastructure.

Lehman Brothers did have a significant presence in the mortgage market. This should not be surprising, though. U.S. residential mortgages are an 11 trillion dollar market, more than twice the size of the U.S. Treasury market, and a serious participant in the fixed-income business, had a significant presence in the mortgage market.

As the environment changed, we took numerous actions to reduce our risk. We strengthened our balance sheet, reduced leverage, improved liquidity, closed our mortgage origination businesses, and reduced our exposure to troubled assets. We also raised over 10 billion dollars in new capital. We explored converting to a back – a bank holding company. We looked at a wide range of strategic alternatives, including spinning off our commercial real estate assets to our shareholders.

We also considered selling part or all of the company. We approached many potential investors, but in a market paralyzed by a crisis in confidence none of these discussions came to fruition. Indeed, contrary to what you may have read, I never turned down an offer to buy Lehman Brothers. Throughout 2008, the SEC [Securities and Exchanges Commission] and the Federal Reserve conducted regular, and at times daily, oversight of our business and our balance sheet. They saw what we saw in real time as they reviewed our liquidity and our funding, our capital risk management and our mark-to-market process.

As the crisis in confidence spread throughout the capital markets, naked short sellers targeted financial institutions and spread rumors and false information. The impact of this market manipulation became self-fulfilling. As short sellers drove down the stock prices of financial firms, the rating agencies lowered their ratings because lower stock prices made it harder to raise capital and reduced financial flexibility. The downgrades in turn caused lenders and counter parties to reduce credit lines and then demand more collateral, which increased liquidity pressures.

At Lehman Brothers, the crisis in confidence that permeated the markets led to an extraordinary run on the bank. In the end, despite all of our efforts, we were overwhelmed. However, what happened to Lehman Brothers could have happened to any financial institution, and almost did happen to others. Bear Stearns, Fannie Mae, Freddie Mac, AIG, Washington Mutual, and Merrill Lynch all were trapped in this vicious cycle. Morgan Stanley and Goldman Sachs also came under attack.

Lehman's demise was brought on by many destabilizing factors: the collapse of the real estate market, naked short attacks, false rumors, widening spreads on credit default swaps, rating agency downgrades, a loss of confidence by clients and counter parties, and buyers sitting on the sidelines waiting for an assisted deal. Again, this is not just a Lehman Brothers story. It's now an all-too-familiar tale. It is too late for Lehman Brothers, but the government has now been forced to dramatically change the rules and provide substantial support to other institutions.

CHAIRMAN WAXMAN: Mr. Fuld, the committee – our committee – requested all the documents relating to your salary, bonuses and stock sales; and the committee staff put together a chart, which I hope will come up on the screen.

This chart will show your compensation for the last 8 years. It shows your base salary, your cash bonuses and your stock sales. In 2000, you received over 52 million dollars. In 2001, that increased to 98 million dollars. It dipped for a few years. And then in 2005, you took home 89 million dollars. In 2006, you made a huge stock sale, and you received over 100 million dollars in that year alone. Are these figures basically accurate?

MR. FULD: Sir, if those are the documents that we provided to you, I would assume they are.

CHAIRMAN WAXMAN: Okay. The bottom line is that, since 2000, you have taken home more than 480 million dollars. That's almost half a billion dollars, and that's difficult to comprehend for a lot of people. Your company is now bankrupt; our economy is in a state of crisis; but you get to keep 480 million dollars. I – I have a very basic question for you: Is this fair?

MR. FULD: Mr. Chairman, your first question was about this slide: Are those numbers accurate? They are accurate the way you have put them up on that slide, but – I believe your number of cash and salary bonuses are accurate. The option exercises – the way you have them portrayed here I believe represent the full option without the strike price. And the only reason I exercised those options was because they came due at maturity. If I had not exercised those, I would have lost it. There was that stock sale, but –

CHAIRMAN WAXMAN: Well...I'll leave the record open for you to give me any changes in that list.

MR. FULD: What I would say to you –

CHAIRMAN WAXMAN: But, basically, didn't you take home around 4 to 500 million dollars as the head of Lehman Brothers for the last – since 2000 to now?

MR. FULD: The majority of my stocks, sir, came – excuse me – the majority of my compensation came in stock. The vast majority of the stock that I got I still owned at the point of our filing.

CHAIRMAN WAXMAN: The stock is in addition to the numbers that I've indicated, because those were your salary and your bonuses. Now, you had bonuses; and, in addition to that, you had some stock sales. You've lost some money of the stock that you've received as compensation, which you received as compensation on top of these other figures. So you've been able to pocket close to half a (billion) dollars. And my question to you is, a lot of people ask, "Is that fair for the CEO of a company that's now bankrupt to have made that kind of money?" It's just unimaginable to so many people.

MR. FULD: I would say to you the 500 number is not accurate. I would say to you that, although it's still a large number, I think for the years that you're talking about here, I believe my cash compensation was close to 60 million, which you have indicated here. And I believe the amount that I took out of the company over and above that was, I believe, a little bit less than 250 million. Still a large number, though.

CHAIRMAN WAXMAN: Still a large amount of money. You have a 14 million dollar ocean front home in Florida. You have a summer vacation home in Sun Valley, Idaho. You and your wife have an art collection filled with million dollar paintings. Your former President, Joe Gregory, used to travel to work in his own private helicopter. I guess people wonder, if you made all this money by taking risks with other people's money, you could have done other things. You had high leverage, 30 to 1 and higher. You didn't pay out billions of dollars in dividends. And you didn't have to pay out these millions of dollars in dividends and bonuses. You could have saved some of these funds for lean times, but you didn't.

Do you think it's fair and do you have any recommendations on fundamental reforms that would bring a new approach to executive compensation? Because it seems that the system worked for you, but it didn't seem to work for the rest of the country and the taxpayers who now have to pay up to 700 billion dollars to bail out our economy.

You can't – We can't continue to have a system where Wall Street executives privatize all the gains and then socialize the losses. Accountability needs to be a two-way street. Do you disagree with that? And do you have any recommendations of what we ought to be doing in this area?

MR. FULD: Mr. Chairman, we had a compensation committee that spent a tremendous amount of time making sure that the interests of the executives and the employees were aligned with shareholders. My employees owned close to 30 percent of our company, and that was because we wanted them to think, act, and behave like shareholders. When the company did well, we did well. When the company did not do well, sir, we did not do well.

Questions

Is there any way that the scale of Fuld's earnings could be justified?
Does Fuld give a picture of a well-managed financial sector, or a sector that is highly unstable?

References

https://www.americanrhetoric.com/speeches/richardfuldlehmanbrosbankruptcytestimony.htm
Permission: AmericanRhetoric/Online Speech Bank

Document 18

President Obama, Speech on Nuclear Weapons, Prague, May 2009

Shortly after North Korea test-launched a long-range rocket, President Obama put forward the ideal of a nuclear-free world in his first major foreign policy speech after his election. Obama had gone to Prague to commemorate the tenth anniversary of the Czech Republic's NATO membership. At the time the Czech Republic, together with Poland, was in the race to host part of NATO's anti-ballistic missile system designed to protect against a missile threat from Iran (see Part I Document 20).

President Obama argued that the US, as the only state that had used nuclear weapons in the past, had a moral responsibility to lead the way towards full disarmament among the seven countries that possessed them. He announced concrete policy measures to achieve that goal, among them strengthening the Nuclear Non-Proliferation Treaty. This treaty had come into force in 1970 and was meant to prevent the spread of nuclear weapons and promote complete nuclear disarmament. It was signed by almost all UN members, including the major nuclear powers, the US, Russia and China. The treaty was not signed, however, by a few states who refused to abandon their nuclear ambitions (North Korea, India, Pakistan and Israel).

[This is an excerpt from the full document]

This marks the 10th year of NATO membership for the Czech Republic. And I know that many times in the 20th century, decisions were made without you at the table. Great powers let you down, or determined your destiny without your voice being heard. I am here to say that the United States will never turn its back on the people of this nation. We are bound by shared values, shared history. We are bound by shared values and shared history and the enduring promise of our alliance. NATO's Article V states it clearly: An attack on one is an attack on all. That is a promise for our time, and for all time.

The people of the Czech Republic kept that promise after America was attacked; thousands were killed on our soil, and NATO responded. NATO's mission in Afghanistan is fundamental to the safety of people on both sides of the Atlantic.

We must strengthen our cooperation with one another, and with other nations and institutions around the world, to confront dangers that recognize no borders. And we must pursue constructive relations with Russia on issues of common concern.

Now, one of those issues that I'll focus on today is fundamental to the security of our nations and to the peace of the world—that's the future of nuclear weapons in the 21st century.

The existence of thousands of nuclear weapons is the most dangerous legacy of the Cold War. No nuclear war was fought between the United States and the Soviet Union, but generations lived with the knowledge that their world could be erased in a single flash of light. Cities like Prague that existed for centuries, that embodied the beauty and the talent of so much of humanity, would have ceased to exist.

DOI: 10.4324/9781003159551-42

Today, the Cold War has disappeared but thousands of those weapons have not. In a strange turn of history, the threat of global nuclear war has gone down, but the risk of a nuclear attack has gone up. More nations have acquired these weapons. Testing has continued. Black market trade in nuclear secrets and nuclear materials abound. The technology to build a bomb has spread. Terrorists are determined to buy, build or steal one. Our efforts to contain these dangers are centered on a global non-proliferation regime, but as more people and nations break the rules, we could reach the point where the center cannot hold.

Now, understand, this matters to people everywhere. One nuclear weapon exploded in one city—be it New York or Moscow, Islamabad or Mumbai, Tokyo or Tel Aviv, Paris or Prague—could kill hundreds of thousands of people. And no matter where it happens, there is no end to what the consequences might be—for our global safety, our security, our society, our economy, to our ultimate survival.

Some argue that the spread of these weapons cannot be stopped, cannot be checked—that we are destined to live in a world where more nations and more people possess the ultimate tools of destruction. Such fatalism is a deadly adversary, for if we believe that the spread of nuclear weapons is inevitable, then in some way we are admitting to ourselves that the use of nuclear weapons is inevitable.

Just as we stood for freedom in the 20th century, we must stand together for the right of people everywhere to live free from fear in the 21st century. And as nuclear power—as a nuclear power, as the only nuclear power to have used a nuclear weapon, the United States has a moral responsibility to act. We cannot succeed in this endeavor alone, but we can lead it, we can start it.

So today, I state clearly and with conviction America's commitment to seek the peace and security of a world without nuclear weapons. I'm not naive. This goal will not be reached quickly—perhaps not in my lifetime. It will take patience and persistence. But now we, too, must ignore the voices who tell us that the world cannot change. We have to insist, "Yes, we can."

Now, let me describe to you the trajectory we need to be on. First, the United States will take concrete steps towards a world without nuclear weapons. To put an end to Cold War thinking, we will reduce the role of nuclear weapons in our national security strategy, and urge others to do the same. Make no mistake: As long as these weapons exist, the United States will maintain a safe, secure and effective arsenal to deter any adversary, and guarantee that defense to our allies—including the Czech Republic. But we will begin the work of reducing our arsenal.

To reduce our warheads and stockpiles, we will negotiate a new Strategic Arms Reduction Treaty with the Russians this year. President Medvedev and I began this process in London, and will seek a new agreement by the end of this year that is legally binding and sufficiently bold. And this will set the stage for further cuts, and we will seek to include all nuclear weapons states in this endeavor.

To achieve a global ban on nuclear testing, my administration will immediately and aggressively pursue U.S. ratification of the Comprehensive Test Ban Treaty. After more than five decades of talks, it is time for the testing of nuclear weapons to finally be banned.

And to cut off the building blocks needed for a bomb, the United States will seek a new treaty that verifiably ends the production of fissile materials intended for use in state nuclear weapons. If we are serious about stopping the spread of these weapons, then we should put an end to the dedicated production of weapons-grade materials that create them. That's the first step.

Second, together we will strengthen the Nuclear Non-Proliferation Treaty as a basis for cooperation.

The basic bargain is sound: Countries with nuclear weapons will move towards disarmament, countries without nuclear weapons will not acquire them, and all countries can access peaceful nuclear energy. To strengthen the treaty, we should embrace several principles. We need more resources and authority to strengthen international inspections. We need real and immediate consequences for countries caught breaking the rules or trying to leave the treaty without cause.

And we should build a new framework for civil nuclear cooperation, including an international fuel bank, so that countries can access peaceful power without increasing the risks of proliferation. That must be the right of every nation that renounces nuclear weapons, especially developing countries embarking on peaceful programs. And no approach will succeed if it's based on the denial of rights to nations that play by the rules. We must harness the power of nuclear energy on behalf of our efforts to combat climate change, and to advance peace opportunity for all people.

But we go forward with no illusions. Some countries will break the rules. That's why we need a structure in place that ensures when any nation does, they will face consequences.

Just this morning, we were reminded again of why we need a new and more rigorous approach to address this threat. North Korea broke the rules once again by testing a rocket that could be used for long range missiles. This provocation underscores the need for action—not just this afternoon at the U.N. Security Council, but in our determination to prevent the spread of these weapons.

Rules must be binding. Violations must be punished. Words must mean something. The world must stand together to prevent the spread of these weapons. Now is the time for a strong international response—(applause)—now is the time for a strong international response, and North Korea must know that the path to security and respect will never come through threats and illegal weapons. All nations must come together to build a stronger, global regime. And that's why we must stand shoulder to shoulder to pressure the North Koreans to change course.

Iran has yet to build a nuclear weapon. My administration will seek engagement with Iran based on mutual interests and mutual respect. We believe in dialogue. But in that dialogue we will present a clear choice. We want Iran to take its rightful place in the community of nations, politically and economically. We will support Iran's right to peaceful nuclear energy with rigorous inspections. That's a path that the Islamic Republic can take. Or the government can choose increased isolation, international pressure, and a potential nuclear arms race in the region that will increase insecurity for all.

So let me be clear: Iran's nuclear and ballistic missile activity poses a real threat, not just to the United States, but to Iran's neighbors and our allies. The Czech Republic and Poland have been courageous in agreeing to host a defense against these missiles. As long as the threat from Iran persists, we will go forward with a missile defense system that is cost-effective and proven. If the Iranian threat is eliminated, we will have a stronger basis for security, and the driving force for missile defense construction in Europe will be removed.

So, finally, we must ensure that terrorists never acquire a nuclear weapon. This is the most immediate and extreme threat to global security. One terrorist with one nuclear weapon could unleash massive destruction. Al Qaeda has said it seeks a bomb and that it would have no problem with using it. And we know that there is unsecured nuclear material across the globe. To protect our people, we must act with a sense of purpose without delay.

So today I am announcing a new international effort to secure all vulnerable nuclear material around the world within four years. We will set new standards, expand our cooperation with Russia, pursue new partnerships to lock down these sensitive materials.

We must also build on our efforts to break up black markets, detect and intercept materials in transit, and use financial tools to disrupt this dangerous trade. Because this threat will be lasting, we should come together to turn efforts such as the Proliferation Security Initiative and the Global Initiative to Combat Nuclear Terrorism into durable international institutions. And we should start by having a Global Summit on Nuclear Security that the United States will host within the next year.

Human destiny will be what we make of it. Together we can do it.

Thank you, Prague.

Questions

Is there a compelling case to be made for the possession of nuclear weapons as part of a nation-state's security strategy?

What could Obama have done to turn the goals of this speech into reality, in terms of US policy?

Reference

https://obamawhitehouse.archives.gov/the-press-office/remarks-president-barack-obama-prague-delivered

Document 19
The Lisbon Treaty, 2009

The Lisbon Treaty amended two previous European treaties: the Treaty of Rome (1957) and the Maastricht Treaty (1992). Lisbon sought to clarify the division of power among the EU institutions, simplified voting procedures in almost all policy areas, and introduced a number of social initiatives such as the legally binding Charter of Fundamental Rights. It also gave member states the right to leave the Union, something that the UK would later make use of (see Part III Document 10). In the field of foreign and security policy it introduced the new position of High Representative of the Union for Foreign Affairs and Security Policy ("Foreign Policy chief"). This Representative also became one of the Vice-Chairs of the European Commission, thereby strengthening the foreign policy focus in the European Commission's work. Below are the most relevant articles regarding EU foreign policy.

[This is an excerpt from the full document. The original numbers of the articles have been kept]

Article 18

1   The European Council, acting by a qualified majority, with the agreement of the President of the Commission, shall appoint the High Representative of the Union for Foreign Affairs and Security Policy. The European Council may end his term of office by the same procedure.
2   The High Representative shall conduct the Union's common foreign and security policy. He shall contribute by his proposals to the development of that policy, which he shall carry out as mandated by the Council. The same shall apply to the common security and defence policy.
3   The High Representative shall preside over the Foreign Affairs Council.
4   The High Representative shall be one of the Vice-Presidents of the Commission. He shall ensure the consistency of the Union's external action. He shall be responsible within the Commission for responsibilities incumbent on it in external relations and for coordinating other aspects of the Union's external action. In exercising these responsibilities within the Commission, and only for these responsibilities, the High Representative shall be bound by Commission procedures to the extent that this is consistent with paragraphs 2 and 3.

Article 21

1   The Union's action on the international scene shall be guided by the principles which have inspired its own creation, development and enlargement, and which it seeks to advance in the wider world: democracy, the rule of law, the universality and indivisibility of human rights and fundamental freedoms, respect for human dignity, the

DOI: 10.4324/9781003159551-43

principles of equality and solidarity, and respect for the principles of the United Nations Charter and international law.

The Union shall seek to develop relations and build partnerships with third countries, and international, regional or global organisations which share the principles referred to in the first subparagraph. It shall promote multilateral solutions to common problems, in particular in the framework of the United Nations.

2   The Union shall define and pursue common policies and actions, and shall work for a high degree of cooperation in all fields of international relations, in order to:

a   safeguard its values, fundamental interests, security, independence and integrity;
b   consolidate and support democracy, the rule of law, human rights and the principles of international law;
c   preserve peace, prevent conflicts and strengthen international security, in accordance with the purposes and principles of the United Nations Charter, with the principles of the Helsinki Final Act [1975] and with the aims of the Charter of Paris [1990], including those relating to external borders;
d   foster the sustainable economic, social and environmental development of developing countries, with the primary aim of eradicating poverty;
e   encourage the integration of all countries into the world economy, including through the progressive abolition of restrictions on international trade;
f   help develop international measures to preserve and improve the quality of the environment and the sustainable management of global natural resources, in order to ensure sustainable development;
g   assist populations, countries and regions confronting natural or man-made disasters; and
h   promote an international system based on stronger multilateral cooperation and good global governance.

3   The Union shall respect the principles and pursue the objectives set out in paragraphs 1 and 2 in the development and implementation of the different areas of the Union's external action covered by this Title and by Part Five of the Treaty on the Functioning of the European Union, and of the external aspects of its other policies.

The Union shall ensure consistency between the different areas of its external action and between these and its other policies. The Council and the Commission, assisted by the High Representative of the Union for Foreign Affairs and Security Policy, shall ensure that consistency and shall cooperate to that effect.

Article 22

1   On the basis of the principles and objectives set out in Article 21, the European Council shall identify the strategic interests and objectives of the Union.

Decisions of the European Council on the strategic interests and objectives of the Union shall relate to the common foreign and security policy and to other areas of the external action of the Union. Such decisions may concern the relations of the Union with a specific country or region or may be thematic in approach. They shall define their duration, and the means to be made available by the Union and the Member States.

The European Council shall act unanimously on a recommendation from the Council, adopted by the latter under the arrangements laid down for each area. Decisions of the

European Council shall be implemented in accordance with the procedures provided for in the Treaties.

2   The High Representative of the Union for Foreign Affairs and Security Policy, for the area of common foreign and security policy, and the Commission, for other areas of external action, may submit joint proposals to the Council.

Article 27

1   The High Representative of the Union for Foreign Affairs and Security Policy, who shall chair the Foreign Affairs Council, shall contribute through his proposals towards the preparation of the common foreign and security policy and shall ensure implementation of the decisions adopted by the European Council and the Council.

2   The High Representative shall represent the Union for matters relating to the common foreign and security policy. He shall conduct political dialogue with third parties on the Union's behalf and shall express the Union's position in international organisations and at international conferences.

3   In fulfilling his mandate, the High Representative shall be assisted by a European External Action Service. This service shall work in cooperation with the diplomatic services of the Member States and shall comprise officials from relevant departments of the General Secretariat of the Council and of the Commission as well as staff seconded from national diplomatic services of the Member States. The organisation and functioning of the European External Action Service shall be established by a decision of the Council. The Council shall act on a proposal from the High Representative after consulting the European Parliament and after obtaining the consent of the Commission.

Questions

Does the Lisbon Treaty give the impression that a united, common foreign policy for the EU is a possibility?

Would it be better for transatlantic relations if the EU, and not separate member states, was able to represent all European policy matters directly with Washington?

Reference

https://eur-lex.europa.eu/legal-content/EN/TXT/?uri=celex%3A12007L%2FTXT

Document 20

Remarks by President Obama at the United Nations Climate Change Conference, Copenhagen, 18 December 2009

From the early 1990s, climate change became a serious political issue for the entire global community. The initial scepticism among world leaders about the urgency of the issue was soon replaced by a generally shared understanding that climate change should be collectively addressed – the disagreements came when deciding who would pay the most costs, and why. Via a series of UN conferences on climate change, starting in 1992 with the UN Framework Convention on Climate Change, the world community succeeded slowly but steadily to outline the way forward for a global accord on controlling carbon emissions. The expectations ran very high for the UN Climate Change Conference in Copenhagen (mockingly referred to as "Hopenhagen") to secure a final agreement. However, the conference ended in an almost complete failure.

The US had never showed any enthusiasm about committing itself to an international legally binding system for reducing greenhouse-gas emissions. President George W. Bush decided in 2001 to reverse the decision taken by his predecessor, President Clinton, to sign the Kyoto protocol (see Part I Document 14). President Obama, on the other hand, sought an active role for the US on the climate change issue and personally attended the Copenhagen conference, with his opening speech included below. The diplomatic process, however, failed completely. "Climate financing" for the developing countries and binding emission reductions for the industrialized world were among the most contested issues on the negotiating table.

The central role of the UN in this process was another one. The premature leak of the draft text of the Copenhagen Agreement, a compromise produced by a number of EU countries, caused a stir among the delegates of the US, China and India, as well as among many of the developing countries. Many felt by-passed or even humiliated, and China above all refused to accept mandatory emission cuts. Thus, no common agreement was reached, merely an 'accord' that was urgently written down by the US and China and kept outside of the multilateral UN negotiating process. Tellingly, this "accord" became publicly known as the "side deal". The conference was unable to reach consensus on this "accord", voting only to take "note" of it. President Obama even left Copenhagen before the text was circulated among the 150 delegations.

[This is an excerpt from the full document]

THE PRESIDENT: We come here in Copenhagen because climate change poses a grave and growing danger to our people. All of you would not be here unless you – like me – were convinced that this danger is real. This is not fiction, it is science. Unchecked, climate change will pose unacceptable risks to our security, our economies, and our planet. This much we know.

The question, then, before us is no longer the nature of the challenge – the question is our capacity to meet it. For while the reality of climate change is not in doubt, I have to

DOI: 10.4324/9781003159551-44

be honest, as the world watches us today, I think our ability to take collective action is in doubt right now, and it hangs in the balance.

I believe we can act boldly, and decisively, in the face of a common threat. That's why I come here today – not to talk, but to act.

Now, as the world's largest economy and as the world's second largest emitter, America bears our responsibility to address climate change, and we intend to meet that responsibility. That's why we've renewed our leadership within international climate change negotiations. That's why we've worked with other nations to phase out fossil fuel subsidies. That's why we've taken bold action at home – by making historic investments in renewable energy; by putting our people to work increasing efficiency in our homes and buildings; and by pursuing comprehensive legislation to transform to a clean energy economy.

These mitigation actions are ambitious, and we are taking them not simply to meet global responsibilities. We are convinced, as some of you may be convinced, that changing the way we produce and use energy is essential to America's economic future – that it will create millions of new jobs, power new industries, keep us competitive, and spark new innovation. We're convinced, for our own self-interest, that the way we use energy, changing it to a more efficient fashion, is essential to our national security, because it helps to reduce our dependence on foreign oil, and helps us deal with some of the dangers posed by climate change.

So I want this plenary session to understand, America is going to continue on this course of action to mitigate our emissions and to move towards a clean energy economy, no matter what happens here in Copenhagen. We think it is good for us, as well as good for the world. But we also believe that we will all be stronger, all be safer, all be more secure if we act together. That's why it is in our mutual interest to achieve a global accord in which we agree to certain steps, and to hold each other accountable to certain commitments.

After months of talk, after two weeks of negotiations, after innumerable side meetings, bilateral meetings, endless hours of discussion among negotiators, I believe that the pieces of that accord should now be clear.

First, all major economies must put forward decisive national actions that will reduce their emissions, and begin to turn the corner on climate change. I'm pleased that many of us have already done so. Almost all the major economies have put forward legitimate targets, significant targets, ambitious targets. And I'm confident that America will fulfill the commitments that we have made: cutting our emissions in the range of 17 percent by 2020, and by more than 80 percent by 2050 in line with final legislation.

Second, we must have a mechanism to review whether we are keeping our commitments, and exchange this information in a transparent manner. These measures need not be intrusive, or infringe upon sovereignty. They must, however, ensure that an accord is credible, and that we're living up to our obligations. Without such accountability, any agreement would be empty words on a page.

I don't know how you have an international agreement where we all are not sharing information and ensuring that we are meeting our commitments. That doesn't make sense. It would be a hollow victory.

Number three, we must have financing that helps developing countries adapt, particularly the least developed and most vulnerable countries to climate change. America will be a part of fast-start funding that will ramp up to $10 billion by 2012. And yesterday, Secretary Hillary Clinton, my Secretary of State, made it clear that we will engage in a global effort to mobilize $100 billion in financing by 2020, if – and only if – it is part of a broader accord that I have just described.

Mitigation. Transparency. Financing. It's a clear formula – one that embraces the principle of common but differentiated responses and respective capabilities. And it adds up to a significant accord – one that takes us farther than we have ever gone before as an international community.

I just want to say to this plenary session that we are running short on time. And at this point, the question is whether we will move forward together or split apart, whether we prefer posturing to action. I'm sure that many consider this an imperfect framework that I just described. No country will get everything that it wants. There are those developing countries that want aid with no strings attached, and no obligations with respect to transparency. They think that the most advanced nations should pay a higher price; I understand that. There are those advanced nations who think that developing countries either cannot absorb this assistance, or that will not be held accountable effectively, and that the world's fastest-growing emitters should bear a greater share of the burden.

We know the fault lines because we've been imprisoned by them for years. These international discussions have essentially taken place now for almost two decades, and we have very little to show for it other than an increased acceleration of the climate change phenomenon. The time for talk is over. This is the bottom line: We can embrace this accord, take a substantial step forward, continue to refine it and build upon its foundation. We can do that, and everyone who is in this room will be part of a historic endeavor – one that makes life better for our children and our grandchildren.

Or we can choose delay, falling back into the same divisions that have stood in the way of action for years. And we will be back having the same stale arguments month after month, year after year, perhaps decade after decade, all while the danger of climate change grows until it is irreversible.

Ladies and gentlemen, there is no time to waste. America has made our choice. We have charted our course. We have made our commitments. We will do what we say. Now I believe it's the time for the nations and the people of the world to come together behind a common purpose.

We are ready to get this done today – but there has to be movement on all sides to recognize that it is better for us to act than to talk; it's better for us to choose action over inaction; the future over the past – and with courage and faith, I believe that we can meet our responsibility to our people, and the future of our planet. Thank you very much.

Questions

Why has it proven so difficult for the US and Europe to agree on a common strategy to deal with climate change?

Why do you think China, following Copenhagen, was considered triumphant by the international press corps?

Reference

https://obamawhitehouse.archives.gov/the-press-office/remarks-president-morning-plenary-session-united-nations-climate-change-conference

Document 21

Remarks by President Obama on a new strategy for Afghanistan and Pakistan, 27 March 2009

Soon after the "9/11" attacks on New York and Washington DC, and the crash of the hijacked plane near Shanksville, Pennsylvania, the Bush administration identified the terrorist organisation al-Qaeda as the main culprit. Although the nineteen hijackers came from different countries (mainly Saudi Arabia), al-Qaeda's leader, Osama bin Laden, was seen as the mastermind behind the meticulously prepared attacks. He and his organisation enjoyed the protection of the Islamic Taliban who had offered them a safe haven in Afghanistan to train and prepare terrorist attacks. The American request to extradite Osama bin Laden was rejected by the Taliban leaders. The US, supported by the UK and local forces, invaded the country in October 2001 and soon removed the Taliban from power, but the al-Qaeda leadership managed to escape to Pakistan.

In December 2001 the UN set up ISAF (the International Security Assistance Force), which from 2003 to December 2014 was led by NATO. ISAF became the largest mission in NATO's history. ISAF's main goals were to provide security while training and equipping national Afghan military and police forces. At its height over fifty NATO countries and partners contributed approximately 130,000 troops to the mission. Major differences existed among the allies in troop contribution and risk-sharing. The US contributed the bulk of the military – 90,000 at its height, followed by the UK with almost 10,000 troops. Casualties varied according to the different national rules of engagement in force and to the particular regions being controlled. The southern part of the country, where the largest Afghan ethnic group, the Pashtun, had its power base, proved to be among the most dangerous areas. Taliban forces were not a regular army and used asymmetric tactics, road bombs in particular.

Reconstruction and development efforts were carried out through twenty-eight Provincial Reconstruction Teams. Afghan parliamentary and presidential elections were frequently held under extremely difficult security circumstances and led to accusations of fraud and corruption among the local politicians. Thus, attempts by ISAF to pacify the country and support the development of a democratic culture was almost impossible. It proved hard to win the "hearts and minds" of the population at large, despite achievements made with special development and civilian-administrative programmes. Most of the country, in particular outside the cities, remained under control of the Taliban. In 2009 President Obama, elected on the promise to end the wars in Iraq and Afghanistan, presented a new strategy designed to enable an exit for US and NATO forces.

Since neither side was able to gain the upper hand, peace talks among the main parties became inevitable. These eventually culminated in a peace agreement between the US and the Taliban in February 2020, but this still did not put an end to the hostilities. Approximately 115,000 military personnel and civilians died in the Afghan war between 2001–2020. Documents published in 2019 by the Washington Post *revealed a staggering picture of often contradictory strategic goals, irresponsible decision-making and incompetence among the*

DOI: 10.4324/9781003159551-45

responsible US officials. In January 2021, NATO still had 11,000 troops in Afghanistan to assist and train the Afghan security forces, but in April President Joe Biden announced the withdrawal of all US forces from the country by September 11 – the twentieth anniversary of 9/11.

[This is an excerpt from the original document]

THE PRESIDENT: Good morning

Today, I'm announcing a comprehensive, new strategy for Afghanistan and Pakistan. The situation is increasingly perilous. It's been more than seven years since the Taliban was removed from power, yet war rages on, and insurgents control parts of Afghanistan and Pakistan. Attacks against our troops, our NATO allies, and the Afghan government have risen steadily. And most painfully, 2008 was the deadliest year of the war for American forces.

Many people in the United States – and many in partner countries that have sacrificed so much – have a simple question: What is our purpose in Afghanistan? After so many years, they ask, why do our men and women still fight and die there? And they deserve a straightforward answer.

So let me be clear: Al Qaeda and its allies – the terrorists who planned and supported the 9/11 attacks – are in Pakistan and Afghanistan. Multiple intelligence estimates have warned that al Qaeda is actively planning attacks on the United States homeland from its safe haven in Pakistan. And if the Afghan government falls to the Taliban – or allows al Qaeda to go unchallenged – that country will again be a base for terrorists who want to kill as many of our people as they possibly can.

The future of Afghanistan is inextricably linked to the future of its neighbor, Pakistan. In the nearly eight years since 9/11, al Qaeda and its extremist allies have moved across the border to the remote areas of the Pakistani frontier. This almost certainly includes al Qaeda's leadership: Osama bin Laden and Ayman al-Zawahiri. They have used this mountainous terrain as a safe haven to hide, to train terrorists, to communicate with followers, to plot attacks, and to send fighters to support the insurgency in Afghanistan. For the American people, this border region has become the most dangerous place in the world.

But this is not simply an American problem – far from it. It is, instead, an international security challenge of the highest order. If there is a major attack on an Asian, European, or African city, it, too, is likely to have ties to al Qaeda's leadership in Pakistan. The safety of people around the world is at stake.

For the Afghan people, a return to Taliban rule would condemn their country to brutal governance, international isolation, a paralyzed economy, and the denial of basic human rights to the Afghan people – especially women and girls. The return in force of al Qaeda terrorists who would accompany the core Taliban leadership would cast Afghanistan under the shadow of perpetual violence.

As President, my greatest responsibility is to protect the American people. We are not in Afghanistan to control that country or to dictate its future. We are in Afghanistan to confront a common enemy that threatens the United States, our friends and our allies, and the people of Afghanistan and Pakistan who have suffered the most at the hands of violent extremists.

So I want the American people to understand that we have a clear and focused goal: to disrupt, dismantle and defeat al Qaeda in Pakistan and Afghanistan, and to prevent their return to either country in the future. That's the goal that must be achieved. That is a cause that could not be more just. And to the terrorists who oppose us, my message is the same: We will defeat you.

To achieve our goals, we need a stronger, smarter and comprehensive strategy. To focus on the greatest threat to our people, America must no longer deny resources to Afghanistan because of the war in Iraq. To enhance the military, governance and economic capacity of Afghanistan and Pakistan, we have to marshal international support. And to defeat an enemy that heeds no borders or laws of war, we must recognize the fundamental connection between the future of Afghanistan and Pakistan – which is why I've appointed Ambassador Richard Holbrooke, who is here, to serve as Special Representative for both countries, and to work closely with General Petraeus to integrate our civilian and military efforts.

Let me start by addressing the way forward in Pakistan.

The United States has great respect for the Pakistani people. The single greatest threat to that future comes from al Qaeda and their extremist allies, and that is why we must stand together. It's important for the American people to understand that Pakistan needs our help in going after al Qaeda. This is no simple task. The tribal regions are vast, they are rugged, and they are often ungoverned. And that's why we must focus our military assistance on the tools, training and support that Pakistan needs to root out the terrorists. And after years of mixed results, we will not, and cannot, provide a blank check.

Pakistan must demonstrate its commitment to rooting out al Qaeda and the violent extremists within its borders. And we will insist that action be taken – one way or another – when we have intelligence about high-level terrorist targets.

The government's ability to destroy these safe havens is tied to its own strength and security. To help Pakistan weather the economic crisis, we must continue to work with the IMF, the World Bank and other international partners. To lessen tensions between two nuclear-armed nations that too often teeter on the edge of escalation and confrontation, we must pursue constructive diplomacy with both India and Pakistan. To avoid the mistakes of the past, we must make clear that our relationship with Pakistan is grounded in support for Pakistan's democratic institutions and the Pakistani people. And to demonstrate through deeds as well as words a commitment that is enduring, we must stand for lasting opportunity.

A campaign against extremism will not succeed with bullets or bombs alone. Al Qaeda's offers the people of Pakistan nothing but destruction. We stand for something different. So today, I am calling upon Congress to pass a bipartisan bill co-sponsored by John Kerry and Richard Lugar that authorizes $1.5 billion in direct support to the Pakistani people every year over the next five years – resources that will build schools and roads and hospitals, and strengthen Pakistan's democracy. I'm also calling on Congress to pass a bipartisan bill co-sponsored by Maria Cantwell, Chris Van Hollen and Peter Hoekstra that creates opportunity zones in the border regions to develop the economy and bring hope to places plagued with violence.

Security demands a new sense of shared responsibility. And that's why we will launch a standing, trilateral dialogue among the United States, Afghanistan and Pakistan. This is just one part of a comprehensive strategy to prevent Afghanistan from becoming the al Qaeda safe haven that it was before 9/11. To succeed, we and our friends and allies must reverse the Taliban's gains, and promote a more capable and accountable Afghan government.

Afghans have suffered and sacrificed for their future. But for six years, Afghanistan has been denied the resources that it demands because of the war in Iraq. Now, we must make a commitment that can accomplish our goals.

I've already ordered the deployment of 17,000 troops that had been requested by General McKiernan for many months. These soldiers and Marines will take the fight to the Taliban in the south and the east, and give us a greater capacity to partner with Afghan security forces and to go after insurgents along the border. This push will also help provide security in advance of the important presidential elections in Afghanistan in August.

At the same time, we will shift the emphasis of our mission to training and increasing the size of Afghan security forces, so that they can eventually take the lead in securing their country. That's how we will prepare Afghans to take responsibility for their security, and how we will ultimately be able to bring our own troops home. We will accelerate our efforts to build an Afghan army of 134,000 and a police force of 82,000 so that we can meet these goals by 2011 – and increases in Afghan forces may very well be needed as our plans to turn over security responsibility to the Afghans go forward.

This push must be joined by a dramatic increase in our civilian effort. Afghanistan has an elected government, but it is undermined by corruption and has difficulty delivering basic services to its people. The economy is undercut by a booming narcotics trade that encourages criminality and funds the insurgency. The people of Afghanistan seek the promise of a better future. Yet once again, we've seen the hope of a new day darkened by violence and uncertainty.

So to advance security, opportunity and justice – not just in Kabul, but from the bottom up in the provinces – we need agricultural specialists and educators, engineers and lawyers. That's how we can help the Afghan government serve its people and develop an economy that isn't dominated by illicit drugs. And that's why I'm ordering a substantial increase in our civilians on the ground. That's also why we must seek civilian support from our partners and allies, from the United Nations and international aid organizations – an effort that Secretary Clinton will carry forward next week in The Hague.

None of the steps that I've outlined will be easy; none should be taken by America alone. As America does more, we will ask others to join us in doing their part. From our partners and NATO allies, we will seek not simply troops, but rather clearly defined capabilities: supporting the Afghan elections, training Afghan security forces, a greater civilian commitment to the Afghan people. For the United Nations, we seek greater progress for its mandate to coordinate international action and assistance, and to strengthen Afghan institutions.

And finally, together with the United Nations, we will forge a new Contact Group for Afghanistan and Pakistan that brings together all who should have a stake in the security of the region – our NATO allies and other partners, but also the Central Asian states, the Gulf nations and Iran; Russia, India and China.

I remind everybody, the United States of America did not choose to fight a war in Afghanistan. Nearly 3,000 of our people were killed on September 11, 2001, for doing nothing more than going about their daily lives. We will use all elements of our national power to defeat al Qaeda, and to defend America, our allies, and all who seek a better future. Because the United States of America stands for peace and security, justice and opportunity. That is who we are, and that is what history calls on us to do once more.

Questions

Why do you think NATO committed its largest mission to Afghanistan, a poor country thousands of miles from the transatlantic region?

Do you think nation-building in Afghanistan could have been more successful using a different strategy?

Reference

https://obamawhitehouse.archives.gov/the-press-office/2012/05/21/remarks-president-nato-press-conference

Document 22

Sarah Palin, Keynote Speech at the Inaugural Tea Party Convention, 6 February 2010

Sarah Palin, governor of Alaska from 2006 to 2010, was the Republican nominee for Vice-President of the US in the 2008 election, alongside presidential nominee John McCain. Following their defeat she became a staunch supporter of the Tea Party movement – named after the Boston Tea Party of 1773 – and a commentator on Fox News, the conservative television channel. She endorsed Donald Trump during the 2016 presidential campaign.

The Tea Party came about largely because of the financial crisis of 2007–2009. Many of its supporters – mainly from the middle classes – had lost their jobs and homes as a result of that crisis. The movement was highly decentralized – some commentators argued that there were multiple Tea Parties, not just one single movement. The membership and agenda was highly conservative in its outlook on society and called for, among other things, lower taxes and a reduction of the national debt. Moreover, it profiled itself as anti-establishment, in particular agitating against the "fat cats" in Washington DC and the whole idea of liberal "big government". But although the movement originated outside the existing American party system, their strategy was aimed at selecting and promoting their own candidates within the Republican Party. In this way the Tea Party succeeded in heavily influencing mainstream politics, promoting its conservative agenda on a national political level. This also contributed to the subsequent election of Donald Trump as President in 2016 (see Part III Document 11).

[This is an excerpt from the original document]

I am a big supporter of this movement. I look forward to attending more Tea Party events. It is just so inspiring to see real people – not politicos, not inside-the-Beltway professionals – come out and stand up and speak out for common-sense conservative principles.

The soul of this movement is the people – everyday Americans who grow our food and run our small businesses, teach our kids, and fight our wars. They're folks in small towns and cities across this great nation who saw what was happening – and they saw and were concerned, and they got involved. You have a vision for the future, one that values conservative principles and common sense solutions.

Washington has now replaced private irresponsibility with public irresponsibility. The list of companies and industries that the government is crowding out and bailing out and taking over, it continues to grow. First it was the banks, mortgage companies, financial institutions, then automakers. Soon, if they had their way, health care, student loans.

So here's some advice for those in D.C. who want to shine in the greatest show on earth. Our government needs to adopt a pro-market agenda that doesn't pick winners and losers, but it invites competition and it levels the playing field for everyone. Washington has got to across the board, lower taxes for small businesses so that our mom and pops can reinvest and hire people so that our businesses can thrive. They should support competition, support innovation, reward hard work.

DOI: 10.4324/9781003159551-46

And they should do all that they can to make sure that the game is fair without that undo corrupt influence. And then they need to get government out of the way. Remember that red reset button that America through Secretary Clinton, she gave to Putin. Remember that? I think we should ask for that back and hand it instead to Congress. And say, no, start all over on this health care scheme and pass meaningful, market-based reforms that incorporate some simple steps that have broad support, the – the best ideas, not back room deals but things like insurance purchases across state lines and the tort reform that we've talked about.

To do so would be a fitting tribute to Ronald Reagan, especially tonight, as he would have turned 99. He knew the best of our country is not all gathered in Washington, D.C.

Questions

How does Palin's speech reflect the right-wing and left-wing tendencies of political populism?

What are the similarities and differences between populism in the United States and in Europe?

References

https://www.americanrhetoric.com/speeches/sarahpalin2010teapartykeynote.htm
Permission: AmericanRhetoric/Online Speech Bank

PART III

2011–2020: disarray?

Document 1

Joint Op-ed by President Obama, Prime Minister Cameron and President Sarkozy, "Libya's Pathway to Peace," April 14 2011

The so-called Arab Spring, a wave of anti-government protests across North Africa and the Arab world, started with the Jasmine Revolution in Tunisia in December 2010 and soon spread to Egypt. In February 2011 the first anti-government meetings in Libya took place, leading soon thereafter to a popular uprising against Libya's dictator Muammar Gaddafi (1942–2011). The anti-Gaddafi forces, working together in the National Transition Council, quickly gathered strength but lacked the military capability to defeat pro-Gaddafi military forces. The international community feared a humanitarian disaster.

On 17 March the UN Security Council adopted resolution 1973, which called for a no-fly zone, an arms embargo and the protection of the civilian population against Gaddafi's military forces. The UN resolution allowed an international coalition led by NATO to intervene. Military intervention started on 19 March. The international coalition acted mainly as a protective air force for the insurgents, destroying Gaddafi's military infrastructure and army units from the air. By the summer Gaddafi had lost control of most of the country. On 20 October Gaddafi was captured and shot by the rebel forces, which put an end to the international intervention. In hindsight the most controversial aspect of the NATO-led operation became the de facto regime change in Libya that it ultimately enabled. China and Russia, who had both abstained in the Security Council, considered this outcome to be a violation of the UN's mandate. After all, they both argued, the resolution had only allowed for the protection of the civilian population. How this circle – intervention without regime change – could ever have been squared by the international community remains a question until today. That the political leaders of the international coalition were well aware of this can be read in their op-ed below. Signed by President Barack Obama, UK Prime Minister David Cameron and President Nicolas Sarkozy of France, it appeared simultaneously in a number of international newspapers.

[This is an excerpt from the full document]

Together with our NATO allies and coalition partners, the United States, France and Britain have been united from the start in responding to the crisis in Libya, and we are united on what needs to happen in order to end it.

We must never forget the reasons why the international community was obliged to act in the first place. As Libya descended into chaos with Colonel Muammar el-Qaddafi attacking his own people, the Arab League called for action. The Libyan opposition called for help. And the people of Libya looked to the world in their hour of need. In an historic resolution, the United Nations Security Council authorized all necessary measures to protect the people of Libya from the attacks upon them. By responding immediately, our countries, together with an international coalition, halted the advance of Qaddafi's forces and prevented the bloodbath that he had promised to inflict upon the citizens of the besieged city of Benghazi.

DOI: 10.4324/9781003159551-48

Tens of thousands of lives have been protected. But the people of Libya are still suffering terrible horrors at Qaddafi's hands each and every day. His rockets and shells rained down on defenseless civilians in Ajdabiya. The city of Misurata is enduring a medieval siege, as Qaddafi tries to strangle its population into submission. The evidence of disappearances and abuses grows daily.

Our duty and our mandate under U.N. Security Council Resolution 1973 is to protect civilians, and we are doing that. It is not to remove Qaddafi by force. But it is impossible to imagine a future for Libya with Qaddafi in power. The International Criminal Court is rightly investigating the crimes committed against civilians and the grievous violations of international law. It is unthinkable that someone who has tried to massacre his own people can play a part in their future government. The brave citizens of those towns that have held out against forces that have been mercilessly targeting them would face a fearful vengeance if the world accepted such an arrangement. It would be an unconscionable betrayal.

Furthermore, it would condemn Libya to being not only a pariah state, but a failed state too. Qaddafi has promised to carry out terrorist attacks against civilian ships and airliners. And because he has lost the consent of his people any deal that leaves him in power would lead to further chaos and lawlessness. We know from bitter experience what that would mean. Neither Europe, the region, or the world can afford a new safe haven for extremists.

There is a pathway to peace that promises new hope for the people of Libya—a future without Qaddafi that preserves Libya's integrity and sovereignty, and restores her economy and the prosperity and security of her people. [S]o long as Qaddafi is in power, NATO must maintain its operations so that civilians remain protected and the pressure on the regime builds. Then a genuine transition from dictatorship to an inclusive constitutional process can really begin, led by a new generation of leaders. In order for that transition to succeed, Qaddafi must go and go for good. At that point, the United Nations and its members should help the Libyan people as they rebuild where Qaddafi has destroyed—to repair homes and hospitals.

This vision for the future of Libya has the support of a broad coalition of countries, including many from the Arab world. These countries came together in London on March 29 and founded a Contact Group which met this week in Doha to support a solution to the crisis that respects the will of the Libyan people.

Today, NATO and our partners are acting in the name of the United Nations with an unprecedented international legal mandate. But it will be the people of Libya, not the U.N., who choose their new constitution, elect their new leaders, and write the next chapter in their history. Britain, France and the United States will not rest until the United Nations Security Council resolutions have been implemented and the Libyan people can choose their own future.

Questions

In what ways did the "Arab Spring" challenge transatlantic security?

Do you think the UNSC's mandate – protection of civilians – could have been performed without causing a regime change in Libya?

Reference

https://obamawhitehouse.archives.gov/the-press-office/2011/04/14/joint-op-ed-president-obama-prime-minister-cameron-and-president-sarkozy

Document 2

Secretary of Defense Robert M. Gates, "Farewell Speech," 10 June 2011

Robert M. Gates served as Secretary of Defense from 2006 to 2011 under both the Republican George W. Bush Administration and the Democratic Obama Administration. He had been CIA Director from 1991 to 1993 and during his long career in national government had served in other security positions. In his "Farewell Speech", his last speech on European soil before his resignation from office, Gates addressed the issue of 'burden sharing' among the NATO Allies. He criticized NATO and in particular the European Allies for their financial and military shortcomings. He feared a "two-tiered" Alliance, with some members focusing on "soft" military missions with low-risk impact and others focusing on "hard" combat missions with high casualty risks. His speech did not come as a complete surprise, since for decades US administrations had been critical of the European political and military commitment to the Alliance or lack thereof.

[This is an excerpt from the full document]

I am glad to share some thoughts with you this morning about the transatlantic security relationship in what will be my last policy speech as U.S. defense secretary.

The security of this continent – with NATO as the main instrument for protecting that security – has been the consuming interest of much of my professional life.

In many ways, today's event brings me full circle. The first major speech I delivered after taking this post nearly four-and-a-half years ago was also on the Continent, at the Munich Security Conference. Today, I would like to share some parting thoughts about the state of the now 60-plus year old transatlantic security project, to include:

- Where the alliance mission stands in Afghanistan as we enter a critical transition phase;
- NATO's serious capability gaps and other institutional shortcomings laid bare by the Libya operation;
- The military – and political – necessity of fixing these shortcomings if the transatlantic security alliance is going to be viable going forward;
- And more broadly, the growing difficulty for the U.S. to sustain current support for NATO if the American taxpayer continues to carry most of the burden in the Alliance.

I share these views in the spirit of solidarity and friendship, with the understanding that true friends occasionally must speak bluntly with one another for the sake of those greater interests and values that bind us together.

First, a few words on Afghanistan. It is no secret that for too long, the international military effort in Afghanistan suffered from a lack of focus, resources, and attention, a situation exacerbated by America's primary focus on Iraq for most of the past decade.

DOI: 10.4324/9781003159551-49

When NATO agreed at Riga in 2006 to take the lead for security across the country, I suspect many allies assumed that the mission would be primarily peacekeeping, reconstruction, and development assistance – more akin to the Balkans. Instead, NATO found itself in a tough fight against a determined and resurgent Taliban returning in force from its sanctuaries in Pakistan.

Soon, the challenges inherent to any coalition operation came to the surface – national caveats that tied the hands of allied commanders in sometimes infuriating ways, the inability of many allies to meet agreed upon commitments and, in some cases, wildly disparate contributions from different member states. Frustrations with these obstacles sometimes boiled into public view. I had some choice words to say on this topic during my first year in office, unfavorably characterized at the time by one of my NATO ministerial colleagues as "megaphone diplomacy."

Yet, through it all, NATO – as an alliance collectively – has for the most part come through for the mission in Afghanistan. Consider that when I became Secretary of Defense in 2006 there were about 20,000 non-U.S. troops from NATO nations in Afghanistan. Today, that figure is approximately 40,000. More than 850 troops from non-U.S. NATO members have made the ultimate sacrifice in Afghanistan. For many allied nations these were the first military casualties they have taken since the end of the Second World War.

The way ahead in Afghanistan is "in together, out together." Then our troops can come home to the honor and appreciation they so richly deserve, and the transatlantic alliance will have passed its first major test of the 21st Century:

- Inflicting a strategic and ideological defeat on terrorist groups that threaten our homelands;
- Giving a long-suffering people hope for a future;
- Providing a path to stability for a critically important part of the world.

Though we can take pride in what has been accomplished and sustained in Afghanistan, the ISAF mission has exposed significant shortcomings in NATO – in military capabilities, and in political will. Despite more than 2 million troops in uniform – NOT counting the U.S. military – NATO has struggled, at times desperately, to sustain a deployment of 25- to 40,000 troops, not just in boots on the ground, but in crucial support assets such as helicopters, transport aircraft, maintenance, intelligence, surveillance and reconnaissance, and much more.

Turning to the NATO operation over Libya [Operation Unified Protector], it has become painfully clear that similar shortcomings – in capability and will –have the potential to jeopardize the alliance's ability to conduct an integrated, effective and sustained air-sea campaign. Consider that Operation Unified Protector is:

- A mission with widespread political support;
- A mission that does not involve ground troops under fire;
- And indeed, is a mission in Europe's neighborhood deemed to be in Europe's vital interest.

To be sure, at the outset, the NATO Libya mission did meet its initial military objectives – grounding Qaddafi's air force and degrading his ability to wage offensive war against his own citizens. And while the operation has exposed some shortcomings caused by underfunding, it has also shown the potential of NATO, with an operation where Europeans are taking the lead with American support. However, while every alliance member voted for Libya mission, less than half have participated at all, and fewer than a third have been willing to participate in the strike mission. Frankly, many of those allies sitting on the sidelines do so not because they do not want to participate, but simply because they can't. The military capabilities simply aren't there.

In particular, intelligence, surveillance, and reconnaissance assets are lacking that would allow more allies to be involved and make an impact. [T]he mightiest military alliance in history is only 11 weeks into an operation against a poorly armed regime in a sparsely populated country – yet many allies are beginning to run short of munitions, requiring the U.S., once more, to make up the difference.

In the past, I've worried openly about NATO turning into a two-tiered alliance: Between members who specialize in "soft' humanitarian, development, peacekeeping, and talking tasks, and those conducting the "hard" combat missions. Between those willing and able to pay the price and bear the burdens of alliance commitments, and those who enjoy the benefits of NATO membership – be they security guarantees or headquarters billets – but don't want to share the risks and the costs. This is no longer a hypothetical worry. We are there today. And it is unacceptable.

Part of this predicament stems from a lack of will, much of it from a lack of resources in an era of austerity. For all but a handful of allies, defense budgets – in absolute terms, as a share of economic output – have been chronically starved for adequate funding for a long time, with the shortfalls compounding on themselves each year. Despite the demands of mission in Afghanistan – the first 'hot' ground war fought in NATO history – total European defense spending declined, by one estimate, by nearly 15 percent in the decade following 9/11. Furthermore, rising personnel costs combined with the demands of training and equipping for Afghan deployments has consumed an ever growing share of already meager defense budgets. The result is that investment accounts for future modernization and other capabilities not directly related to Afghanistan are being squeezed out – as we are seeing today over Libya.

I am the latest in a string of U.S. defense secretaries who have urged allies privately and publicly, often with exasperation, to meet agreed-upon NATO benchmarks for defense spending. However, fiscal, political and demographic realities make this unlikely to happen anytime soon, as even military stalwarts like the U.K have been forced to ratchet back with major cuts to force structure. Today, just five of 28 allies – the U.S., U.K., France, Greece, along with Albania – exceed the agreed 2% of GDP spending on defense.

Despite the pressing need to spend more on vital equipment and the right personnel to support ongoing missions – needs that have been evident for the past two decades – too many allies been unwilling to fundamentally change how they set priorities and allocate resources. The non-U.S. NATO members collectively spend more than $300 billion U.S. dollars on defense annually which, if allocated wisely and strategically, could buy a significant amount of usable military capability. Instead, the results are significantly less than the sum of the parts. This has both shortchanged current operations but also bodes ill for ensuring NATO has the key common alliance capabilities of the future.

[T]o avoid the very real possibility of collective military irrelevance, member nations must examine new approaches to boosting combat capabilities – in procurement, in training, in logistics, in sustainment. While it is clear NATO members should do more to pool military assets, such "Smart Defense" initiatives are not a panacea. In the final analysis, there is no substitute for nations providing the resources necessary to have the military capability the Alliance needs when faced with a security challenge. Ultimately, nations must be responsible for their fair share of the common defense.

Let me conclude with some thoughts about the political context in which all of us must operate. As you all know, America's serious fiscal situation is now putting pressure on our defense budget, and we are in a process of assessing where the U.S. can or cannot accept more risk as a result of reducing the size of our military. Tough choices lie ahead affecting every part of our government, and during such times, scrutiny inevitably falls on the cost of overseas commitments – from foreign assistance to military basing, support, and guarantees.

President Obama and I believe that despite the budget pressures, it would be a grave mistake for the U.S. to withdraw from its global responsibilities. And in Singapore last week, I outlined the many areas where U.S. defense engagement and investment in Asia was slated to grow further in coming years, even as America's traditional allies in that region rightfully take on the role of full partners in their own defense.

With respect to Europe, for the better part of six decades there has been relatively little doubt or debate in the United States about the value and necessity of the transatlantic alliance. The benefits of a Europe whole, prosperous and free after being twice devastated by wars requiring American intervention was self evident. Thus, for most of the Cold War U.S. governments could justify defense investments and costly forward bases that made up roughly 50 percent of all NATO military spending. But some two decades after the collapse of the Berlin Wall, the U.S. share of NATO defense spending has now risen to more than 75 percent – at a time when politically painful budget and benefit cuts are being considered at home.

The blunt reality is that there will be dwindling appetite and patience in the U.S. Congress – and in the American body politic writ large – to expend increasingly precious funds on behalf of nations that are apparently unwilling to devote the necessary resources or make the necessary changes to be serious and capable partners in their own defense. Nations apparently willing and eager for American taxpayers to assume the growing security burden left by reductions in European defense budgets.

Indeed, if current trends in the decline of European defense capabilities are not halted and reversed, future U.S. political leaders – those for whom the Cold War was *not* the formative experience that it was for me – may not consider the return on America's investment in NATO worth the cost.

What I've sketched out is the real possibility for a dim, if not dismal future for the transatlantic alliance. Such a future is possible, but not inevitable. The good news is that the members of NATO – individually, and collectively – have it well within their means to halt and reverse these trends, and instead produce a very different future:

- By making a serious effort to protect defense budgets from being further gutted in the next round of austerity measures;
- By better allocating (and coordinating) the resources we do have; and
- By following through on commitments to the alliance and to each other.

It is not too late for Europe to get its defense institutions and security relationships on track. But it will take leadership from political leaders and policy makers on this continent. It cannot be coaxed, demanded or imposed from across the Atlantic.

Over the life of the transatlantic alliance there has been no shortage of squabbles and setbacks. But through it all, we managed to get the big things right over time. We came together to make the tough decisions in the face of dissension at home and threats abroad. And I take heart in the knowledge that we can do so again.

Questions

Explain the discussion among NATO Allies about "burden sharing" (go to https://www.nato.int/ to check the defense expenditures of the NATO Allies)

What did Gates mean to imply with the phrase "a two-tiered Alliance"?

Reference

www.voltairenet.org/article170425.html [originally on Department of Defense website]

Document 3

Remarks by the President to the White House Press Corps, 20 August 2012 (Syrian "Red Line")

The use of the phrase "red line" by President Barack Obama in 2012 in relation to the Syrian civil war came to represent a major shift in US strategic thinking and political calculation. The Syrian civil war had broken out in mid-March 2011 in the context of widespread pro-tests against autocratic and authoritarian regimes in North Africa and the Middle East. The war, which involved a variety of factions (Kurdish forces, Sunni rebels, and jihadi groups) opposing the regime of Syrian president Bashar al-Assad, had led to involvement from Iran, Hezbollah and Russia on the side of the government forces, and the United States and Turkey (sometimes together, sometimes opposed) for the opposition. Calls for direct US military intervention to end the war and propel a democratic transition began to escalate in 2012 as the level of violence escalated and the numbers of civilian casualties and refugees increased. In the wake of the UN-sanctioned NATO intervention in Libya in March–April 2011 that ultimately led to the end of the Gaddafi regime, such an option seemed very real. Despite the devastating war in Iraq after 2003, humanitarian intervention was still a major plank of US foreign policy. In August 2012, President Obama was asked during a press conference what would trigger such an intervention, to which he replied that the use of chemical weapons by any party involved in the war would "change my calculation significantly." Almost exactly a year later, on 21 August 2013, reports of a sarin gas attack in a rebel-held suburb of Da-mascus prompted debate in the US National Security Council, Congress, and with European allies as to the legality and possible effectiveness of a military strike. But such a strike lacked both UN authorization and the claim that it would be in self-defence, and the vote of the British parliament on 30 August against joining US-led strikes ultimately led to rejecting the option. Instead, a joint venture between the US and Russia led to the securing and destruction of the Syrian government's chemical weapons stockpile. But the failure to act once the 'red line' was breached marked a turning point in US backing for humanitarian intervention, and further erosion of transatlantic solidarity in pursuing it. The false claims of the Iraq war had led many to mistrust the reasons behind US military action, and in subsequent years the polit-ical turmoil and civil war in Libya would also strengthen criticism against such interventions, particularly from Russia and China.

[Only the excerpt of the press conference concerning Syria is included]

Q: Mr. President, could you update us on your latest thinking of where you think things are in Syria, and in particular, whether you envision using U.S. military, if simply for nothing else, the safe keeping of the chemical weapons, and if you're confident that the chemical weapons are safe?

THE PRESIDENT: On Syria, obviously this is a very tough issue. I have indicated repeat-edly that President al-Assad has lost legitimacy, that he needs to step down. So far, he hasn't gotten the message, and instead has double downed in violence on his own

DOI: 10.4324/9781003159551-50

people. The international community has sent a clear message that rather than drag his country into civil war he should move in the direction of a political transition. But at this point, the likelihood of a soft landing seems pretty distant.

What we've said is, number one, we want to make sure we're providing humanitarian assistance, and we've done that to the tune of $82 million, I believe, so far. And we'll probably end up doing a little more because we want to make sure that the hundreds of thousands of refugees that are fleeing the mayhem, that they don't end up creating – or being in a terrible situation, or also destabilizing some of Syria's neighbors.

The second thing we've done is we said that we would provide, in consultation with the international community, some assistance to the opposition in thinking about how would a political transition take place, and what are the principles that should be upheld in terms of looking out for minority rights and human rights. And that consultation is taking place.

I have, at this point, not ordered military engagement in the situation. But the point that you made about chemical and biological weapons is critical. That's an issue that doesn't just concern Syria; it concerns our close allies in the region, including Israel. It concerns us. We cannot have a situation where chemical or biological weapons are falling into the hands of the wrong people.

We have been very clear to the Assad regime, but also to other players on the ground, that a red line for us is we start seeing a whole bunch of chemical weapons moving around or being utilized. That would change my calculus. That would change my equation.

Q: So you're confident it's somehow under – it's safe?

THE PRESIDENT: In a situation this volatile, I wouldn't say that I am absolutely confident. What I'm saying is we're monitoring that situation very carefully. We have put together a range of contingency plans. We have communicated in no uncertain terms with every player in the region that that's a red line for us and that there would be enormous consequences if we start seeing movement on the chemical weapons front or the use of chemical weapons. That would change my calculations significantly.

Questions

What explains the reluctance of the American President to act once he had drawn a clear "red line"?

Should NATO have intervened in the Syrian civil war because of its security implications or due to humanitarian needs?

Reference

https://obamawhitehouse.archives.gov/the-press-office/2012/08/20/remarks-president-white-house-press-corps

Document 4

Establishment of a Committee of Inquiry (regarding Internet and telecommunications surveillance), German Bundestag, 18 March 2014

On 26 October 2013 the German magazine Der Spiegel *announced that the US Embassy in the centre of Berlin was being used as a location for the National Security Agency (NSA) and the CIA to listen in on German government communications, including conversations conducted by Chancellor Angela Merkel via her own mobile phone. Such surveillance had been taking place since 2002, so it was claimed, and Merkel's phone had most recently been monitored in June 2013 when President Obama himself visited Germany. In the wake of information concerning NSA surveillance activity leaked by former NSA contractor Edward Snowden,* Der Spiegel *referred to an NSA-CIA joint venture termed the Special Collection Service that operated communications surveillance in 80 locations around the world, including 19 in Europe. In May 2013 Snowden had fled his NSA post in Hawaii via Hong Kong for Moscow, taking with him documents that indicated massive surveillance of both political and private communications around the world. Central to this operation was the "Five Eyes" intelligence-sharing coalition of the US, Canada, Britain, Australia, and New Zealand, which dated from Second World War agreements that were then solidified in the war's aftermath.*

The revelations rocked US-German relations and undermined the up-till-then close relationship between Merkel and Obama. The fact that Obama denied knowledge of the operation also created the impression that US security services were out of control. A cross-party coalition in the German parliament initiated a full-scale investigation of the practices, but eventually in June 2015 Federal Prosecutor Harald Range declared that there was not enough evidence to justify any legal action, mainly due to lack of cooperation from the NSA. There is evidence to suggest that the "Merkel cellphone" episode may have been a Russian act of propaganda, an "active measure" designed to disrupt German-American relations. Yet it was also one of several stories in the early- to mid-2010s that indicated constant surveillance and spying going on between the transatlantic allies, such as the hacking of the Belgacom telecommunications network by Britain's equivalent to the NSA, GCHQ (General Communications Headquarters). Belgacom had been targeted because of its role as one of Europe's most extensive telecommunications networks, with huge intercontinental traffic and major clients such as the European Commission and NATO. Snowden's release of hundreds of documents had exposed the fact that behind the public scenes of unity and diplomatic respect, the transatlantic relationship really rested on mistrust and competition.

German Bundestag   Printed paper 18/843
18th electoral term   18.03.2014

Motion tabled by the CDU/CSU, SPD, The Left Party and Alliance 90/The Greens parliamentary groups

Establishment of a committee of inquiry

DOI: 10.4324/9781003159551-51

The Bundestag is requested to adopt the following motion:

A   Establishment

I   A committee of inquiry shall be established.
II   The committee of inquiry is to consist of eight members and the same number of substitute members.

B   Task

The committee of inquiry should – triggered in particular by press coverage following the revelations by Edward Snowden regarding Internet and telecommunications surveillance – clarify for the period from 2001 onwards:

I   whether, in what way and on what scale the intelligence services of the "Five Eyes" states (United States of America, United Kingdom, Canada, Australia and New Zealand) collected or are collecting data on communication activities (including content-related, subscriber and traffic data), their content and other data-processing actions (including internet use and stored address directories) from, to and in Germany for data retention or used or are using such data collected by public companies or private third parties and to what extent federal agencies, in particular the Federal Government, intelligence services or the Federal Office for Information Security had knowledge of such practices, were involved in them, combated them or possibly exploited them. To this end, the committee should examine the following specific points:

1   Was data collected and retained, checked and analysed by surveillance programmes of the US intelligence service, the National Security Agency (NSA), and of the British Government Communications Headquarters (GCHQ) or by companies on their behalf (in particular on telecommunications activities, including text messages, Internet use, email correspondence – "C2C", use of social networks and electronic payment transactions) which also affected communication and data-processing activities from, to and in Germany? Were German nationals residing on the territory of one of the countries cited in point I or in any EU Member State subject to such surveillance? Were such activities carried out by other services of the countries listed under point I? Since when, how and on what scale and, if applicable, on what legal basis did this take place?
2   To what extent were and are diplomatic missions and military sites used or being used to collect data on such communication and data-processing activities and the content thereof?
3   If applicable, which laws at German, European and international level did or do such activities contravene?
4   Do the Federal Government, its subordinate agencies or those they have entrusted with security-relevant tasks (including IT tasks) have indications or affirmative knowledge of the activities cited in points I. or 1. and if so for how long has this been the case? Did they know of, approve, support or order the participation of federal agencies or those they entrusted with security-relevant tasks (including IT tasks) in this?
5   Do the Federal Government, its subordinate agencies or those they have entrusted with security-relevant tasks (including IT tasks) have indications or affirmative knowledge of the activities cited in points I. or 1. against other Member States of the EU or NATO, their population or businesses located there, and if so for how long

has this been the case? If so, how was this knowledge viewed and what conclusions were drawn from it?

6 What precautions or measures did federal agencies take or initiate or, as the case may be, should have taken or initiated in order to identify the activities cited in points I. and 1. and their extent and to put a stop to them? In the latter event, up until when and why did this not happen and who bears responsibility for this?

7 Did federal agencies or those entrusted by them with security-relevant tasks (including IT tasks) acquire or use data from the activities cited in points I. or 1. or possibly provide services in kind in exchange? Were federal agencies or those entrusted by them with security-relevant tasks (including IT tasks) part of a systematic mutual or "circular" intelligence exchange, in which the other side receives data or findings which they are not allowed to collect themselves under the laws applicable at the location of the data collection? If so, on what legal basis and for what purpose was or is such data acquired or used? If so, how was it ensured that the information in question can be acquired and used under German law as well? How was it ensured, if applicable, that information was not or is not acquired or used that would not have been allowed to be collected under German law?

8 Were federal agencies or those entrusted by them with security-relevant tasks (including IT tasks) involved in any way in the development or technical implementation or use of programmes such as "PRISM", "TEMPORA", "XKeyscore" or other programmes used by the services of the countries listed in point I. or used on their behalf for the activities cited in points I. or 1.? If so, who on the German side was involved, for how long and in what specifically?

9 Did federal agencies or those entrusted by them with security-relevant tasks (including IT tasks) receive, test or use programmes developed by the NSA, GCHQ or other services of the countries listed in point I. themselves or on their behalf and, in doing so, did they also access data records originating from the communication and data-processing activities stated in points I. or 1.? If so, who on the German side received which programmes, tested or used them for how long and accessed which of the said data records?

10 What knowledge regarding the type and scale of such activities geared against business enterprises located in the Federal Republic of Germany did federal agencies have at what time?

11 Could or should federal agencies possibly already have gained knowledge of such measures at an earlier point in time? If so, which bodies and when?

12 To what extent was the Federal Commissioner for Data Protection and Freedom of Information notified immediately of knowledge and information suited to providing grounds for suspicion that data protection law provisions were being violated? Or, as the case may be, why and due to what circumstances and influences did this not happen?

13 Which IT security concepts has the Federal Government applied in its area of responsibility to secure the organisation and operation of telecommunications and IT structures, files, indexes and administration processes against unauthorised data removal and access by third parties?

14 Have US bodies carried out or initiated telecommunications surveillance, arrests, or targeted killings through the deployment of combat drones on or from German territory? If so, what knowledge did German federal agencies have of this at what time? If applicable, were they involved in the preparation or implementation of such measures in any form whatsoever or did they approve them? If applicable, what action should they have taken in response to such knowledge and what action was actually taken?

15   To what extent did the German Federal Government and its subordinate departments enable US security authorities to take part in the questioning of asylum seekers or to question asylum seekers themselves?

16   What action did the Federal Government and its subordinate departments take and when in order to bring to light, prosecute and end these practices, or if not, why and due to what circumstances and influences did this fail to happen?

17   Was the information the Federal Government provided to the general public on the aforesaid questions correct? Was the information the Federal Government provided to members of parliament or parliamentary institutions on the aforesaid questions correct and comprehensive? Did the Federal Government fulfil all its statutory duties of information towards the Parliamentary Control Panel, the G10 Commission and the Federal Commissioner for Data Protection and Freedom of Information? Was any relevant information withheld from these scrutiny and oversight bodies?;

II   whether and to what extent data on communication activities and the contents thereof (in the form of telecommunication or conversations including their subject matter, such as draft legislation or negotiation strategies) of members of the Federal Government, federal staff and members of the German Bundestag or other constitutional bodies of the Federal Republic of Germany was collected or analysed for intelligence purposes by the intelligence services of the states named in point I. To this end, the committee should examine the following points:

1   Was the data traffic from federal agencies recorded or subject to surveillance by intelligence services of the said countries? Did this also affect German diplomatic missions abroad? If so, since when, how and on what scale?

2   Was telecommunication (telephone conversations, text messages, emails, etc.) or Internet use by members of the Federal Government, federal staff and members of the German Bundestag or other constitutional bodies of the Federal Republic of Germany recorded or analysed by intelligence services of the said states? As of when and on what scale did this happen?

3   If so, why did federal agencies not notice earlier that this type of recording of communication was happening and put an end to it?

4   What strategy did the Federal Government pursue to protect the IT systems of the German Federation from data being accessed or removed without authorisation in the period under inquiry and how has this been further developed?

5   Was the information the Federal Government provided to the general public on the aforesaid questions correct? Was the information the Federal Government provided on the aforesaid questions to members of parliament or parliamentary institutions correct and comprehensive? Has the Federal Government met all its statutory duties of information towards the Parliamentary Control Panel, the G10 Commission and the Federal Commissioner for Data Protection and Freedom of Information? Was any relevant information withheld from these scrutiny and oversight bodies?;

III   whether recommendations to ensure the protection enshrined in the constitution of the right to determine the disclosure and use of one's own personal data, to privacy, to the secrecy of telecommunications and the integrity and confidentiality of IT systems and confidential communication in the state sphere are required. To this end, the committee should clarify the following:

1   Are legal and technical changes required to the German system of foreign surveillance carried out by the intelligence services in order to ensure that German authorities comply fully with fundamental and human rights, and if so, which?
2   Are legal and technical changes regarding transmission, receipt and exchange of information with foreign security authorities necessary in order to ensure the Federal Government and all German authorities comply fully with fundamental and human rights, and if so, which?
3   Which measures of a legal, organisational or technical nature can be used to ensure that the guaranteed protection of the confidentiality of electronic communication from, to and in Germany is realised to the fullest extent possible, so that citizens as well as those subject to professional secrecy, those holding the right to refuse testimony and custodians of trade and commercial secrets are protected against electronic communication activities and the content thereof being recorded by foreign intelligence services irrespective of whether there are grounds for suspicion or not?
4   What measures are necessary in order to ensure confidential electronic communication for state bodies as well?
5   Are changes necessary to protect telecommunication and IT security when awarding public contracts in the future?
6   What measures are required to ensure the best possible protection of the privacy of electronic communication at European and international level? The findings of the inquiry by the Civil Liberties, Justice and Home Affairs (LIBE) Committee of the European Parliament as well as the work at the level of the United Nations should be incorporated into this.
7   What measures are necessary to provide better protection for the population, businesses and public administration against Internet and telecommunications surveillance by foreign authorities?
8   How can the executive, parliamentary, judicial and independent data-protection oversight of the federal security authorities be ensured fully and effectively?
9   What other legal, technical infrastructure and political action must be taken?

Berlin, 18 March 2014

Volker Kauder, Gerda Hasselfeldt and the CDU/CSU parliamentary group, Thomas Oppermann and the SPD parliamentary group, Dr Gregor Gysi and the Left Party parliamentary group, Katrin Göring-Eckardt, Dr Anton Hofreiter and the Alliance 90/The Greens parliamentary group.

Questions

How does this enquiry express concerns not only about the American surveillance activities, but also about the German government?
To what extent did Edward Snowden single-handedly undermine the transatlantic alliance?

Reference

https://www.bundestag.de/resource/blob/284528/a89d6006f28900c4f46e56f5e0807ddf/einsetzungsantrag_englisch-docx-data.pdf

Document 5

Vladimir Putin, Speech on the Accession of the Republic of Crimea to the Russian Federation, 18 March 2014

In February 2014 Russia announced it would not recognize the new Ukrainian government, which came to power after pro-Western political forces ousted the pro-Russian President Yanukovych. Russia feared losing its naval base on the Crimean peninsula, use of which by its Black Sea fleet had been granted for twenty years in a series of treaties from 1997. On the basis of a new treaty in April 2010 the lease of the port of Sebastopol had been extended until 2042 in return for a discount on Russian energy supplies to Ukraine. The Russian Black Sea Fleet in Sebastopol, one of Russia's four major fleets, plays a highly important role in Russia's military strategic options in the Mediterranean basin and the Middle East.

In late February 2014 Russia undertook a swift military action to conquer the Crimean peninsula, making use of unorthodox tactical means, such as so-called "little green men" (special forces in unmarked green uniforms). In the same period, hostilities between Russian-supported separatists in East Ukraine (Donbass) and the regular Ukraine military broke out. Soon thereafter Russia announced the annexation of the Crimean peninsula via an agreement with the newly founded Republic of Crimea. The Agreement between Russia and the Republic of Crimea on the "Accession of the Republic of Crimea in the Russian Federation and on Forming New Constituent Entities within the Russian Federation" was signed on 18 March 2014.

Dear friends,

This is a very joyful and happy day for us!

Citizens of Russia, residents of Crimea and Sevastopol!

After a long, hard and exhausting voyage, Crimea and Sevastopol are returning to their harbour, to their native shores, to their home port, to Russia!

I would like to thank the residents of Crimea and Sevastopol for their consistent and decisive stance and for their clearly expressed will to be with Russia. We all felt for them, and Russia gave them its warmth, turned towards them and opened up its heart to them.

We are gravely concerned over the developments in Ukraine. But I believe that Ukraine will overcome all the hardships. We are not just neighbours, we are family and our future success depends on both of us, Russia and Ukraine.

I would again like to thank the residents of Crimea and Sevastopol for their courage and persistence, for staying true to the memory of their heroic ancestors and for carrying their love for our motherland, for Russia over decades.

Together we have done a lot, but a lot more remains to be done, more tasks to resolve. However, I am certain that we will overcome all the problems, and we will do it because we are together.

Long live Russia!

DOI: 10.4324/9781003159551-52

Questions

Was the Russian involvement in Ukraine a direct challenge to transatlantic security?
In what ways was the Russian annexation of the Crimean peninsula a Pyrrhic victory?

Reference

http://en.kremlin.ru/events/president/news/20607

Document 6

Greece: Article IV Consultation, IMF Country Report No. 13/154, 5 June 2013

The financial crisis that unfolded in 2008 went on to become a "Eurozone crisis" from 2009. European nations that had relied on steady inflows of capital to sustain their current account deficits suddenly faced a serious decline in their ability to borrow. Following the introduction of the Euro, the European Central Bank (ECB) had maintained low interest rates to encourage investment transfers from northern eurozone members to the southern nations, who in turn were encouraged to borrow in order to stimulate increased growth. Much of this investment went into property development, creating inflated prices and the likelihood of market collapse. In late 2009, with the banking sector in turmoil and creditors no longer providing capital inflows, Greece was the first southern Eurozone member to signal that its budget deficits were reaching unsustainable levels. Calling for external support, in May 2010 the so-called "Troika" of the European Commission, the European Central Bank (ECB), and the International Monetary Fund (IMF) introduced a rescue package for Greece that involved large-scale cut-backs in public spending in order to bring the ballooning deficits under control. Even though Greece had been allowed to borrow huge sums during 2000–2008, the responsibility of the reforms – and so the socio-economic costs of austerity – fell on the Greek governments and the Greek people. Its two main business sectors, tourism and shipping, had both been hit hard by the decline in world spending and trade after 2007, and by 2014 Greek public debt had reached over 180% of GDP, three times the expected debt-to-GDP ratio for a Eurozone member economy. By June 2013 the unemployment rate had soared to 27.9%, youth unemployment was reckoned to be much higher, and between 2008–2012 the economy as a whole had contracted by 22%. The Greece situation therefore exposed the lack of political solidarity within the European Union, and the unequal measures applied to solve the financial crises of its smaller economies.

Greece received three bailouts arranged by the Troika, in 2010, 2012, and from 2015 onwards, totalling around €310bn. The IMF would issue Article IV Consultation reports, named after Article IV of the IMF's Articles of Agreement, which allows for the Fund to surveille and assess a national economy's performance. The excerpts from the report below, compiled following the second bailout, indicate that the assumptions of returning Greece to a situation of economic growth were far wide of the mark due to the social and political turmoil caused by the severe austerity measures. The bailouts kept Greece in the Eurozone, but at great social cost, and also damage to the credibility of the EU as an economic bloc and the IMF as a guarantor of financial stability.

[This is an excerpt from the full document]

KEY ISSUES

In the midst of a sharp and socially painful recession, Greece is making important progress in overcoming deep-seated problems. Progress on fiscal adjustment has been

DOI: 10.4324/9781003159551-53

exceptional by any standard, with the cyclically-adjusted primary balance having improved cumulatively by about 15 percent of GDP during 2010–12. Labor market reforms are helping to realign nominal wages and productivity; this internal devaluation has reduced the competitiveness gap by about half since 2010. And financial stability has been preserved, notwithstanding public debt restructuring and the recession. This progress has been facilitated by considerable European and international support.

But Greece is adjusting mainly through recession, not through productivity-enhancing reforms. Beyond the labor market, broader structural reforms have fallen well short of the critical mass required to transform the investment climate and boost potential growth. With fiscal adjustment set to weigh on demand for several more years, growth must come from private investment and exports. Thus, restoring growth and reducing unacceptably high unemployment will require full and timely implementation of ambitious reforms that firmly puts to rest uncertainty about the authorities' willingness to tackle vested interests. The key priorities:

- Undertaking structural reforms to lower barriers to entry would reduce product prices and facilitate re-allocation of resources to more productive activities.
- Reinforcing the governance framework in the financial sector and reversing the rising tide of non-performing loans are key to effective financial intermediation.
- Broadening the tax base and strengthening revenue and public administration would improve the quality of adjustment (the burden has fallen excessively on those earning a salary or pension) and underpin further fiscal effort to reach medium-term targets.
- Ensuring that debt sustainability concerns do not continue to weigh on investment requires timely delivery of Greece's European partners' undertakings on debt relief.

The last Article IV consultation was concluded in July 2009. This report focuses on developments since then and on policies to overcome current challenges.

Crisis Response

3   In response, an ambitious multi-year adjustment program was put in place. The May 2010 EC/ECB/IMF supported program had two broad aims: to make fiscal policy and the fiscal and debt position sustainable, and to improve competitiveness. Given an overall fiscal deficit of 13.5 percent of GDP in 2009 (revised to 15.5 percent of GDP shortly after program approval), the program entailed significant front-loaded fiscal consolidation (with provisions to shield low-income households from the brunt of the adjustment), in addition to comprehensive structural reforms to boost productivity and a strategy to backstop the banking system. In this regard, the authorities were convinced when the program was put in place that Greece's large potential for catch-up gains in productivity—together with the expectation that the crisis would mobilize broad political support for comprehensive structural reforms to unlock this potential—meant that direct measures to force down wages and achieve accelerated internal devaluation would not be necessary.

4   Growth underperformed considerably. Although nominal GDP was from the outset assumed to contract substantially in 2011–12, actual performance was worse than projected. Several adverse and mutually reinforcing factors combined to undermine investor sentiments during this period, of which the following stand out:
   - Bouts of political turmoil left increasing doubts about support for reforms. The program was from the outset not supported by all mainstream parties and increasing opposition began to emerge from inside the governing party in early 2011. A

government reshuffle in mid-2011, followed by an aborted attempt at galvanizing public support through a referendum, failed to mobilize broader political support. Such support was only achieved after the Cannes Summit in November 2011, when European leaders explicitly raised the euro exit option, prompting the two main political parties to support a technocratic interim government. By then, however, the deep recession had already seriously undermined public support, and the two parties' share of the vote in two rounds of elections in early 2012 fell from 80 to 42 percent. At present, the program is supported only by a slim majority of pro-program parties in a fragile coalition.

- Structural reforms stalled. Against a backdrop of political turmoil, vested interests opposed to reforms were increasingly emboldened. After a strong start in 2010, and aside from labor market reforms in early 2012 by the technocratic interim government, reforms were hesitant and piecemeal, falling well short of the critical mass needed to transform the investment climate.
- Investors were unsettled by increasing uncertainty about the external financing strategy. In a reversal of the initial strategy, key euro area member states started calling for a bail-in of investors at the Deauville Summit in October 2010. The reduction in spreads achieved during the previous months was quickly lost, and by the time consensus among Greece's European partners had shifted firmly in favor of a PSI one year later, spreads had risen to near default levels.
- Debt sustainability concerns were increasing. Under the program's baseline in May 2010, public debt-to-GDP was expected to increase dramatically—peaking at about 155–160 percent (including an expected data revision)—as a result of the contraction in nominal GDP. In the event, the much deeper-than-expected recession caused an even sharper increase in the debt ratio, and debt sustainability concerns were increasingly weighing on sentiment.

These mutually reinforcing factors contributed to a steady deterioration in investor sentiment and a large outflow of deposits, especially as the increasing doubts about political support for the program gradually raised the specter of euro exit. The assumed recovery in the investment climate failed to take hold. Instead, a continued contraction in investment amplified the negative output effect of the large upfront fiscal impulse and deepened the recession (1). Thus, Greece has adjusted mainly through recession, rather than through productivity-enhancing reforms.

(1) As a result, with the benefit of hindsight, the macroeconomic assumptions at the initiation of the program proved optimistic. In this regard, an earlier debt restructuring exercise—if it had been feasible—could have provided for a somewhat more gradual fiscal adjustment path.

Questions

The IMF is one of the central pillars of transatlantic economic management. In what ways is this report critical of the response to the Greek economic crisis?

In what ways was the economic collapse of Greece a direct challenge to the transatlantic economy?

Reference

https://www.imf.org/en/Publications/CR/Issues/2016/12/31/Greece-2013-Article-IV-Consultation-40637

Document 7

Michael Rühle, NATO Enlargement and Russia: Myths and Realities (NATO Fact Sheet), 1 July 2014

After the end of the Cold War, the proposal to expand NATO membership met not only with fierce diplomatic resistance from Moscow, but also became a hotly disputed issue among policy planners and academics on both sides of the Atlantic. Among the opponents of enlargement was former American diplomat George Kennan, the author of the famous "Long Telegram" (February 1946) and the founding father of the US containment strategy. He argued that NATO enlargement would unnecessarily provoke Russia and would make future cooperation more complicated. Enlargement was indeed a thorn in the side of Russia. To this day, Moscow has never accepted the fact that (Central) European countries have the sovereign right to join any international organisation that they choose (and that will accept them), despite this being sanctioned by the 1975 Helsinki Accords. Moscow has claimed that Russia's legitimate security interests are violated by NATO enlargement, referring to earlier promises not to expand NATO made by Western leaders to the Soviet Communist leader Gorbachev at the time of German reunification in 1990. Particular emphasis is put on the 2+4 Treaty of 1990, which saw the four occupying powers renounce all rights and laying the path for a fully sovereign united Germany. This NATO document responds to the Russian claims and attempts to set the record straight. At the time, Michael Rühle was Head of NATO's Energy Security section and a former speechwriter to the NATO Secretary General.

In his address to the Russian Parliament on 18 April 2014, in which President Putin justified the annexation of the Crimea, he stressed the humiliation Russia had suffered due to many broken promises by the West, including the alleged promise not to enlarge NATO beyond the borders of a reunited Germany. Putin touched a responsive chord among his audience. For more than 20 years the narrative of the alleged "broken promise" of not enlarging NATO eastward is part and parcel of Russia's post-Soviet identity. It is hardly surprising, therefore, that this narrative has resurfaced in the context of the Ukraine crisis. Dwelling on the past remains the most convenient tool to distract from the present.

But is there any truth to these claims? Over recent years countless records and other archival material has become available, allowing historians to go beyond the interviews or autobiographies of those political leaders who were in power during the crucial developments between the fall of the Berlin Wall in November 1989 and the Soviet acceptance of a reunified Germany in NATO in July 1990. Yet even these additional sources do not change the fundamental conclusion: there have never been political or legally binding commitments of the West not to extend NATO beyond the borders of a reunified Germany. That such a myth could nevertheless emerge should not come as a surprise, however. The rapid pace of political change at the Cold War's end produced its fair share of confusion. It was a time where legends could easily emerge.

DOI: 10.4324/9781003159551-54

The origins of the myth of the "broken promise" lie in the unique political situation in which the key political actors found themselves in 1990, and which shaped their ideas about the future European order. Former USSR leader, Mikhail Gorbachev's reform policies had long spun out of control, the Baltic countries were demanding independence, and the countries of Central and Eastern Europe were showing signs of upheaval. The Berlin Wall had fallen; Germany was on the road to reunification. However, the Soviet Union still existed, as did the Warsaw Pact, who's Central and Eastern European member countries did not talk about joining NATO, but rather about the "dissolution of the two blocks".

Thus, the debate about the enlargement of NATO evolved solely in the context of German reunification. In these negotiations Bonn and Washington managed to allay Soviet reservations about a reunited Germany remaining in NATO. This was achieved by generous financial aid, and by the "2+4 Treaty" ruling out the stationing of foreign NATO forces on the territory of the former East Germany. However, it was also achieved through countless personal conversations in which Gorbachev and other Soviet leaders were assured that the West would not take advantage of the Soviet Union's weakness and willingness to withdraw militarily from Central and Eastern Europe.

It is these conversations that may have left some Soviet politicians with the impression that NATO enlargement, which started with the admission of the Czech Republic, Hungary and Poland in 1999, had been a breach of these Western commitments. Some statements of Western politicians – particularly German Foreign Minister Hans Dietrich Genscher and his American counterpart James A. Baker – can indeed be interpreted as a general rejection of any NATO enlargement beyond East Germany. However, these statements were made in the context of the negotiations on German reunification, and the Soviet interlocutors never specified their concerns. In the crucial "2+4" negotiations, which finally led Gorbachev to accept a unified Germany in NATO in July 1990, the issue was never raised. As former Soviet Foreign Minister Eduard Shevardnadze later put it, the idea of the Soviet Union and the Warsaw Pact dissolving and NATO taking in former Warsaw Pact members was beyond the imagination of the protagonists at the time.

Yet even if one were to assume that Genscher and others had indeed sought to forestall NATO's future enlargement with a view to respecting Soviet security interests, they could never have done so. The dissolution of the Warsaw Pact and the end of the Soviet Union in 1991 later created a completely new situation, as the countries of Central and Eastern Europe were finally able to assert their sovereignty and define their own foreign and security policy goals. As these goals centered on integration with the West, any categorical refusal of NATO to respond would have meant the de facto continuation of Europe's division along former Cold War lines. The right to choose one's alliance, enshrined in the 1975 Helsinki Charter, would have been denied – an approach that the West could never have sustained, neither politically nor morally.

The NATO enlargement conundrum

Does the absence of a promise not to enlarge NATO mean that the West never had any obligations vis-à-vis Russia? Did the enlargement policy of Western institutions therefore proceed without taking Russian interests into account? Again, the facts tell a different story. However, they also demonstrate that the twin goals of admitting Central and Eastern European countries into NATO while at the same time developing a "strategic partnership" with Russia were far less compatible in practice than in theory.

When the NATO enlargement debate started in earnest around 1993, due to mounting pressure from countries in Central and Eastern Europe, it did so with considerable controversy. Some academic observers in particular opposed admitting new members into NATO, as this would inevitably antagonise Russia and risk undermining the positive achievements since the end of the Cold War. Indeed, ever since the beginning of NATO's post-Cold War enlargement process, the prime concern of the West was how to reconcile this process with Russian interests. Hence, NATO sought early on to create a cooperative environment that was conducive for enlargement while at the same time building special relations with Russia. In 1994 the "Partnership for Peace" programme established military cooperation with virtually all countries in the Euro-Atlantic area. In 1997 the NATO-Russia Founding Act established the Permanent Joint Council as a dedicated framework for consultation and cooperation. In 2002, as Allies were preparing the next major round of NATO enlargement, the NATO-Russia Council was established, giving the relationship more focus and structure. These steps were in line with other attempts by the international community to grant Russia its rightful place: Russia was admitted to the International Monetary Fund, the World Bank, the G7 and the World Trade Organisation.

The need to avoid antagonising Russia was also evident in the way NATO enlargement took place in the military realm. As early as 1996, Allies declared that in the current circumstances they had "no intention, no plan, and no reason to deploy nuclear weapons on the territory of new members". These statements were incorporated into the 1997 NATO-Russia Founding Act, together with similar references regarding substantial combat forces and infrastructure. This "soft" military approach to the enlargement process was supposed to signal to Russia that the goal of NATO enlargement was not Russia's military "encirclement", but the integration of Central and Eastern Europe into an Atlantic security space. In other words, the method was the message.

Russia never interpreted these developments as benignly as NATO hoped. For Russian Foreign Minister Primakov, the signing of the NATO-Russia Founding Act in 1997 was merely "damage limitation": As Russia had no means to stop NATO enlargement, it might as well take whatever the Allies were willing to offer, even at the risk of appearing to acquiesce in the enlargement process. The fundamental contradiction of all NATO-Russia bodies – that Russia was at the table and could co-decide, but could not veto, on key issues – could not be overcome.

However, these institutional weaknesses paled against the background of real political conflicts. NATO's military intervention in the Kosovo crisis was interpreted in Moscow as a geopolitical coup by a West that was bent on marginalising Russia's status as a permanent member of the UN Security Council. NATO's missile defence approach, though directed at third countries, was interpreted by Moscow as an attempt to undermine Russia's nuclear second strike capability. Worse, the "Orange Revolution" in Ukraine and the "Rose Revolution" in Georgia brought to power elites who envisioned the future of their respective countries in the EU and NATO.

Against this background, Western arguments about the benevolence of NATO enlargement never had – and probably never will have – much traction. Appealing to Russia to acknowledge the benign nature of NATO's enlargement misses a most essential point: NATO enlargement – as well as the enlargement of the European Union – is designed as a continental unification project. It therefore does not have an "end point" that could be convincingly defined either intellectually or morally. In other words, precisely because the two organisations' respective enlargement processes are not intended as anti-Russian projects, they are open-ended and – paradoxically – are bound to be perceived by Russia as a permanent assault on its status and influence. As long as Russia shirks an honest debate about why so many of its neighbors seek to orient themselves towards the West, this will not change – and the NATO-Russia relationship will remain haunted by myths of the past instead of looking to the future.

Questions

How convincing is Rühle's argument against Russian claims, in your opinion?
Why is it difficult to include Russia in an overarching Euro-Atlantic security architecture?

Reference

https://www.nato.int/docu/review/articles/2014/07/01/nato-enlargement-and-russia-myths-and-realities/index.html

Document 8

Statement by Geert Wilders, Press Conference of the Europe of Nations and Freedom, Milan, 29 January 2016

In the 2010s the political parties that were pushing a nationalist-populist Eurosceptic agenda began to organize as a visible bloc within European politics. This began with the formation of the European Alliance for Freedom (EAF) in 2010, which involved individual politicians in the European Parliament (EP) from mainly Austria, Belgium, France, and Malta. After the 2014 EP elections, efforts were made to form an official parliamentary group, with support from the French Front Nationale, the Dutch Party for Freedom, the Flemish Vlaams Belang, the Austrian Freedom Party, and the Italian Northern League. At the time the Eurosceptic right was divided on the issue of anti-Semitism (which excluded the Hungarian Jobbik and the Greek Golden Dawn) and the rivalry between the EAF and the Europe of Freedom and Democracy group led by the UK Independence Party's Nigel Farage (who regarded the Front Nationale as too extreme). Since seven member states need to be represented in any EP group, the EAF fell short, and instead they formed the Europe of Nations and Freedom (ENF) on 16 June 2015, with the Polish Congress of the New Right also joining. Through 2015–2016 the ENF organized many events to demonstrate cross-party solidarity and common ground as they sought to capitalize on popular disillusionment with the EU. Geert Wilders, leader of the Dutch Party for Freedom (PVV), has been a prominent member of both the EAF and the ENF, and both groups initially revolved around the close relations between him and Marine Le Pen (who renamed the Front Nationale as Rassemblement national in 2018), although Vlaams Belang played a key organizational role. Wilders has always maintained a strong anti-Islamic stance, opposing the "Islamization" of Europe through immigration and liberal policies towards freedom of religion. This has been put forward within a wider call for regaining national sovereignty and identity, and reducing the powers of EU institutions. In 2019 the ENF was renamed the Identity and Democracy group and other parties such as Alternative for Germany, the Danish People's Party, and the Finns party were by then also associated.

I am extremely happy to be in Milan. Because this is the city which in 2005 awarded the late Oriana Fallaci, a true Italian hero, Milan's highest award, the Ambrogino d'Oro.

She deserved it. She was one of Italy's greatest and most courageous women and journalists. Whenever I come to Italy, I do so in honor of her: Oriana Fallaci, whose bravery in warning against the dangers of Islamization I greatly admire. Her book The Force of Reason – La Forza Della Ragione – was one the best books I have ever read. It was published in 2004 and inspired me to start my own political party that same year, a party that today – twelve years later – is by far the biggest party in all the polls in The Netherlands with almost 30 percent of the votes.

Thank you Italy, thank you Oriana for the inspiration. I am very proud to have been awarded the Oriana Fallaci prize in Rome in 2009.

DOI: 10.4324/9781003159551-55

Today our civilization is still in danger, as a matter of fact worse than ever before. We are facing an existential threat.

You can see it everywhere, in all Western European countries. Our borders have been opened to Islamic mass immigration. And the consequences are terrible.

The costs are gigantic, the attacks horrible and the threat of terrorism has never been higher.

So we need to act.

That is why we are here today in Milan. With a message of strength and unity.

Together with my good friends from Italy, France, Austria, Belgium, the U.K. and other countries we have forged an alliance. An alliance with a historic mission.

Our mission is to save and defend our nations and our Western civilization, built on the legacy of Rome, Athens and Jerusalem. The survival of our freedom, identity and values are at stake.

My colleagues and I, we ring the bells of the revolution. A democratic and peaceful revolution to regain our national sovereignty. To stop the invasion.

To protect our own people, our women, our culture. We have to become the masters again of our own borders, our own budgets, our own destiny.

Our mission is to do what our governments fail to do. We say: Basta! Finita la commedia!

And there is good news. Ever more people – millions of people – join us. A patriot spring is on its way. The European elites are running our nations into the ground. We will not allow that. We will not accept that. The people will not accept that. The people will resist that.

The people no longer want politicians who are selling out their nation, ignoring the wishes of its citizens, and acting like politically correct appeasers and cowards.

What we need today is real leadership. Brave politicians, unlike the ones that currently misrepresent the people in so many fake parliaments, where they do exactly the opposite of what the majority of the people want. We say: enough is enough.

Most of us here are leading in the polls in our respective countries.

We are politically successful because we stand for the following five principles.

The principles of the new patriotism.

One, we want to close our borders for mass immigration from Islamic countries and the asylum tsunami.

If I would become Prime Minister of the Netherlands next year, I will close the Dutch borders at once.

Two, we must protect ourselves against the terrorist threat.

We do not want jihadis in our countries. And we must restore the safety of our citizens, especially our women. No more rape, no more sexual jihad. On New Year's Eve in Cologne alone, over 1,000 women were assaulted, groped, raped. So far, 30 suspects have been caught. All of them North-Africans, and half of those asylum seekers.

This is unacceptable. Closing our borders is a major step towards more safety too.

Three, we do not want billions of taxpayers' money to be spent on Brussels, bailouts and asylum seekers. We want that money to be spent on our own people. In our own country.

Four, we choose national sovereignty instead of the EU. The Capitol [sic] of The Netherlands is Amsterdam not Brussels. We will regain national sovereignty and get rid of the unelected European bureaucrats.

And five, last but not least, we want to stop the Islamization of our free societies. I say: no more. We chose freedom and will not compromise anymore.

It is time to halt the elite's march of folly and save our countries. That is what people expect of us, that is why people support us, that is what needs to be done, and that is what we will do. That is our duty as true political leaders.

We will make our countries safe, sovereign and great again. And we will succeed. Because the people and the truth are on our side.

Let me remind you of something Oriana Fallaci once said. I quote: "It is a lie to say that the truth stays in the middle. No sir: Sometimes truth stays on one side only." End of quote.

The truth, ladies and gentlemen, indeed, is on one side only. It is on our side. So, get used to it: We are the future.

Questions

What are the main threats facing Europe, according to Wilders?
How has populism challenged the transatlantic relationship?

References

https://canadafreepress.com/article/statement-geert-wilders-press-conference-europe-of-nations-and-freedom
Permission: Geert Wilders

Document 9

EU-Turkey Agreement on Refugees, 18 March 2016

In 2015 it is estimated that 1.015,078 migrants reached the EU by crossing the Mediterranean, while thousands more died making the journey.* Around 800,000 of them travelled from Turkey to Greece, from there they often continued onwards to Germany and other destinations. Between 2014 and 2017 Italy received around 650,000 migrants in total. This large-scale human movement was driven by a variety of factors: the Syrian civil war from 2011 onwards, ongoing civil unrest and violence in Iraq and Afghanistan, the negative effects of climate change in Africa, and the general desire to capitalize on the opportunities for a better life in Europe. The death toll also rose due to the shifting routes – while Turkey-Greece is a relatively short distance, the increasing numbers travelling between Libya and Italy, often in overcrowded and makeshift vessels, from 2016 greatly raised the danger levels. While Germany took by far the most migrants (around 1 million), the effects of this migration could be felt in society and politics throughout Europe, fuelling support for Euro-skeptic populist parties and exposing the inability of the EU to establish common ground on the issue among its member states. In 2015 the European Commission estimated that there were more than 2 million illegal residents in the EU.

The agreement with Turkey was meant to strengthen the external border of the EU and stem the largest flow of migrants from Turkey to Greece, and in strictly numerical terms it largely succeeded. Cooperation between EU and Turkish authorities improved, and all irregular migrants arriving in Greece could from then on be returned to Turkey, in return for two tranches of €6bn to sustain support and processing procedures in Turkey itself. Since Turkey was at the time host to around 2.7m Syrian refugees, the deal was important for the Turkish government, as were additional features such as visa-free travel for Turkish citizens to the EU. But the human cost has been high. Flouting international norms on refugee protection, Greece changed all refugee camps on its islands into temporary detention centres. As a result, these people became stuck in a legal grey area, rejected by the EU and unwanted in Turkey. Basic conditions in the camps and relations with the local Greek population deteriorated, leading to catastrophes such as the fire that destroyed the Moria camp on Lesbos in September 2020. As a result, the credibility of the EU as an upholder of human rights and ethical values in international politics has been severely undermined.

*The term "migrant" is used here to describe collectively migrants, refugees and asylum seekers. The EU document below refers to "migrants" throughout, even though it is entitled as an agreement on refugees.

Today the Members of the European Council met with their Turkish counterpart. This was the third meeting since November 2015 dedicated to deepening Turkey-EU relations as well as addressing the migration crisis.

DOI: 10.4324/9781003159551-56

The Members of the European Council expressed their deepest condolences to the people of Turkey following the bomb attack in Ankara on Sunday. They strongly condemned this heinous act and reiterated their continued support to fight terrorism in all its forms.

Turkey and the European Union reconfirmed their commitment to the implementation of their joint action plan activated on 29 November 2015. Much progress has been achieved already, including Turkey's opening of its labour market to Syrians under temporary protection, the introduction of new visa requirements for Syrians and other nationalities, stepped up security efforts by the Turkish coast guard and police and enhanced information sharing. Moreover, the European Union has begun disbursing the 3 billion euro of the Facility for Refugees in Turkey for concrete projects and work has advanced on visa liberalisation and in the accession talks, including the opening of Chapter 17 last December. On 7 March 2016, Turkey furthermore agreed to accept the rapid return of all migrants not in need of international protection crossing from Turkey into Greece and to take back all irregular migrants intercepted in Turkish waters. Turkey and the EU also agreed to continue stepping up measures against migrant smugglers and welcomed the establishment of the NATO activity on the Aegean Sea. At the same time Turkey and the EU recognise that further, swift and determined efforts are needed.

In order to break the business model of the smugglers and to offer migrants an alternative to putting their lives at risk, the EU and Turkey today decided to end the irregular migration from Turkey to the EU. In order to achieve this goal, they agreed on the following additional action points:

1   All new irregular migrants crossing from Turkey into Greek islands as from 20 March 2016 will be returned to Turkey. This will take place in full accordance with EU and international law, thus excluding any kind of collective expulsion. All migrants will be protected in accordance with the relevant international standards and in respect of the principle of non-refoulement. It will be a temporary and extraordinary measure which is necessary to end the human suffering and restore public order. Migrants arriving in the Greek islands will be duly registered and any application for asylum will be processed individually by the Greek authorities in accordance with the Asylum Procedures Directive, in cooperation with UNHCR [UN High Commissioner for Refugees]. Migrants not applying for asylum or whose application has been found unfounded or inadmissible in accordance with the said directive will be returned to Turkey. Turkey and Greece, assisted by EU institutions and agencies, will take the necessary steps and agree any necessary bilateral arrangements, including the presence of Turkish officials on Greek islands and Greek officials in Turkey as from 20 March 2016, to ensure liaison and thereby facilitate the smooth functioning of these arrangements. The costs of the return operations of irregular migrants will be covered by the EU.

2   For every Syrian being returned to Turkey from Greek islands, another Syrian will be resettled from Turkey to the EU taking into account the UN Vulnerability Criteria. A mechanism will be established, with the assistance of the Commission, EU agencies and other Member States, as well as the UNHCR, to ensure that this principle will be implemented as from the same day the returns start. Priority will be given to migrants who have not previously entered or tried to enter the EU irregularly. On the EU side, resettlement under this mechanism will take place, in the first instance, by honouring the commitments taken by Member States in the conclusions of Representatives of the Governments of Member States meeting within the Council on 20 July 2015, of which 18.000 places for resettlement remain. Any further need for resettlement will be carried out through a similar voluntary arrangement up to a limit of an additional

54.000 persons. The Members of the European Council welcome the Commission's intention to propose an amendment to the relocation decision of 22 September 2015 to allow for any resettlement commitment undertaken in the framework of this arrangement to be offset from non-allocated places under the decision. Should these arrangements not meet the objective of ending the irregular migration and the number of returns come close to the numbers provided for above, this mechanism will be reviewed. Should the number of returns exceed the numbers provided for above, this mechanism will be discontinued.

3   Turkey will take any necessary measures to prevent new sea or land routes for illegal migration opening from Turkey to the EU, and will cooperate with neighbouring states as well as the EU to this effect.

4   Once irregular crossings between Turkey and the EU are ending or at least have been substantially and sustainably reduced, a Voluntary Humanitarian Admission Scheme will be activated. EU Member States will contribute on a voluntary basis to this scheme.

5   The fulfilment of the visa liberalisation roadmap will be accelerated vis-à-vis all participating Member States with a view to lifting the visa requirements for Turkish citizens at the latest by the end of June 2016, provided that all benchmarks have been met. To this end Turkey will take the necessary steps to fulfil the remaining requirements to allow the Commission to make, following the required assessment of compliance with the benchmarks, an appropriate proposal by the end of April on the basis of which the European Parliament and the Council can make a final decision.

6   The EU, in close cooperation with Turkey, will further speed up the disbursement of the initially allocated 3 billion euros under the Facility for Refugees in Turkey and ensure funding of further projects for persons under temporary protection identified with swift input from Turkey before the end of March. A first list of concrete projects for refugees, notably in the field of health, education, infrastructure, food and other living costs, that can be swiftly financed from the Facility, will be jointly identified within a week. Once these resources are about to be used to the full, and provided the above commitments are met, the EU will mobilise additional funding for the Facility of an additional 3 billion euro up to the end of 2018.

7   The EU and Turkey welcomed the ongoing work on the upgrading of the Customs Union.

8   The EU and Turkey reconfirmed their commitment to re-energise the accession process as set out in their joint statement of 29 November 2015. They welcomed the opening of Chapter 17 on 14 December 2015 and decided, as a next step, to open Chapter 33 during the Netherlands presidency. They welcomed that the Commission will put forward a proposal to this effect in April. Preparatory work for the opening of other Chapters will continue at an accelerated pace without prejudice to Member States' positions in accordance with the existing rules.

9   The EU and its Member States will work with Turkey in any joint endeavour to improve humanitarian conditions inside Syria, in particular in certain areas near the Turkish border which would allow for the local population and refugees to live in areas which will be more safe.

All these elements will be taken forward in parallel and monitored jointly on a monthly basis.

The EU and Turkey decided to meet again as necessary in accordance with the joint statement of 29 November 2015.

Questions

In what ways did this agreement indicate the EU turning away from its commitment to human rights?

In what ways is migration a major challenge for the transatlantic region?

Reference

https://www.consilium.europa.eu/en/press/press-releases/2016/03/18/eu-turkey-statement/

Document 10

Statement by Prime Minister David Cameron, EU Referendum outcome, 24 June 2016

The deeper background to the "Brexit" (British exit) referendum involves the long-running problematic relationship between the UK and the EU. Differences of opinion on fundamental issues such as the goals of European integration and the functioning of its institutions had existed right from the start of British membership in 1973. The two major political parties in the UK were both divided on the merits of EU membership. The Labour party had always included leftist critics who argued that European integration limited the ability of a nation-state to control its own socio-economic policies. For the Conservative party, the main problem was a determined challenge from the outspoken anti-EU party, UKIP (UK Independence Party). In early 2013, the Conservative Prime Minister David Cameron promised to renegotiate membership in the EU should he win the next election. When his party won a landslide victory in 2015, he kept his promise and announced a referendum to be held in June 2016. Cameron led the "Remain" camp, while the "Leave" campaign was led by former London mayor Boris Johnson, also a Conservative, and UKIP's Nigel Farage (see Part III, Document 8). Labour, to try and overcome its own divisions, chose a course of "tactical ambiguity," expressing no clear preference to remain or leave. As a result, Labour failed to exploit the Conservatives' own divisions, and did not lead a convincing campaign to argue for "Remain". Ultimately, the "Leave" camp won the referendum with a narrow majority of 52%. It was the first time an EU member had voted to end its membership, causing a shock wave in European politics. Immediately following the announcement of the result Prime Minister David Cameron made the following statement from Downing Street.

[This is an excerpt from the full document]

The country has just taken part in a giant democratic exercise – perhaps the biggest in our history. Over 33 million people – from England, Scotland, Wales, Northern Ireland and Gibraltar – have all had their say.

We should be proud of the fact that in these islands we trust the people with these big decisions.

We not only have a parliamentary democracy, but on questions about the arrangements for how we are governed, there are times when it is right to ask the people themselves, and that is what we have done.

The British people have voted to leave the European Union and their will must be respected.

I want to thank everyone who took part in the campaign on my side of the argument, including all those who put aside party differences to speak in what they believed was the national interest.

And let me congratulate all those who took part in the Leave campaign – for the spirited and passionate case that they made.

DOI: 10.4324/9781003159551-57

The will of the British people is an instruction that must be delivered. It was not a decision that was taken lightly, not least because so many things were said by so many different organisations about the significance of this decision.

So there can be no doubt about the result.

Across the world people have been watching the choice that Britain has made. I would reassure those markets and investors that Britain's economy is fundamentally strong.

And I would also reassure Brits living in European countries, and European citizens living here, that there will be no immediate changes in your circumstances. There will be no initial change in the way our people can travel, in the way our goods can move or the way our services can be sold.

We must now prepare for a negotiation with the European Union. This will need to involve the full engagement of the Scottish, Welsh and Northern Ireland governments to ensure that the interests of all parts of our United Kingdom are protected and advanced.

But above all this will require strong, determined and committed leadership.

I am very proud and very honoured to have been Prime Minister of this country for 6 years.

I believe we have made great steps, with more people in work than ever before in our history, with reforms to welfare and education, increasing people's life chances, building a bigger and stronger society, keeping our promises to the poorest people in the world, and enabling those who love each other to get married whatever their sexuality.

But above all restoring Britain's economic strength, and I am grateful to everyone who has helped to make that happen.

I have also always believed that we have to confront big decisions – not duck them.

That's why we delivered the first coalition government in 70 years to bring our economy back from the brink. It's why we delivered a fair, legal and decisive referendum in Scotland. And why I made the pledge to renegotiate Britain's position in the European Union and hold a referendum on our membership, and have carried those things out.

I fought this campaign in the only way I know how – which is to say directly and passionately what I think and feel – head, heart and soul.

I held nothing back.

I was absolutely clear about my belief that Britain is stronger, safer and better off inside the European Union, and I made clear the referendum was about this and this alone – not the future of any single politician, including myself.

But the British people have made a very clear decision to take a different path, and as such I think the country requires fresh leadership to take it in this direction.

I do not think it would be right for me to try to be the captain that steers our country to its next destination.

This is not a decision I have taken lightly, but in my view we should aim to have a new Prime Minister in place by the start of the Conservative party conference in October.

A negotiation with the European Union will need to begin under a new Prime Minister, and I think it is right that this new Prime Minister takes the decision about when to trigger Article 50 and start the formal and legal process of leaving the EU.

I will attend the European Council next week to explain the decision the British people have taken and my own decision.

Now the decision has been made to leave, we need to find the best way, and I will do everything I can to help.

I love this country – and I feel honoured to have served it.

And I will do everything I can in future to help this great country succeed.

Questions

Assess the use of a referendum as a policy instrument. What are the benefits and draw-backs, based on the Brexit experience?
In what ways has Brexit challenged the norms of transatlantic relations?

Reference

https://www.gov.uk/government/speeches/eu-referendum-outcome-pm-statement-24-june-2016

Document 11

Inaugural Address by President Trump, "America First," 20 January 2017

The 45th President of the US, who had never held public office before, did not disappoint his rank-and-file when he delivered his inaugural speech. Trump continued with the themes he had put forward during his election campaign, such as the negative impact of globalization on the American people. The "forgotten man and woman" – the American worker – occupied a central position in his address. Here Trump echoed the 19th-century libertarian thinker William Graham Sumner, who coined the notion "Forgotten Man" (1883), a popular metaphor for those at the bottom of society and used widely in American political discourse since then. From the address, which used simple and direct language, it was difficult to ascertain what the "new vision" and actual priorities of the administration would be. Investments in infrastructure, tariffs to protect American economic production and disengagement from international affairs were among Trump's most persuasive key points.

We, the citizens of America, are now joined in a great national effort to rebuild our country and to restore its promise for all of our people.

Together, we will determine the course of America and the world for years to come.

We will face challenges. We will confront hardships. But we will get the job done.

Every four years, we gather on these steps to carry out the orderly and peaceful transfer of power, and we are grateful to President Obama and First Lady Michelle Obama for their gracious aid throughout this transition. They have been magnificent.

Today's ceremony, however, has very special meaning. Because today we are not merely transferring power from one Administration to another, or from one party to another – but we are transferring power from Washington, D.C. and giving it back to you, the American People.

For too long, a small group in our nation's Capital has reaped the rewards of government while the people have borne the cost.

Washington flourished – but the people did not share in its wealth.

Politicians prospered – but the jobs left, and the factories closed.

The establishment protected itself, but not the citizens of our country.

Their victories have not been your victories; their triumphs have not been your triumphs; and while they celebrated in our nation's Capital, there was little to celebrate for struggling families all across our land.

That all changes – starting right here, and right now, because this moment is your moment: it belongs to you.

It belongs to everyone gathered here today and everyone watching all across America.

This is your day. This is your celebration.

And this, the United States of America, is your country.

What truly matters is not which party controls our government, but whether our government is controlled by the people.

DOI: 10.4324/9781003159551-58

January 20th 2017, will be remembered as the day the people became the rulers of this nation again.

The forgotten men and women of our country will be forgotten no longer.

Everyone is listening to you now.

You came by the tens of millions to become part of a historic movement the likes of which the world has never seen before.

At the center of this movement is a crucial conviction: that a nation exists to serve its citizens.

Americans want great schools for their children, safe neighborhoods for their families, and good jobs for themselves.

These are the just and reasonable demands of a righteous public.

But for too many of our citizens, a different reality exists: Mothers and children trapped in poverty in our inner cities; rusted-out factories scattered like tombstones across the landscape of our nation; an education system, flush with cash, but which leaves our young and beautiful students deprived of knowledge; and the crime and gangs and drugs that have stolen too many lives and robbed our country of so much unrealized potential.

This American carnage stops right here and stops right now.

We are one nation – and their pain is our pain. Their dreams are our dreams; and their success will be our success. We share one heart, one home, and one glorious destiny.

The oath of office I take today is an oath of allegiance to all Americans.

For many decades, we've enriched foreign industry at the expense of American industry;

Subsidized the armies of other countries while allowing for the very sad depletion of our military;

We've defended other nation's borders while refusing to defend our own;

And spent trillions of dollars overseas while America's infrastructure has fallen into disrepair and decay.

We've made other countries rich while the wealth, strength, and confidence of our country has disappeared over the horizon.

One by one, the factories shuttered and left our shores, with not even a thought about the millions upon millions of American workers left behind.

The wealth of our middle class has been ripped from their homes and then redistributed across the entire world.

But that is the past. And now we are looking only to the future.

We assembled here today are issuing a new decree to be heard in every city, in every foreign capital, and in every hall of power.

From this day forward, a new vision will govern our land.

From this moment on, it's going to be America First.

Every decision on trade, on taxes, on immigration, on foreign affairs, will be made to benefit American workers and American families.

We must protect our borders from the ravages of other countries making our products, stealing our companies, and destroying our jobs. Protection will lead to great prosperity and strength.

I will fight for you with every breath in my body – and I will never, ever let you down.

America will start winning again, winning like never before.

We will bring back our jobs. We will bring back our borders. We will bring back our wealth. And we will bring back our dreams.

We will build new roads, and highways, and bridges, and airports, and tunnels, and railways all across our wonderful nation. We will get our people off of welfare and back to work – rebuilding our country with American hands and American labor.

We will follow two simple rules: Buy American and Hire American.

We will seek friendship and goodwill with the nations of the world – but we do so with the understanding that it is the right of all nations to put their own interests first.

We do not seek to impose our way of life on anyone, but rather to let it shine as an example for everyone to follow.

We will reinforce old alliances and form new ones – and unite the civilized world against Radical Islamic Terrorism, which we will eradicate completely from the face of the Earth.

At the bedrock of our politics will be a total allegiance to the United States of America, and through our loyalty to our country, we will rediscover our loyalty to each other.

When you open your heart to patriotism, there is no room for prejudice.

The Bible tells us, "how good and pleasant it is when God's people live together in unity."

We must speak our minds openly, debate our disagreements honestly, but always pursue solidarity.

When America is united, America is totally unstoppable.

There should be no fear – we are protected, and we will always be protected.

We will be protected by the great men and women of our military and law enforcement and, most importantly, we are protected by God.

Finally, we must think big and dream even bigger.

In America, we understand that a nation is only living as long as it is striving.

We will no longer accept politicians who are all talk and no action – constantly complaining but never doing anything about it.

The time for empty talk is over.

Now arrives the hour of action.

Do not let anyone tell you it cannot be done. No challenge can match the heart and fight and spirit of America.

We will not fail. Our country will thrive and prosper again.

We stand at the birth of a new millennium, ready to unlock the mysteries of space, to free the Earth from the miseries of disease, and to harness the energies, industries and technologies of tomorrow.

A new national pride will stir our souls, lift our sights, and heal our divisions.

It is time to remember that old wisdom our soldiers will never forget: that whether we are black or brown or white, we all bleed the same red blood of patriots, we all enjoy the same glorious freedoms, and we all salute the same great American Flag.

And whether a child is born in the urban sprawl of Detroit or the windswept plains of Nebraska, they look up at the same night sky, they fill their heart with the same dreams, and they are infused with the breath of life by the same almighty Creator.

So to all Americans, in every city near and far, small and large, from mountain to mountain, and from ocean to ocean, hear these words:

You will never be ignored again.

Your voice, your hopes, and your dreams, will define our American destiny. And your courage and goodness and love will forever guide us along the way.

Together, We Will Make America Strong Again.

We Will Make America Wealthy Again.

We Will Make America Proud Again.

We Will Make America Safe Again.

And, Yes, Together, We Will Make America Great Again. Thank you, God Bless You, And God Bless America.

Questions

Who was President's Trump target audience?

"We will reinforce old alliances" – are there elements in this inaugural speech that could be positive for transatlantic relations?

Reference

https://www.whitehouse.gov/briefings-statements/the-inaugural-address/

Document 12

Presidential Memorandum regarding Withdrawal of the United States from the Trans-Pacific Partnership Negotiations and Agreement, 23 January 2017

One of President Trump's main election themes concerned the negative effects of international trade agreements, signed by his predecessors. For the President, globalization represented a loss of control over the national economy, the loss of jobs overseas, and the generation of profits for unaccountable elites. He promised to renegotiate these agreements and, if necessary, to withdraw from them. Two major treaties, one with the EU and the other with the Pacific partners of the US, were examples of major commercial treaties with geo-political implications. The TTIP (Transatlantic Trade and Investment Partnership) with the EU was still being negotiated at the time Trump took office, but was soon mothballed due to no grounds for an agreement being found. The TPP (Trans Pacific Partnership) originally involved Australia, Brunei, Canada, Chile, Japan, Malaysia, Mexico, New Zealand, Peru, Singapore, the United States, and Vietnam, and collectively they represented 40% of global GDP. The Office of the US Trade Representative calculated in 2013 that US goods exports to TPP partners were worth $698bn, representing 44% of US global goods exports. US agricultural exports to TPP nations were worth $63bn, 42% of the global total. It had the intention to strengthen trans-Pacific economic activity, and in particular position the United States at the centre of those economic channels as a balance to increasing Chinese dominance of the Asia-Pacific region. Negotiations were concluded in October 2015 and the agreement was signed on 4 February 2016, with the approval of each participating nation's legislature the next step. However, already during the election campaign in 2016, Trump had announced his intention to withdraw from TPP if elected. He considered the treaty harmful to the American economy and independence, and was, in short, an unfair trade deal. Withdrawal from the TPP would be his first act as President.

[This is an excerpt from the full document]

It is the policy of my Administration to represent the American people and their financial well-being in all negotiations, particularly the American worker, and to create fair and economically beneficial trade deals that serve their interests. Additionally, in order to ensure these outcomes, it is the intention of my Administration to deal directly with individual countries on a one-on-one (or bilateral) basis in negotiating future trade deals. Trade with other nations is, and always will be, of paramount importance to my Administration and to me, as President of the United States.

Based on these principles, and by the authority vested in me as President by the Constitution and the laws of the United States of America, I hereby direct you to withdraw the United States as a signatory to the Trans-Pacific Partnership (TPP), to permanently withdraw the United States from TPP negotiations, and to begin pursuing, wherever possible, bilateral trade negotiations to promote American industry, protect American workers, and raise American wages.

DOI: 10.4324/9781003159551-59

You are directed to provide written notification to the Parties and to the Depository of the TPP, as appropriate, that the United States withdraws as a signatory of the TPP and withdraws from the TPP negotiating process.

You are authorized and directed to publish this memorandum in the Federal Register.

Donald J. Trump

Questions

Why was Trump's withdrawal from the TPP a major reversal of US policy up to that point? What message did this send to US allies on the issue of US leadership?

Reference

https://www.whitehouse.gov/presidential-actions/presidential-memorandum-regarding-withdraw-al-united-states-trans-pacific-partnership-negotiations-agreement/

Document 13
Celebrating Four Years of Black Lives Matter, 2017

In the 2010s Black Lives Matter (BLM) came to symbolize the popular anger and protest against institutional racism and violence against black people by the US police and judicial system. A decentralized social movement focused on civil disobedience, it originated in response to the killing of 17-year-old Trayvon Martin in Miami Gardens, Florida, by local community watch member George Zimmerman on 26 February 2012. Zimmerman's claim of self-defence and subsequent acquittal for both murder and manslaughter triggered widespread protest rallies that gathered national media attention. BLM was founded by three female activists, Alicia Garza, Patrisse Cullors, and Opal Tometi, although since the founding BLM has been criticized for giving less attention to the experiences of black women. The movement was fully galvanized in response to the 2014 killings of Michael Brown in Ferguson, Missouri, and Eric Garner in New York, with the shooting of Brown leading to several days of rioting that were met with tear gas and rubber bullets as part of a heavily militarized police response. From 2014 onwards BLM established a network of chapters in urban centres across the United States in order to maintain the spotlight on ongoing police violence. Further notoriety for the cause was generated when quarterback Colin Kaepernick of the San Francisco 49ers began kneeling in September 2016 when the US national anthem was played prior to a game of American Football, stating that "I am not going to stand up to show pride in a flag for a country that oppresses black people and people of colour." Supported at the time as a legitimate form of protest by President Obama, President Trump's hard-line declaration in 2017 that those who took the knee should be fired generated wider sympathy for Kaepernick and turned the gesture into a common form of non-violent protest at BLM demonstrations.

In 2020 BLM again came to national attention following the brutal death of George Floyd in Minneapolis by police officer Derek Chauvin on 25 May 2020. Floyds's last words – "I can't breathe" – as he lay on the ground with Chauvin's knee on his neck became the keywords for both national and worldwide protests. Chauvin was charged with second-degree unintentional murder and manslaughter and all four officers who were present were dismissed. The nonchalant violence of Chauvin, captured on film by passersby, caused a groundswell of disgust and support across US society for BLM that had not been present before. Polls run by the Pew Research Center in June 2020 found that 60% of white, 77% of Hispanic, 75% of Asian and 86% of black people either strongly or somewhat supported BLM. Counter-movements such as All Lives Matter arose to try and move the focus away from racial divisions and protest against all forms of injustice and brutality. While BLM members often referred to 'white supremacy' as the cause, President Obama responded more moderately in October 2015 that BLM still respected all lives but that it was highlighting the specific problems faced by black Americans and that this needed to be addressed. Increasing polarization in US society occurred during the Trump presidency, most notably demonstrated by the Unite the Right rally at Charleston on 11–12 August 2017 that brought together alt-right, far right, and neo-nazi

DOI: 10.4324/9781003159551-60

white supremacy groups around a broad nativist-racist agenda that centred on the protection of Confederate monuments from removal from public spaces.

[This is an excerpt from the full document]

Introduction

Four years ago, what is now known as the Black Lives Matter Global Network began to organize. It started out as a Black-centered political will and movement building project turned chapter-based, member-led organization whose mission is to build local power and to intervene when violence was inflicted on Black communities by the state and vigilantes. In the years since, we've committed to struggling together and to imagining and creating a world free of anti-Blackness, where every Black person has the social, economic, and political power to thrive.

Black Lives Matter began as a call to action in response to state-sanctioned violence and anti-Black racism. Our intention from the very beginning was to connect Black people from all over the world who have a shared desire for justice to act together in their communities. The impetus for that commitment was, and still is, the rampant and deliberate violence inflicted on us by the state.

Enraged by the death of Trayvon Martin and the subsequent acquittal of his killer, George Zimmerman, and inspired by the 31-day takeover of the Florida State Capitol by POWER U and the Dream Defenders, we took to the streets. A year later, we set out together on the Black Lives Matter Freedom Ride to Ferguson, in search of justice for Mike Brown and all of those who have been torn apart by state-sanctioned violence and anti-Black racism. Forever changed, we returned home and began building the infrastructure for the Black Lives Matter Global Network, which, even in its infancy, has become a political home for many.

We've accomplished a lot in four short years. Ferguson helped to catalyze a movement to which we've all helped give life. Organizers who call this network home have ousted anti-Black politicians, won critical legislation to benefit Black lives, and changed the terms of conversations around Blackness globally. Through movement and relationship building, we have also helped catalyze other movements and shifted culture with an eye toward the dangerous impacts of anti-Blackness.

Herstory

In 2013, three radical Black organizers—Alicia Garza, Patrisse Khan-Cullors, and Opal Tometi—created a Black-centered political will and movement building project called #BlackLivesMatter. It was in response to the acquittal of Trayvon Martin's murderer, George Zimmerman.

The project is now a member-led global network of more than 40 chapters. Our members organize and build local power to intervene in violence inflicted on Black communities by the state and vigilantes. Black Lives Matter is an ideological and political intervention in a world where Black lives are systematically and intentionally targeted for demise. It is an affirmation of Black folks' humanity, our contributions to this society, and our resilience in the face of deadly oppression.

As organizers who work with everyday people, BLM members see and understand significant gaps in movement spaces and leadership. Black liberation movements in this country have created room, space, and leadership mostly for Black heterosexual, cisgender men—leaving women, queer and transgender people, and others either out of the movement or in the background to move the work forward with little or no recognition. As a network, we have always recognized the need to center the leadership of women and queer and trans people. To maximize our movement muscle, and to be intentional about not replicating harmful practices that excluded so many in past movements for liberation, we made a commitment to placing those at the margins closer to the center.

As #BlackLivesMatter developed throughout 2013 and 2014, we utilized it as a platform and organizing tool. Other groups, organizations, and individuals used it to amplify anti-Black racism across the country, in all the ways it showed up. Tamir Rice, Tanisha Anderson, Mya Hall, Walter Scott, Sandra Bland—these names are inherently important. The space that #BlackLivesMatter held and continues to hold helped propel the conversation around the state-sanctioned violence they experienced. We particularly highlighted the egregious ways in which Black women, specifically Black trans women, are violated. #BlackLivesMatter was developed in support of all Black lives.

In 2014, Mike Brown was murdered by Ferguson police officer Darren Wilson. It was a guttural response to be with our people, our family—in support of the brave and courageous community of Ferguson and St. Louis as they were being brutalized by law enforcement, criticized by media, tear gassed, and pepper sprayed night after night. Darnell Moore and Patrisse Khan-Cullors organized a national ride during Labor Day weekend that year. We called it the Black Life Matters Ride. In 15 days, we developed a plan of action to head to the occupied territory to support our brothers and sisters. Over 600 people gathered. We made two commitments: to support the team on the ground in St. Louis, and to go back home and do the work there. We understood Ferguson was not an aberration, but in fact, a clear point of reference for what was happening to Black communities everywhere. When it was time for us to leave, inspired by our friends in Ferguson, organizers from 18 different cities went back home and developed Black Lives Matter chapters in their communities and towns— broadening the political will and movement building reach catalyzed by the #BlackLivesMatter project and the work on the ground in Ferguson.

It became clear that we needed to continue organizing and building Black power across the country. People were hungry to galvanize their communities to end state-sanctioned violence against Black people, the way Ferguson organizers and allies were doing. Soon we created the Black Lives Matter Global Network infrastructure. It is adaptive and decentralized, with a set of guiding principles. Our goal is to support the development of new Black leaders, as well as create a network where Black people feel empowered to determine our destinies in our communities. The Black Lives Matter Global Network would not be recognized worldwide if it weren't for the folks in St. Louis and Ferguson who put their bodies on the line day in and day out, and who continue to show up for Black lives.

Who We Are

The Black Lives Matter Global Network is a chapter-based, member-led organization whose mission is to build local power and to intervene in violence inflicted on Black communities by the state and vigilantes.

We are expansive. We are a collective of liberators who believe in an inclusive and spacious movement. We also believe that in order to win and bring as many people with us along the way, we must move beyond the narrow nationalism that is all too prevalent in Black communities. We must ensure we are building a movement that brings all of us to the front.

We affirm the lives of Black queer and trans folks, disabled folks, undocumented folks, folks with records, women, and all Black lives along the gender spectrum. Our network centers those who have been marginalized within Black liberation movements.

We are working for a world where Black lives are no longer systematically targeted for demise.

We affirm our humanity, our contributions to this society, and our resilience in the face of deadly oppression.

The call for Black lives to matter is a rallying cry for ALL Black lives striving for liberation.

Every day, we recommit to healing ourselves and each other, and to co-creating alongside comrades, allies, and family a culture where each person feels seen, heard, and supported.

Questions

How has BLM opened up new grounds for reconsidering transatlantic relations?
What would "decolonising the transatlantic" mean in practice?

Reference

https://blacklivesmatter.com/resources/
Permission: Shanelle Matthews (author)

Document 14

In Spite of it All, America: A Transatlantic Manifesto in Times of Donald Trump, A German Perspective, October 2017

The manifesto was written by a large number of German and American experts on German-American relations and first published in the German weekly Die Zeit. *The background of this manifesto reflects two fundamental notions. The first one is the belief that stable German-American relations and constructive cooperation are at the heart of transatlantic stability and security. The second one is the conviction that American engagement is needed in a multilateral world order. The fundamental differences of opinion between the German government under Angela Merkel and the Trump administration were of great concern to the authors, who saw the arrival of Trump as a serious signal that the US commitment to European security and stability could no longer be taken for granted. The manifesto acknowledged that there was a serious gap opening up in terms of diverging interests on both sides of the Atlantic, but since the US was still considered an indispensable ally, a way out had to be found even if it meant making some hard choices.*

[This is an excerpt from the full document]

International Order—the new German–American conflict of interests

- One of the new German government's premier challenges will be to manage the transatlantic relationship of German government under Donald Trump's presidency. Its success in this endeavor will be one way to measure its overall performance. We, a group of foreign policy experts from civil society, would like to offer some ideas.
- The liberal world order with its foundation in multilateralism, its global norms and values, its open societies and markets—is in danger. It is exactly this order on which Germany's freedom and prosperity depends. The order is being challenged from various directions and sources: rising powers strive for influence; illiberal governments and authoritarian regimes are ascending; anti-modern thinking is gaining traction and influence even within Western democracies; Russia is challenging the peaceful European order; and new technologies are disrupting old economic structures.
- Lastly, the United States, inventor and—until recently—guardian of the liberal order, currently does not see itself as system guarantor. Donald Trump is the first U.S. president since World War II to fundamentally question the ideas and institutions of the liberal international order. He opposes this order by advocating a system of raw power and national interest. In his alternative system, small and medium sized countries play a role as dependent and secondary actors. Donald Trump is skeptical of any and all of the United States' commitments to multilateral institutions and norms.
- With its preference for stable treaty-based alliances and long term, multilateral commitments, Germany sees the current international order as a cornerstone of its foreign

DOI: 10.4324/9781003159551-61

policy. For Germany, Donald Trump's foreign policy creates a previously unknown conflict of interest with its most important ally.

- Since Germany's as well as Europe's security and affluence rest upon the current international order even as President Trump charts a different course for the United States, an increased responsibility falls to the European Union and its member state Germany to safeguard and strengthen the international order.

A president *sui generis*

- It is impossible to ignore that President Trump was able to attract the support of 60 million voters. It is also true that unilateral foreign policy, protectionist moods, and periodic calls for "America First" policies have a long tradition in the United States. Still, Donald Trump is a president *sui generis* whose ideas about international order do not fit within the modern American politician tradition. These ideas are supported by few in the United States. His disdain for international alliances and institutions is not even shared by many in the government he leads, much less by those outside of government. Donald Trump's positions on global order are outside the mainstream of the foreign policy expert community in the United States. It is unclear, maybe even unlikely, that his strategy of undermining the international order will ever succeed in the United States and become his country's policy.

Dangerous consequences

Some analysts and political actors in Germany would like to draw far-reaching conclusions from this period of uncertainty about the direction of the United States. They endorse a strategic reorientation for Germany. Some strive to decouple Europe's foreign and security policy from the United States. Others place their faith in a German–French mini version of Europe. Sometimes, European aspirations only disguise German nationalism as a response to American nationalism. Some recommend that Germany should focus on ad hoc coalitions or maintain equidistance between Russia and the United States. Some even recommend that Germany should go further, and align itself with Russia or China in the future.

All of these propositions are costly or dangerous—or both.

The United States remains indispensable

- Turning away from the United States would bring insecurity to Germany and ultimately to Europe.
- The bond with the United States was born from dependence, but it has long been in Germany's core national interest. Today, no other actor in the world can offer the same advantages to Germany that it gains from its alliance with the United States. No other power takes on such far-reaching security guarantees and offers such comprehensive political resources.
- As a liberal hegemon, the United States made European integration possible. The majority of the political establishment in the United States continues to see the country as a supporter of European integration—also because it suits its own interest. The country needs allies that share its values and interests.
- If Germany wants to be an effective actor in Europe, it needs the United States. If the ties to the United States are cut, with them go the reassurance that other European

countries need in order to accept a strong Germany in the center of the continent. The more leadership that Germany can and should take on, the closer the coordination must be with the United States.

- Decoupling from the United States would fundamentally question one of the most important political and cultural achievements of the past 70 years: Germany's integration in the West.
- In aligning itself with the West Germany also committed itself to the values of freedom and democracy, and to cooperation with all those who stand for these values. Freedom is the precondition for human beings to lead a self-determined and dignified live. Germany has committed itself to this set of ideas in its constitution, the Basic Law. Its anchoring in the West gave Germany the steadfastness to resist the Communist regimes and make possible German and European reunification. A departure from this transatlantic orientation will renew the threat of a special path (*Sonderweg*) of Germany, it will strengthen nationalists on the left and the right, and it will endanger the peaceful European order.
- The West, even today, does not exist without the United States, neither as a concept, nor as a political subject America is the anchor of liberal universalism and the open world order. Even if Donald Trump's presidency carries significant risks for the liberal order, these perils will not diminish if Germany puts its strategic partnership with the United States at stake. A strategic decoupling from the United States would ultimately endanger the liberal international order more than prudent cooperation with a United States whose leadership currently rattles this order. Autocracies such as China and Russia can be important ad hoc partners for single projects; the United States, however, must remain the strategic partner for a democratic and European Germany.

The relationship with the United States is a values-based partnership built on our democratic political systems. Even if the current U.S. president challenges significant elements of the political system, the United States remains a democracy. President Trump is not America, nor is the illiberal movement for which he stands a solely American phenomenon. In Europe too it has made its mark. What we see today is not a divergence between Europe and the United States; it is a conflict within the West unfolding on both sides of the Atlantic.

Finally, the economic, scientific, and cultural linkages with the United States are far stronger than with any other region in the world. The interplay with the United States remains a central element of Europe's capacity for innovation.

Yet, no business as usual

So, how do we engage with the United States in times of Donald Trump?

Even if turning away from the United States is not a responsible option for Germany, business as usual is not an option with the current presidency either. It would be equally unhelpful to stay silent and look the other way, waiting until this presidency is finally over and a successor occupies the White House. Four or even eight years is too long to sit it out, especially since there will not be a return to the supposed good old times.

Ideas for a new U.S. Strategy

- German policy now requires something that it did not need before: a U.S. strategy. A responsible policy toward the United States must be long-term and build a bridge into the post-Trump age. This policy must look beyond an exceptional period of U.S. skepticism toward any multilateral commitment. However, Germany must not fall prey to the illusion that there will be a return to the *status quo ante* following the Trump Presidency. Several political trends in the United States will outlive Trump's time in office—for example, the demand for more balanced burden-sharing between Europe and the United States within NATO. However, the end of the Trump presidency should be the end of the inner Western conflict about the fundamentals of the world order. Once this fundamental consensus is reestablished policy disagreements can be resolved or bridged more easily and more constructively.

- This long-term goal must be the point of reference for Germany's short-term engagement with the Trump administration.
- In the short term, Germany must learn to distinguish between the problems that are solvable, those that are unsolvable, and those in between that require pragmatic management.
- It goes without saying that the German government should double down on those policy areas where it finds common ground with the current U.S. administration. But successful relationship management in times of Donald Trump may also require to adjust an increasingly untenable position or—vice versa—to enter into a limited conflict. Finally, we will need to look for partners not only at the highest federal levels, but elsewhere in the administration, in the U.S. Congress, in the states, in civil society, and in business.
- It will be more important than ever to manage differences responsibly. In its own long-term interest, Germany should attempt to handle these differences with the Trump administration in such a way that does not escalate them or allow them to spiral out of control.
- Germany should not succumb to illusions: large-scale joint projects with the Trump government will have little chance for success in policy areas that are central to President Trump's populist agenda. Trying to do too much in these key policy areas will only cause new disagreements.
- In short, Germany's U.S. strategy must allow for multitasking: to actively pursue key national interests in collaboration with the United States, to moderate conflicts, to avoid unrealistic ambitions, and to thus build a bridge to a better future for transatlantic relations.
- This nuanced approach will have different consequences for the different policy areas.

Trade policy—aim only for conflict management

Soberingly, the signs are not favorable for larger projects in several policy areas that would actually be vital, such as trade policy. Despite all controversies, the strategic and economic reasons for a transatlantic free trade agreement (TTIP) have not disappeared since November 2016. Some in Berlin and Brussels hope that one can resurrect TTIP in an adapted version. This idea is illusory, maybe even dangerous. A president who castigates all free trade agreements as unfair toward the United States will not easily compromise in international negotiations. A negotiating failure will be more devastating to the project than a long hibernation.

There are signs already that the United States and the European Union might be headed toward trade disputes. The European Union must react to punitive tariffs. But it should do so exclusively in a legal, proportional, and symmetrical manner. Everything else could trigger an unwanted escalation.

International refugee policy—no chance for a joint vision

- Joint initiatives regarding international refugee policy do not look very promising either. The global system of protection, however, urgently needs to be reformed to cope with modern conditions. The rights of refugees need to be protected while illegal migration needs to be curtailed, organized trafficking should be combatted so that the universal refugee regime is not undermined. Equally important will be a push toward new and improved United Nations' resettlement programs. However, it appears difficult to imagine that the Trump administration will agree to such initiatives. Consequently, Europe must become active itself here—as best as it can.
- Therefore, *trade and refugee policies* fall in the category of currently difficult, hardly resolvable issues. The best we can expect is limited progress, but no large-scale initiatives.

Security policy—strive for progress, also with President Trump

- Security policy is a different matter. Without the United States there will be no security for and in Germany for the foreseeable future. This applies to territorial as well as Alliance defense within NATO, but also to nuclear deterrence, to combatting cyber crimes and money laundering, and finally to counterterrorism and the cooperation of intelligence agencies. No single European country, not Germany, not any other country, and not the European Union, can provide the necessary resources to guarantee the continent's security. Therefore, the existing cooperation must be strengthened. Remaining committed to NATO also provides a way to integrate the United States into the structures of multilateral security policy and may dissuade Washington from going it alone.
- Alliance defense is the most cost-effective form of defense. Germany should thus take seriously the call for fairer burden-sharing within the Alliance. Acting against its own core interest, Germany has not done enough in this respect. Germany still has a long way to go until it's NATO goals and commitments are met. To be clear: Germany agreed to increase its defense expenditures toward 2 percent of its GDP. Germany should keep its word. To present this commitment as a threat to the military balance in European is to get it backwards. It is precisely our European neighbors and partners who are asking for more German commitment within the NATO framework and within European defense policy.
- It would be even better if Germany were to invest an extra percentage point of GDP into development assistance, international police operations, UN missions, conflict prevention, and diplomacy. With this linkage, non-military aspects of security would also be upgraded. This would substantially strengthen European defense capabilities within the transatlantic alliance. Germany would do something that is in its own interest and would stabilize the transatlantic alliance at the same time. It would address concerns of the Trump administration and build goodwill for the time after Donald Trump. The chances of success for this strategy are high: Despite all of the skeptical rhetoric about NATO, the Trump administration has fulfilled America's NATO commitments so far.

Security policy cooperation with the Trump government should be central to Germany and should also include security guarantees for the central and eastern European NATO members, support for an independent Ukraine, as well as the stabilization of the North African coast.

Energy security policy—giving up Nord Stream 2 is in Germany's interest

- There is one more policy area in which the German government should reconsider its position to open the door for productive cooperation: *energy security policy.* The United States has identified Nord Stream 2, the planned pipeline running through the Baltic Sea to Russia, as a geostrategic project. They are correct. More importantly: This pipeline project is not in the joint European interest. Nord Stream 2 contradicts a policy of greater energy independence and undermines the envisaged European Energy Union. We should try to identify a joint approach with our European partners and the United States.

Climate, energy, and digital policy—manage conflicts responsibly

- After having addressed the solvable issues and set aside the unsolvable issues for now, one will need to turn to those policy areas that require responsible conflict management. It would be useless to try to convince the U.S. administration of the importance of the Paris Climate Agreement, but it is equally wrong-headed to isolate President Trump on international climate and energy policy. Necessary criticism should not turn into dogmatism.
- Instead, Germany should seek concrete steps forward in climate protection together with the United States. Germany does not need President Trump in order to engage with partners who are interested in climate policy cooperation. A number of states (not just California) and large cities are already rapidly reducing their CO_2 emissions. Political, scientific, and technical cooperation with local partners is possible. There is no shortage of potent allies on climate policy in the United States, in the private sector as well as in civil society. Here, the key is to be proactive, to invest money, and to build networks that will endure and outlast the Trump administration.
- *Digital policy* is another policy area where confrontation is possible—about regulatory questions as well as about market shares. It is important to identify points of contention as soon as possible and to avoid unnecessary escalation. Sealing off Europe's and the United States' digital markets from each other will seriously damage the outlook for jobs and growth on both sides of the Atlantic. European consumer and data protection standards might be able to be maintained globally if they have U.S. support, but certainly not without it.

Final point—more Europe within the Alliance

- Making progress with the Trump administration wherever possible, moderating conflicts and avoiding escalation, expanding the spectrum of transatlantic partners beyond the current U.S. administration—these are all core aims of a U.S. strategy that can preserve the transatlantic partnership with and if necessary against this American President, and function beyond his time in office. The United States has proven its capacity for self-correction repeatedly. America remains the indispensible power for those countries that stand for freedom and democracy and strive for an open world order. But Europe—and thus Germany—must do more to support and preserve these values. More European self-reliance is imperative. It would be an error of historical proportions to play out "more Europe" against the transatlantic alliance. The new German government's foreign policy will be measured by how clearly it pursues this course.

Questions

According to the authors, are there grounds for a continuing strong transatlantic relationship?

Why do the authors still consider the US as an indispensable ally for Germany?

References

https://www.gmfus.org/publications/spite-it-all-america-transatlantic-manifesto-times-donald-trump-german-perspective
Permission: German Marshall Fund

Document 15

Appendix: Memorandum from the Foreign and Commonwealth Office (Global Britain), March 2018

From the start it was clear that the negotiations between the UK and the EU regarding Brexit would involve a complicated political and economic puzzle with divergent interests on both sides of the Channel. On 29 March 2017 the UK first invoked the so-called withdrawal notice under article 50 of the EU Treaty. This article provides for a two-year negotiation period, unless the parties agree to extend it. Given the complexity of the negotiations and the political instability in the British parliament, the negotiating period was delayed several times. On 31 January 2020 the UK officially left the EU, with the specifics of the deal to be agreed (or not) by 1 January 2021. A deal was ultimately reached in the last days of December 2020 in order to prevent a "hard Brexit", but several key policy issues still needed to be resolved. Foreign policy was not central to the Brexit debate, but it was obvious that the UK would need a post-Brexit foreign policy strategy. Prime Minister Theresa May (2016–2019) first set out the idea of a "Global Britain" in October 2016, emphasizing a new role for the UK in international affairs. The Foreign Office's memorandum throws further light on the idea of Global Britain and the role of the various government institutions in implementing it.

[This is an excerpt from the full document]

1. This memorandum explains the Government's (HMG) vision of Global Britain and the role of the Foreign and Commonwealth Office (FCO) in supporting and enabling government departments to deliver this vision. It covers the UK's overseas presence, influence and capability.

Context: "Global Britain"

5 Britain has always taken a leading role in responding to global challenges and in making the most of opportunities for this country. However, the pace of change in an ever more challenging global environment, where information and influence are dispersed and contested amongst many more actors, both state and non-state, inevitably has a significant impact on how the UK projects influence and protects its national interests.

6 Some elements of our interaction with the rest of the world will change once we leave the European Union (EU). Although we will lose some elements of the force multiplier advantages of EU membership, we will gain more flexibility and agility to react, and our foreign policy capability broadly drawn will ensure we are one of the major global players as now.

7 The concept of "Global Britain" is shorthand for our determination to adjust to these changes, to continue to be a successful global foreign policy player, and to resist any sense that Britain will be less engaged in the world in the next few years. It is intended

DOI: 10.4324/9781003159551-62

to signal that the UK will, as Ministers have put it, continue to be open, inclusive and outward facing; free trading; assertive in standing up for British interests and values; and resolute in boosting our international standing and influence. It is a Britain with global presence, active in every region; global interests, working with our allies and partners to deliver the global security and prosperity that ensures our own; and global perspectives, engaging with the world in every area, influencing and being influenced.

8   Our strategic foreign policy objectives have not changed: to protect our people, project our influence and promote our prosperity. Nor have our commitments to being a steadfast partner to our allies, ensuring our adversaries are aware of our capacity for protecting our national interest, remaining an activist global player in projecting our values, supporting the rules-based international order, and leading efforts to ensure global peace and security. But the shifting global context, a new relationship with Europe, and the need to deliver more with finite resources, requires us to evolve and enhance how we achieve our goals, using HMG assets more cohesively and efficiently to maintain our global standing.

9   The scale and range of complexity means the UK cannot always rely on tried and tested methods. HMG will need to understand the local and international context sufficiently to take and manage risks, and experiment with new approaches. This includes working not just across departmental boundaries and with other governments but also building stronger partnerships with other sectors.

10 Our ability to do this depends on whether we can analyse, act and influence, across the world and across the breadth of the Government's international priorities. In turn it depends on the range and depth of our bilateral and regional relationships and our influence in global and regional institutions. We have a wide range of assets to deploy in this context through our diplomatic, defence, development and trade activity.

11 As regards bilateral and regional relationships, our alliance with the United States remains our top priority and cornerstone of what we wish to achieve in the world. We maintain relationships as equals with the other P5 members of the UN Security Council. We aim to remain key players in the Middle East, in collaboration with the EU in Wider Europe, and to put new emphasis on the Indo-Pacific region, the centre of the world's growth. We have the huge advantage of being part of the Commonwealth, allowing us to engage with a wide network of countries across the world with a similar history, legal heritage, and institutions.

12 Our relationship with the EU will of course always be a major priority, and we aim to establish a new, deep and special partnership with the EU and European states to ensure that our work together continues in defending the international order and our shared values. In this way we aim it to become obvious to all that our departure from the EU does not signal a lessening of our international ambition and commitment.

13 Our support for the rules-based international system; for free markets; our values and the rule of law; and our meeting of the 2% NATO target and the 0.7% ODA target give us tremendous influence within international institutions. Our leadership and collaboration on issues such as modern slavery; countering terrorism; and migration make a real impact, as do our efforts in multilateral fora to shift the dial on climate change, to emphasise gender equality—with a particular focus on girls' education, to reform multilateral institutions, and to clamp down on the Illegal Wildlife Trade (IWT).

14 Finally, Britain has constitutional and legal responsibility for the 14 UK Overseas Territories (OTs). The overarching objective is for more effective cross-government support to improve security, good governance and climate resilience, and in the short run to protect their interests as we leave the EU.

15   To make a success of Global Britain, our international posture must reflect all these interests and all our policy ambitions: ie, strategic alignment of our external policies in the national interest.

16   In doing so, we have broader assets available to few other countries and which hugely reinforce our soft power: our high ranking in most international indices of power or attractiveness; our highly competitive business environment; the City of London financial centre; and our renowned legal system. Our institutions such as the BBC World Service and British Council, our cultural heritage, our language, our universities and our record of achievement in science and innovation all hugely reinforce our international strength.

UK influence overseas

17   The three centres of the global economy and political influence are in North America, overwhelmingly the United States, in Europe and its neighbourhood; and in the Indo-Pacific region. Maintaining influence in these areas is essential to making Global Britain a success. At the same time, to realise fully the vision of Global Britain means being active and influential in all regions, the institutions of the rules-based international order and key global issues.

The United States

18   The UK-US relationship represents our most vital bilateral partnership. It has been, for over a century, the most significant and history-defining international partnership. It is a relationship that transcends personalities and party politics—a relationship that matters hugely to both our countries, and which has been a driver of peace and prosperity and provided security to both our countries and beyond. In an age of geopolitical turbulence and uncertainty, the UK-US relationship continues to be of the highest importance to UK interests. In future, after we leave the EU, we can further deepen our already close UK-US ties in the area of trade.

19   As with previous administrations, the Government is working closely with the US on areas of key mutual concern and interest. The UK and United States continue to work as leaders within, and proponents of, the rules-based international system. This system, albeit imperfect, has been the driving force behind an unparalleled period of relative stability and prosperity.

20   The UK stands together with the United States in facing a resurgent Russia and new forms of threat across the world, as well as the implications of an increasingly assertive China. We have shared great successes in the last year, for example in the fight against Daesh, and we continue our incomparable co-operation on intelligence issues and our shared commitment to NATO and the collective defence of our allies.

21   The current Administration has set new directions for US policy in several areas, some of which differ from our own. That is not unusual and there have always been some differences of perspective in this strong relationship. These do not prevent us working together to maximise our joint work for common goals and global interests.

Europe and its Neighbourhood

22   Many of our closest and most like-minded partners are members of the European Union, and our national interests will align in many areas with the interests of our European friends. We will remain unconditionally committed to Europe's security.

Investment in all our relationships across Europe will therefore continue. We will need to maintain a significant presence in Brussels in order to engage effectively with the EU institutions and member state representations, and we are developing bilateral strategies aimed at securing our long-term partnerships with our European neighbours. With France, Germany and Ireland, in particular, we must build comprehensive relationships, recognising that our partnership will be important on a vast range of issues and we must have the relationships, structures and network to support this. The recent UK-France summit set the tone for the kind of relationships we wish to achieve beyond EU Exit.

23 NATO is vital to Britain's and Europe's security at a time of increasing threats, including from cyber, hybrid and information warfare, across the globe. Behind the US, the UK is the most influential member of the Alliance and among the small group that meets the 2% target for defence spending. In September 2017, Chief of the Defence Staff, Air Chief Marshal Sir Stuart Peach, was elected as the next Chairman of NATO's Military Committee. The UK has stood by allies by leading an Enhanced Forward Presence battlegroup in Estonia and contributing troops in Poland, contributing to NATO Maritime Groups, committing Typhoons to Air Policing Missions in Romania, and training thousands of Armed Forces in Ukraine.

24 Our readiness to work with partners in Europe and Wider Europe is shown by our commitment to promote democracy and economic growth in the Western Balkans. The UK will host the Western Balkans Summit in July 2018. This is a firm demonstration of our support for much-needed reform to improve the region's security, boost the economy, and to combat challenges such as illegal drugs and human trafficking.

25 Russia has become more aggressive, authoritarian and nationalist, increasingly defining itself in opposition to the West. Russia uses a range of overt and covert powers to pursue its policies—including propaganda, espionage, cyber interference and subversion. In the cyber sector, Russia has targeted the UK media, telecommunication and energy sectors. The Foreign Secretary's recent visit to Moscow—together with our joint attribution of the NotPetya cyber-attack, in concert with allies and partners—underscored the UK's firm position on malign cyber activity. Working with European partners, the UK supports the Centre of Excellence for Countering Hybrid Threats in Helsinki, convening allies for diplomatic engagement on resisting malign interference.

26 We remain severely concerned by the evolving spectrum of threats emanating from Russia. We are resolved to meet these challenges while remaining open to appropriate dialogue; we want to reduce risk, talk about our differences, and make clear that interference with sovereign states is not acceptable. As P5 members, we want to engage constructively with Russia in the interests of security and stability, including on pressing issues such as DPRK and Iran. We are also working with Russia to ensure a safe and secure World Cup for visiting fans, with UK-Russia police cooperation underway ahead of the tournament.

27 Many of the most intractable problems on the current world scene are in the Middle East—notably Yemen, Syria, Libya, the set of interlinked issues in the Gulf, Iran's intentions to boost its interests, and the long-running Middle East Peace Process (MEPP). Our long-term objective is to see the Middle East return to stability, addressing conflict and failures in governance, which have led to political and regional turbulence and humanitarian catastrophe. Our policy in the Middle East must be credible and consistent. Central to this approach will be maintaining strong relationships with stable countries in the region, particularly in the Gulf where we have both security and prosperity interests.

28   Our core short-term interests are tackling security threats from the region, including: the extant terrorist threats from Daesh and Al-Qaida; migration, from Syria and through Libya; and prosperity—the Gulf collectively is a larger market for the UK than either China or India. We are supporting the Saudi Vision 2030 and other Gulf reform programmes.

29   We are increasing our effort across North Africa to help their governments stay ahead of their demographic and security challenges—manifested in different ways in migration through Libya and the Sousse terrorist attack. In 2016, we established an FCO/DFID North Africa Joint Unit, which oversees the new North Africa Good Governance Fund (£40 million this year).

Indo-Pacific

30   The UK has an All of Asia policy, working with our many different partners in the region on areas of mutual interest. We are continually looking for opportunities to expand our engagement.

31   With China we have a strong economic and global partnership. Central to our approach is the Global Comprehensive Strategic Partnership, established in 2015. It includes engagement through Prime Ministerial summits—most recently the Prime Minister's January 2018 visit—three annual Cabinet-level dialogues; and a wide range of other Ministerial and senior official exchanges.

32   We aim to encourage and support China's greater cooperation in helping resolve global challenges. Both bilaterally and as fellow permanent members of the UN Security Council, we engage extensively with China on a range of threats to international security, for example from North Korea, and on challenges such as global health security and climate change. At the same time, we are robust in defending our position on areas of difference, including on issues of human rights and values, on the South China Sea, and on the importance of Hong Kong's high degree of autonomy and freedoms.

33   China is a hugely important partner for UK trade as the UK's third largest trading partner, after the EU and the USA. In 2016, UK-China bilateral trade in goods and services reached £59.3bn, up 9.4% on 2015. Recent bilateral visits have delivered major economic benefits, generating billions of pounds of commercial deals. Through the UK-China Infrastructure Alliance, we are aiming to deepen UK-China infrastructure project and finance collaboration. We welcome the opportunities provided by China's Belt and Road Initiative to further prosperity and sustainable development across Asia and the wider world.

34   The UK's enduring relationship with India is also central to our aspirations. India is an economic powerhouse, with a growing role in Asian and international geopolitics. A shared past and strong people-to-people links give us influence and access, helping us to tackle security threats, encourage stability, and exploit prosperity opportunities.

35   The UK-India relationship has grown closer in recent years, with Prime Minister Modi's November 2015 UK visit and the Prime Minister's India visit a year later, key milestones. In 2016, UK-India bilateral trade was £15.6bn. India is the fourth largest investor in the UK. UK investment contributes around 8% of India's FDI. Financial services and a Defence and International Security Partnership are central to the relationship, buttressed by cooperation across government and beyond. The next important moment in the relationship will be the Commonwealth summit in April, which we expect PM Modi to attend.

36   South East Asia is a dynamic region where there are opportunities for greater UK engagement across a variety of sectors, e.g. education, prosperity and regional resilience.

More broadly, we have a strong and long-term commitment to the Five Power Defence Arrangements (FPDA) between the UK, Australia, New Zealand, Malaysia and Singapore. The FPDA is an important part of our commitment to peace and security in the Asia Pacific region. We will contribute further, in particular through exercises, including with our new aircraft carriers, and joint training, alongside investing in our strong bilateral defence relationships.

37   Finally, the UK is a partner country in the Asia-Europe Meeting (ASEM), an intergovernmental process to foster dialogue and cooperation between Asia and Europe with biennial summits of the 53 partners. The UK has Dialogue Partner (DP) status with ASEAN, via the EU, and we are committed to strengthening our relationship with it as an institution after EU Exit.

Multilateral institutions and global issues

43   Global Britain involves thinking and acting globally. Our support for the rules-based international system; for free markets; our values and the rule of law; and our meeting of the 2% NATO target and the 0.7% ODA target give us tremendous influence.

44   The UK also enjoys an influential position, including as a Permanent Member of the UNSC and an active member of other key bodies, for example the Commonwealth, NATO, G7, G20, counter-proliferation regimes and international financial institutions. The UN and other multilateral bodies often provide the UK and our allies with the legal and moral basis for action, and the UN in particular has unique global convening power. The UK is committed to the reform and modernisation of global institutions to ensure they can meet 21st century challenges and will step up its efforts to secure the appointment of senior UK experts to key international positions, building on lessons learned from the loss of our seat on the International Court of Justice (ICJ).

45   Our commitment to the UN will remain core to our foreign policy. As a P5 member, we have a key role in all aspects of the Council's work. We play an important part in efforts to reform the Security Council, improve the UN's finances and strengthen the UN's capacity to deal with economic and social issues, peacekeeping and conflict prevention. We will compete more effectively for senior international appointments where our expertise and capacity for innovation is widely acknowledged and appreciated.

46   The Commonwealth is a unique global network: home to one third of the world's population, some of its fastest growing economies and accounting for one-fifth of global trade. It has a diverse membership committed to a set of values founded on democracy and rule of law, embodied in the Commonwealth Charter. It stimulates a wide range of political, non-governmental and people-to-people engagement across different regional and cultural environments. The enduring nature of these relationships, combined with its global and diverse character, offers the UK and its members potential, long term, to reinforce the international rules-based order, and to complement and enhance UK engagement in other multilateral fora. It has a particular strength in addressing shared global challenges across a wide geographical basis – for example, new cross-border security threats, the effects of climate change on small and other vulnerable states, barriers to trade and threats to democracy, good governance and inclusivity.

48   Our leadership and collaboration on issues such as modern slavery; countering terrorism; and migration make a real impact, as do our efforts multilateral fora to shift the dial on climate change; to emphasise gender equality—with a particular focus on girls' education; to reform multilateral institutions and clamp down on the Illegal Wildlife Trade (IWT).

49   The UK is rightly proud of its leadership on international development. We were one of only 6 countries to meet the UN's 0.7% GNI [Gross National Income] ODA target in 2016, the third largest contributor of global ODA overall. We are, as the manifesto commitment makes clear, committed to ensuring that ODA remains fit for purpose and fully supports and helps deliver the UN's Sustainable Development Goals in which we played a full part in securing. Our development budget not only helps us to champion the poor but—alongside the diplomatic network—gives us access and insight on key global issues that matter to partners and are important to UK national interests.

Questions

Explain the goal of this Memorandum. What does it intend to achieve?
What are some of the potential implications of Global Britain for transatlantic relations?

Reference

https://publications.parliament.uk/pa/cm201719/cmselect/cmfaff/780/780.pdf

Document 16

Remarks by President Trump on the Joint Comprehensive Plan of Action, 8 May 2018

Before his election as President, Donald Trump made no secret of his strong disapproval of the so-called Iran Deal, officially known as the Joint Comprehensive Plan of Action (JCPOA), that had been reached in July 2015. The JCPOA was backed by Iran, the five permanent members of the UN Security Council, and Germany and the EU, with the goal to keep Iran's nuclear programme solely focused on civilian purposes. Limits were set to the number of centrifuges Iran could operate, and the amount and type of enriched uranium that it could hold at any one time. This had the intention of preventing Iran's development of a nuclear weapon, a process that requires highly enriched uranium to succeed. The International Atomic Energy Agency (IAEA) would be responsible for the process of verification, involving an inspections regime to ensure that specific nuclear sites were not being used for weapons-type research. The JCPOA was meant to cover a period of 15 years, after which no further restrictions would apply, unless a new agreement could be reached. This would be enough to keep Iran as a signatory to the Non-Proliferation Treaty for that 15-year period, which it would have to leave should it develop a nuclear weapon. The overall goal of the Plan was to contribute to the gradual normalization of relations between Iran, the West, and its regional neighbours, which were deeply suspicious of Iran's nuclear ambitions. In return for signing, economic and financial sanctions against Iran would be lifted by the UN, the EU, and (partially) the US, so long as the IAEA verified Iranian compliance. Trump had tweeted criticism of the JCPOA even before it was signed and promised to withdraw from the treaty once he was elected to the White House.

[This is an excerpt from the full document]

THE PRESIDENT: My fellow Americans: Today, I want to update the world on our efforts to prevent Iran from acquiring a nuclear weapon.

   The Iranian regime is the leading state sponsor of terror. It exports dangerous missiles, fuels conflicts across the Middle East, and supports terrorist proxies and militias such as Hezbollah, Hamas, the Taliban, and al Qaeda.

   Over the years, Iran and its proxies have bombed American embassies and military installations, murdered hundreds of American service members, and kidnapped, imprisoned, and tortured American citizens. The Iranian regime has funded its long reign of chaos and terror by plundering the wealth of its own people.

   No action taken by the regime has been more dangerous than its pursuit of nuclear weapons and the means of delivering them.

   In 2015, the previous administration joined with other nations in a deal regarding Iran's nuclear program. This agreement was known as the Joint Comprehensive Plan of Action, or JCPOA.

DOI: 10.4324/9781003159551-63

In theory, the so-called "Iran deal" was supposed to protect the United States and our allies from the lunacy of an Iranian nuclear bomb, a weapon that will only endanger the survival of the Iranian regime. In fact, the deal allowed Iran to continue enriching uranium and, over time, reach the brink of a nuclear breakout.

The deal lifted crippling economic sanctions on Iran in exchange for very weak limits on the regime's nuclear activity, and no limits at all on its other malign behavior, including its sinister activities in Syria, Yemen, and other places all around the world.

In other words, at the point when the United States had maximum leverage, this disastrous deal gave this regime—and it's a regime of great terror—many billions of dollars, some of it in actual cash—a great embarrassment to me as a citizen and to all citizens of the United States.

A constructive deal could easily have been struck at the time, but it wasn't. At the heart of the Iran deal was a giant fiction that a murderous regime desired only a peaceful nuclear energy program.

Today, we have definitive proof that this Iranian promise was a lie. Last week, Israel published intelligence documents long concealed by Iran, conclusively showing the Iranian regime and its history of pursuing nuclear weapons.

The fact is this was a horrible, one-sided deal that should have never, ever been made. It didn't bring calm, it didn't bring peace, and it never will.

In the years since the deal was reached, Iran's military budget has grown by almost 40 percent, while its economy is doing very badly. After the sanctions were lifted, the dictatorship used its new funds to build nuclear-capable missiles, support terrorism, and cause havoc throughout the Middle East and beyond.

The agreement was so poorly negotiated that even if Iran fully complies, the regime can still be on the verge of a nuclear breakout in just a short period of time. The deal's sunset provisions are totally unacceptable. If I allowed this deal to stand, there would soon be a nuclear arms race in the Middle East. Everyone would want their weapons ready by the time Iran had theirs.

Making matters worse, the deal's inspection provisions lack adequate mechanisms to prevent, detect, and punish cheating, and don't even have the unqualified right to inspect many important locations, including military facilities.

Not only does the deal fail to halt Iran's nuclear ambitions, but it also fails to address the regime's development of ballistic missiles that could deliver nuclear warheads.

Finally, the deal does nothing to constrain Iran's destabilizing activities, including its support for terrorism. Since the agreement, Iran's bloody ambitions have grown only more brazen.

Over the past few months, we have engaged extensively with our allies and partners around the world, including France, Germany, and the United Kingdom. We have also consulted with our friends from across the Middle East. We are unified in our understanding of the threat and in our conviction that Iran must never acquire a nuclear weapon.

After these consultations, it is clear to me that we cannot prevent an Iranian nuclear bomb under the decaying and rotten structure of the current agreement.

The Iran deal is defective at its core. If we do nothing, we know exactly what will happen. In just a short period of time, the world's leading state sponsor of terror will be on the cusp of acquiring the world's most dangerous weapons.

Therefore, I am announcing today that the United States will withdraw from the Iran nuclear deal.

In a few moments, I will sign a presidential memorandum to begin reinstating U.S. nuclear sanctions on the Iranian regime. We will be instituting the highest level of economic sanction. Any nation that helps Iran in its quest for nuclear weapons could also be strongly sanctioned by the United States.

As we exit the Iran deal, we will be working with our allies to find a real, comprehensive, and lasting solution to the Iranian nuclear threat. This will include efforts to eliminate the threat of Iran's ballistic missile program; to stop its terrorist activities worldwide; and to block its menacing activity across the Middle East. In the meantime, powerful sanctions will go into full effect. If the regime continues its nuclear aspirations, it will have bigger problems than it has ever had before.

Finally, I want to deliver a message to the long-suffering people of Iran: The people of America stand with you. It has now been almost 40 years since this dictatorship seized power and took a proud nation hostage. Most of Iran's 80 million citizens have sadly never known an Iran that prospered in peace with its neighbors and commanded the admiration of the world.

But the future of Iran belongs to its people. They are the rightful heirs to a rich culture and an ancient land. And they deserve a nation that does justice to their dreams, honor to their history, and glory to God.

Iran's leaders will naturally say that they refuse to negotiate a new deal; they refuse. And that's fine. I'd probably say the same thing if I was in their position. But the fact is they are going to want to make a new and lasting deal, one that benefits all of Iran and the Iranian people. When they do, I am ready, willing, and able.

Great things can happen for Iran, and great things can happen for the peace and stability that we all want in the Middle East.

There has been enough suffering, death, and destruction. Let it end now.

Thank you. God bless you. Thank you.

Questions

Why were the European signatories to the Plan more willing to try and keep it than Trump? In what ways was Iran a threat to transatlantic security?

Reference

https://www.whitehouse.gov/briefings-statements/remarks-president-trump-joint-comprehensive-plan-action/

Document 17

Remarks by President Trump, Press Conference after NATO Summit, 12 July 2018

*One of President Trump's foreign policy priorities concerned the European Allies' finan-
cial contributions to NATO. He followed in the footsteps of former presidents who had also
complained about decreasing European defence budgets since the end of the Cold War and
even more so since the 2008 banking crisis. The "burden-sharing" issue had been a subject
of continuous discussion since the 1950s, it being shorthand for the huge gap in both defence spending and military capabilities that existed between the US and its European allies.
Trump, however, added a new dimension to this heated debate by expressing doubts about the
continuing value of NATO for US security interests, even going so far as to allude privately
that the US might pull out. Trump also suggested there would be severe consequences should
the Europeans not take his message seriously and start paying more for defence. Germany
in particular was heavily criticized since the country did not fulfill the promise made by all
member states at the NATO summit in Wales (2014) to commit at least 2% of GDP for
defence by 2024. In 2018 the US (3.5%) was still only joined by Greece (2.2%), Estonia
(2.4%) and the UK (2.1%) among the 28 NATO members with defence budgets above
2% of GDP. At the same time, President Trump also observed that the US-German trade
balance was tilted strongly in favour of Germany, a fact that supported his argument that
the Germans were profiting from US defence spending without contributing sufficiently for
their own security needs.*

[This is an excerpt from the full press conference]

THE PRESIDENT: Well, thank you very much, everybody. Appreciate it. We've had a very
amazing two-day period in Brussels. And we really accomplished a lot, with respect
to NATO. For years, Presidents have been coming to these meetings and talked about
the expense—the tremendous expense for the United States. And tremendous progress has been made; everyone has agreed to substantially up their commitment.
They're going to up it at levels that they've never thought of before.

Prior to last year, where I attended my first meeting, it was going down—the
amount of money being spent by countries was going down and down very substantially. And now, it's going up very substantially. And commitments were
made. Only 5 of 29 countries were making their commitment. And that's now
changed. The commitment was at 2 percent. Ultimately, that'll be going up quite
a bit higher than that.

So we are—we made a tremendous amount of progress today. It's been about, at
a minimum, they estimate—and they're going to be giving you exact numbers—but
since last year, they've raise an additional $33 billion that's been put up by the various
countries, not including the United States.

DOI: 10.4324/9781003159551-64

And the United States' commitment to NATO is very strong, remains very strong, but primarily because everyone—the spirit they have, the amount of money they're willing to spend, the additional money that they will be putting up has been really, really amazing to see it. To see the level of spirit in that room is incredible.

And I hope that we're going to be able to get along with Russia. I think that we probably will be able to. The people in the room think so, but they nevertheless—they really stepped up their commitment, and stepped it up like they never have before.

So took in an addition $33 [billion]. The number could actually be higher than $40 [billion] when they give you the final number. The Secretary General, Stoltenberg, will be giving those numbers sometime today, probably in his concluding press statement. But we are doing numbers like they've never done before or ever seen before. And you'll be seeing that, and I guess you'll be hearing that a little bit later.

Q: Mr. President, I'm Tara McKelvey with the BBC. Can you tell us whether or not you warned people that the U.S. would pull out of NATO if they weren't meeting their spending goals?

THE PRESIDENT: I told people that I'd be very unhappy if they didn't up their commitments very substantially, because the United States has been paying a tremendous amount, probably 90 percent of the cost of NATO. And now, people are going to start and countries are going to start upping their commitments. So I let them know yesterday, actually. I was surprised that you didn't pick it up; it took until today. But yesterday, I let them know that I was extremely unhappy with what was happening, and they have substantially upped their commitment, yeah. And now we're very happy and have a very, very powerful, very, very strong NATO, much stronger than it was two days ago.

Q: Hi, President Trump.

THE PRESIDENT: Yes, hi. How are you?

Q: I'm the White House Correspondent for PBS—

THE PRESIDENT: I know. You're very famous on television.

Q: I have a question, again, about—did you ever, at any point, say that the U.S., though, might stop engaging with NATO? And do you think that your rhetoric helps NATO cohesion, or are you worried that people might think that U.S. might not be as committed to NATO? There are a lot of people who say they were worried and stressed by what you did yesterday.

THE PRESIDENT: Well, they were probably worried because the United States was not being treated fairly, but now we are, because the commitment has been upped so much. So now they are. And I was very firm yesterday.

You have to understand, I know a lot of the people in the room. I was here last year. I let them know last year—in a less firm manner, but pretty firm—and they raised an additional $33 billion, I think going to $40 billion. But it's $33 billion as of today. And then today and yesterday, I was probably a little bit more firm.

But I believe in NATO. I think NATO is a very important—probably the greatest ever done. But the United States was paying for anywhere from 70 to 90 percent of it, depending on the way you calculate. That's not fair to the United States.

In addition to that, as you know, we're in negotiations with the EU, and we're going to be meeting with them next week. We've been treated very unfairly on trade. Our farmers have been shut out of the European Union. Now, you could say they're different, but basically, to a large extent, they're the same countries.

So I think we're going to be ultimately treated fairly on trade. We'll see what happens, but I can tell you that NATO now is really a fine-tuned machine. People are paying money that they never paid before. They're happy to do it. And the United States is being treated much more fairly.

Frankly, we were carrying too much of a burden. That's why we call it "burden-sharing." I was using the term a lot today. "Burden-sharing." We had a fantastic meeting at the end—29 countries. And they are putting up a lot. Germany has increased very substantially their time period, and Germany is coming along.

Q: Hi. Thank you. Margaret Talev from Bloomberg.

THE PRESIDENT: Yes. After all these years, I know, Margaret. Go ahead.

Q: Thank you. Maybe I'm being dense here, but could you just clarify: Are you still threatening to potentially pull the United States out of NATO for any reason? And do you believe you can do that without Congress's explicit support and approval?

THE PRESIDENT: I think I probably can, but that's unnecessary. And the people have stepped up today like they've never stepped up before. And remember the word—$33 billion more, they're paying. And you'll hear that from the Secretary General in a little while. He thanked me actually. He actually thanked me. And everybody in the room thanked me. There's a great collegial spirit in that room that I don't think they've had in many years. They're very strong. So, yeah, very unified, very strong. No problem. Right?

Q: Hi, Tomas LeCrass from (inaudible) journalist Croatia Daily Newspaper. We understand your message—

THE PRESIDENT: Congratulations, by the way.

Q: Thank you.

THE PRESIDENT: On soccer.

Q: Thank you. We understand your message, but some people ask themselves, will you be tweeting differently once you board the Air Force One? Thank you.

THE PRESIDENT: No, that's other people that do that. I don't. I'm very consistent. I'm a very stable genius. (Laughter.) Go ahead. Yeah, go ahead.

Q: Thank you, sir. Jeremy Diamond with CNN. How are you?

THE PRESIDENT: Hi, Jeremy.

Q: Quick question with regards to Germany and the comments that you made yesterday. Do you feel like given the threats that you made about potentially leaving NATO, about insulting Germany's sovereignty, it appears, by suggesting that they're totally controlled by Russia—do you feel like that's an effective way to conduct diplomacy? And secondly, would you be able to be a little bit more specific about the commitments that you secured today with regards to increasing the financial commitment? Is there an updated timeline? Are there specific countries you could cite? Because a majority of them were already planning to meet that 2 percent threshold by 2024.

THE PRESIDENT: No, many of them—in fact, Germany was going to be in the year 2028 or '30. Yeah, I think it's a very effective way to deal, but I didn't deal exactly the way you said. I have great respect for Germany. My father is from Germany. Both of my parents are from the EU, despite the fact they don't treat us well on trade.

But I think that will change also, and I think we'll see that—because on the 25th of July, they're coming in to start negotiations with me. We'll see. And if they don't negotiate in good faith, we'll do something having to do with all of the millions of cars that are coming into our country and being taxed at a virtually zero level, at a very low level.

But, Jeremy, I think it's been a very effective way of negotiating. But I'm not negotiating; I just want fairness for the United States. We're paying for far too much of NATO. NATO is very important. But NATO is helping Europe more than it's helping us. At the same time, it's very good for us.

So we have now got it to a point where people are paying a lot more money, and that's starting—really, last year. It really had—you were there last year. And last year we had a big impact. Again, we took in $33 billion more. And if you ask Secretary

General Stoltenberg, he gives us total credit—meaning me, I guess, in this case, total credit—because I said it was unfair.

Now, what has happened is, presidents over many years, from Ronald Reagan to Barack Obama, they came in, they said, "Okay, hey, do the best you can," and they left. Nobody did anything about it. And it got to a point where the United States was paying for 90 percent of NATO. And that's not fair. So it's changed. We had a really good meeting today. We had a great meeting in terms of getting along. I know most of the people in the room because of last year, because of the year and a half that we've been in office—year and a half-plus. But we have a great relationship. Everybody in that room, by the time we left, got along. And they agreed to pay more, and they agreed to pay it more quickly.

Q: (Inaudible.) We are in the NATO, the quarters—the cost (inaudible) the double (inaudible) before. I would like to know if you are planning to guarantee the taxpayers that the new money that is flowing into NATO will be spent in the best possible way, especially the money coming from country that have several problem with the public finances.

THE PRESIDENT: Well, the money will be spent properly. And one of the things that we have—we have many wealthy countries with us today, but we have some that aren't so wealthy. And they did ask if they could buy the military equipment and could I help them out. And we will help them out a little bit. We're not going to finance it for them, but we'll make sure that they're able to get payments and various other things so they can buy.

Because the United States makes, by far, the best military equipment in the world. The best jets, the best missiles, the best guns. The best everything—we make, by far. I mean, that's one thing—I guess I assumed it prior to taking office, but I really learned, since being President, our equipment is so much better than anybody else's equipment when you look at our companies—Lockheed and Boeing and Grumman. The material—the equipment that we make is so far superior, everybody wants to buy our equipment. In fact, it's the question, can they make it? Because they are doing very well. Can they make it for so many people?

So we are helping some of those countries get on line and buy the best equipment.

Thank you very much, everybody. Thank you. I'm going to be going—leaving in about a half an hour. Thank you.

Questions

If burden-sharing has been such a consistent issue within NATO since the 1950s, why do you think it has never been properly resolved?

What is your impression of Trump's style of diplomacy?

Reference

https://www.whitehouse.gov/briefings-statements/remarks-president-trump-press-conference-na-to-summit-brussels-belgium/

Document 18

EU Agency for Fundamental Rights, "Being Black in the EU: Second European Union Minorities and Discrimination Survey," 28 November 2018

While the problem of racial discrimination and violence was most acute in the United States, within Europe the situation was also of serious concern. Article 21 of the EU's Charter of Fundamental Rights (2000) recognized the right to be free from discrimination on the basis of race, ethnic or social origin, religion or belief, or political or any other opinion, and following its introduction the EU acted to combat racism in member states. The Racial Equality Directive of 2000 implemented the principle of equal treatment in labour laws regardless of racial or ethnic identity. 2008's Framework Decision on Racism and Xenophobia outlawed public incitement to violence or hatred based on race, colour, religion, or national/ethnic origin, and in 2012 the Victims' Rights Directive established the minimum rights, support, and protection to be provided for victims of crime. In 2018 the EU's Agency for Fundamental Rights issued this report based on a survey of around 6000 people of African descent in 12 member states. Based on these results, it was clear that levels of discrimination and violence across the EU varied from state to state, but that it nevertheless represented a Union-wide problem.

Protests against racial violence became a transatlantic phenomenon in 2020, although there had already been associative actions taking place in the UK in 2016 (in connection with the fifth anniversary of the shooting of Mark Duggan by London police). In May-June BLM UK held demonstrations in London, Manchester, Cardiff, and Bristol in solidarity with the US-based protests following George Floyd's death in Minneapolis on 25 May, and similar large demonstrations took place in France, Germany, and Denmark. The Premier League added the BLM logo to all club shirts for the rest of the 2019–2020 season. European BLM groups expanded the focus of protest by attacking the ongoing legacies of colonialism and the violence of racial hierarchies enforced by slavery, which they regarded as the foundation for the continuation of racial discrimination and violence. In Bristol on 7 June 2020 BLM protestors toppled a statue of Edward Colston (1636–1721), a local politician and slave trader, and dumped into Bristol Harbour (it was retrieved four days later by the city council). Winston Churchill's statue in Parliament Square, London, was also defaced with graffiti. These events showed that whereas the level of political unity within transatlantic relations was deeply fractious during the late 2010s, there were powerful issues such as racial equality and climate change that continued to unite peoples in North America and Europe around shared causes.

[This is an excerpt from the full document]

Harassment motivated by racism

* Nearly one in three respondents of African descent (30%) experienced what they perceived as racist harassment in the five years before the survey; one in five (21%) experienced such harassment in the 12 months before the survey (20% of women and 23% of men).

DOI: 10.4324/9781003159551-65

* The rates of racist harassment in the five years before the survey vary considerably between EU Member States, ranging from 20% of respondents in Malta and 21% in the United Kingdom, up to 63% of respondents in Finland.
* Experiences of racist harassment most commonly involve offensive non-verbal cues (22%) or offensive or threatening comments (21%), followed by threats of violence (8%).
* Young respondents are more likely to experience racist harassment. The risk of making such experiences decreases with age.
* Merely 14% of the most recent incidents of racist harassment were reported to police or other services (16% of incidents against women, 12% of incidents against men), meaning that the overwhelming majority of incidents were never reported.

Violence motivated by racism

* In the five years before the survey, some 5% of respondents experienced what they perceived as racist violence (including assault by a police officer). The highest rates were recorded in Finland (14%) and in Ireland and Austria (both 13%), followed by Luxembourg (11%). The lowest rates were observed in Portugal (2%) and the United Kingdom (3%). In the same period, 127 respondents (2%) – mainly young men – experienced a racist assault by a police officer; the highest rate was recorded in Austria (5%).
* In the year before the survey, 3% experienced a racist physical attack (including assault by a police officer). The highest rate was recorded for respondents in Austria (11%).
* There are no notable differences in the rates of racist violence towards men and women (7% vs. 5%). Men who wear traditional or religious clothing in public are, however, twice as likely to experience racist violence compared to men who do not (12% vs. 5%). Such differences are not observed among women.
* Most victims (61%) do not know the perpetrators, but generally identify them as not having a minority background (65%). Some 38% of the victims identified the perpetrators as having a minority ethnic background other than their own. One in 10 of those who experience racist violence say that a law enforcement officer was the perpetrator (11%).

Police stops and perceived racial profiling

* One in four (24%) respondents of African descent were stopped by the police in the five years before the survey; 11% were stopped in the 12 months before the survey.
* Among those stopped in the 12 months before the survey, 44% believe the last stop they experienced was racially motivated. This view was shared at the highest rates by respondents in Italy (70%) and Austria (63%), and at the lowest rates by respondents in Finland (18%).
* The rates of police stops and of perceived racial profiling vary substantially among countries. In both periods – five years and 12 months before the survey – respondents were stopped at the highest rates in Austria (5 years: 66%, 12 months: 49%) and Finland (5 years: 38%, 12 months: 22%). However, in Austria, the rate at which the latest police stop was perceived as ethnic profiling is almost eight times higher than that in Finland (31% vs. 4%), when looking at the 12-month period before the survey.
* Men are three times more likely to be stopped than women (22% vs. 7%) and four times more likely to perceive the most recent stop as racial profiling (men: 17%, women: 4%).
* With respect to age, results show a linear trend, with younger respondents more likely to perceive the most recent stop as racially motivated. Specifically, every second respondent aged 16 to 24 (50%) stopped in the five years before the survey perceives the most recent stop as having been racially motivated. By contrast, every third respondent (35%) aged 45 to 59 holds this view.

Treatment by the police and trust

* A majority (60%) of respondents who were stopped by the police in the five years before the survey say that they were treated respectfully during the most recent stop. Meanwhile, 16% say the police treated them disrespectfully. Larger proportions of respondents believe they were treated disrespectfully in Denmark (30%) and Austria (29%).
* Only 9% of respondents who said they were treated disrespectfully reported or made a complaint about this.
* Overall, respondents' level of trust in the police is 6.3 on a scale from 0 to 10, where 0 means 'no trust at all' and 10 indicates 'complete trust'. Respondents in Finland trust the police the most (8.2). By contrast, respondents in Austria have the lowest level of trust in the police (3.6).
* The results show that levels of trust in the police are not affected by a police stop itself, but by whether the stop is perceived as racial profiling. The lowest average level of trust in the police is found among respondents who view the most recent police stop they experienced as racial profiling (4.8).

Labour market participation – not a level playing field

* One in four (25%) respondents felt racially discriminated against when looking for work in the five years before the survey. The highest levels were observed in Austria (46%), Luxembourg (47%) and Italy (46%).
* Eight in 10 respondents (82%) believe skin colour or physical appearance is the main reason for experiencing discrimination when looking for work.
* One in four (24%) respondents felt racially discriminated against at work in the five years before the survey, with slightly higher rates observed for men than for women (26% vs. 22%). Respondents identify skin colour or physical appearance as the main ground for discrimination at work (81%).
* Seven in 10 (69%) respondents of working-age (aged 20 to 64) are in paid work, with the rate higher among men (76%) than among women (63%). The highest paid work rates are observed in Portugal (76%) and the United Kingdom (75%), and the lowest in Denmark (41%), Austria (45%), Ireland and Malta (48% each).
* The paid work rate among respondents with tertiary education is lower than that of the general population.
* One in five (18%) respondents aged 16 to 24 years are neither in paid work nor in education or training, with substantial differences between countries. The share of young respondents who are neither in paid work nor in education or training is highest in Austria (76%), Malta (70%), and Italy (42%), with significant differences when compared to the rate for the general population (Austria: 8%, Malta: 8%, Italy: 20%).
* Almost twice as many respondents with tertiary education (9%) are employed in elementary occupations – usually manual work involving physical effort – than the general population (5%).

Skin colour affects access to adequate housing

* One in five respondents of African descent (21%) felt racially discriminated against in access to housing in the five years before the survey. The highest rates were observed in Italy and Austria (39% each), Luxembourg (36%) and Germany (33%). The lowest were observed in Denmark and the United Kingdom, where less than 10% of respondents mentioned such experiences.

* Eight in 10 respondents (84%) identify their skin colour or physical appearance as the main reason behind the most recent incident of discrimination they experienced when looking for housing. Other reasons include respondents' first or last names (16%) and their citizenship (15%).
* More than one in 10 respondents (14%) of African descent say they were prevented from renting accommodation by a private landlord because of their racial or ethnic origin. The highest rates are observed in in Austria (37%), Italy (31%), Luxembourg (28%) and Germany (25%). The lowest rate is observed in the United Kingdom (3%).
* Some 6% of respondents say that they were prevented from renting municipal/social housing because of their racial or ethnic origin. Meanwhile, 5% were asked to pay a higher rental rate because of their racial or ethnic origin, with respondents in Italy (20%) and Austria (18%) particularly affected.
* Among the general population in the EU, 7 out of 10 persons own the accommodation in which they live, making ownership the most prevalent tenancy status. By contrast, 15% of respondents of African descent own their dwelling.
* One in two respondents live in overcrowded housing (45%), compared to 17% of the general population in the EU-28. One in 10 (12%) respondents experience housing deprivation, which includes living in a dwelling without a bath and toilet or in a dwelling that is too dark, has rot in the walls or windows, or has a leaking roof.
* More than one in two respondents (55%) have a household income below the at-risk-of-poverty threshold after social transfers in the country where they live. The highest rates are observed in Austria (88%), Malta (82%) and Luxembourg (71%). By contrast, this is the case for 14% of the general population in Austria, and 17% of the general population in both Malta and Luxembourg.
* More than one in 10 (13%) respondents of African descent say that they have great difficulties in making ends meet – more so than the general population in the countries surveyed, except for Denmark, Ireland and the United Kingdom. This rate is highest in Austria, where one in two respondents (50%) say they have great difficulties in making ends meet. By contrast, 4% of the general population indicates having such difficulties in Austria.

Questions

Do you think that the details provided in this document indicate a Europe-wide problem in racial discrimination, or are these problems more localized?

How might this document lead you to think differently about transatlantic relations?

References

https://fra.europa.eu/sites/default/files/fra_uploads/fra-2018-being-black-in-the-eu_en.pdf
Permission: © European Union Agency for Fundamental Rights, 2018.

Document 19

Angela Merkel, Speech at the Intergovernmental Conference to Adopt the Global Compact for Safe, Orderly and Regular Migration, Marrakech, 10 December 2018

Migration, be it voluntary or forced, has been on the increase since the end of the Cold War. On the one hand there are more practical opportunities for people to move, while on the other forces such as climate change, civil unrest and war have pushed many thousands to leave their homelands. The downside of increased human traffic around the world, however, has been a lack of common rules, standards and procedures to manage migration in an orderly fashion, or to deal with security concerns. In response, the Global Compact for Safe, Orderly and Regular Migration, an intergovernmental agreement, aimed to bring order to "all dimensions of international migration in a holistic and comprehensive manner". The UN General Assembly formally endorsed the compact in December 2018. Non-binding under international law, the agreement did not distinguish between illegal and legal migrants but referred to "regular" and "irregular" migrants. Nor did the agreement distinguish between economic migrants and refugees. All this raised severe concerns among critics from the right, who felt that it would facilitate increased migration, and the left, who felt that it did not go far enough to protect the human rights of the migrant. The fact that German chancellor Angela Merkel spoke at the Intergovernmental Conference is not without particular significance. Her famous, canonized words of welcome ("Wir schaffen das") to the many asylum seekers at the height of the European migration crisis in 2015 gave her voice a special status on this issue.

[This is an excerpt from the full document]

I am delighted to be here with you in Marrakech today.

Today is a very important day. For we are adopting a comprehensive political agreement on migration at global level for the first time. The United Nations General Assembly was right to focus on two issues in 2016 – on the one hand the topic of refugees, the legal basis of which is the Convention relating to the Status of Refugees, and on the other hand the topic of migration, an issue affecting millions of people throughout our world. A clear distinction has been made here between refugees and migration, which is particularly significant. That is why two Compacts have been drawn up as a result. And both are to be adopted by the General Assembly before the end of December.

Today, on the 70th anniversary of the adoption of the Universal Declaration of Human Rights by the United Nations General Assembly, it is particularly appropriate that we are also considering the fate of the many millions of migrants across the globe and reiterating our conviction that universal human rights apply to every individual in every country of the earth.

Ladies and gentlemen, today we are adopting this Compact, which expressly states that its focus is on safe, orderly and regular migration. The very title of the Compact therefore describes its goal very specifically. It has become clear, and it also makes sense that this

DOI: 10.4324/9781003159551-66

goal can only be achieved through multilateral cooperation. We could therefore say that 70 years after adoption of the International Bill of Human Rights it is high time that we also turned our joint attention to the issue of migration. Migration is a natural and frequent occurrence, and it is a good thing when it takes place legally.

Germany is a member of the European Union. Within the European Union we enjoy freedom of movement for the purposes of taking up employment. That is one aspect of our single market, and it brings us greater prosperity. That is why labour migration within the European Union is clearly regulated, also reflecting the principles of this Compact. It is all about equal pay for the same work. It is about reasonable standards. All this is something we take for granted within the European Union.

Due to its demographic development, Germany is a country that in future will continue to require higher numbers of qualified experts, including more experts from countries outside the European Union. We therefore have an interest in legal migration. And what is in our interests is also subject to our sovereign right to selfdetermination. The Compact states specifically that the Member States have the sovereign right to determine their own policies. At the same time, the Compact is not legally binding. So we will be reliant on legal migration as far as qualified experts are concerned and will need to talk to other countries about what is in our interests.

Nonetheless, we are aware that even within the context of legal migration as it exists in the world today, some people are exposed to extremely unfair working conditions. Child labour is still a reality. Dire working conditions are a reality. The Compact tackles these issues. And rightly so.

The Compact is also expressly intended to prevent and counter illegal migration. It expresses the commitment to border management. It expresses the commitment to fighting human trafficking. It expresses the conviction that every individual should have adequate documentation. And it raises the issue of the readmission of nationals residing illegally in another state.

We are all aware of the risks to which people who fall into the hands of human traffickers and smugglers are exposed. I would like to take this opportunity to thank the International Organization for Migration, which will play a major role in connection with the implementation of this Compact, for its work, which it performs in many countries and which prevents many people from suffering an even worse fate.

We cannot allow human traffickers and smugglers to decide on whether someone from one country should enter another, robbing poor people of their money in the process. Ultimately, this money is then used for drug trafficking or the purchasing of weapons, which in turn makes these countries even more unsafe. Our goal must be for states themselves to regulate migration issues legally. It is crucial that we join forces to fight illegal migration in the interests of our citizens. It must be clear to everyone that states acting single-handedly will not be able to resolve this problem, but that it must be tackled through multilateral cooperation, and that this is indeed the only way to do so.

We all know that we will only be able to tackle illegal migration if all countries in the world have opportunities for development. That is why the Compact goes hand in hand with implementation of the 2030 Agenda [The UN 2030 Agenda for Sustainable Development]. It has already been said here today that if the goals in the areas of education, health, security and nutrition are not achieved, neither will we manage to get to grips with illegal migration and truly put a stop to it. That means that the development and implementation of this Compact and its content are inextricably linked. And all countries of the world need to have fair development opportunities if we are to shape globalisation humanely.

Now we all know that illegal migration due to the unequal development opportunities in the world sparks considerable fear in our countries in some quarters. These fears are exploited by opponents of the Compact to spread false rumours. But in essence, all discussion of this Compact and whether or not it is the right approach centres around the principle of multilateral cooperation.

Ladies and gentlemen, it is worth reminding ourselves that the United Nations was founded as a result of the Second World War. As German Chancellor, I stand here as a representative of a country that brought immeasurable suffering on humanity as a consequence of National Socialism. The response to pure nationalism was the establishment of the United Nations and a commitment to work together to resolve the issues that concern us. All debate surrounding this Compact – and that is why I made a very deliberate decision to come to Morocco today – concerns the very foundation of our international cooperation, no more and no less.

That is why it is worth fighting for this Compact – both because of the many people who will thereby be able to have a better life, and because of its clear commitment to multilateralism. This is the only way that we will be able to make our world a better place. Germany is committed to this task. We have held intensive discussions in our parliament. There was a large parliamentary majority in favour of supporting this Compact. Germany will continue to play an active role in its further implementation for the benefit of the people on our planet.

Thank you very much.

Questions

How has the issue of migration challenged the human rights that form an essential part of the value system of the transatlantic region?

In what way could migrants possibly benefit from this Global Compact agreement?

Reference

https://www.un.org/en/conf/migration/assets/pdf/GCM-Statements/germany.pdf

Document 20

Under Secretary of Defense for Acquisition and Sustainment Ellen M. Lord and Deputy Under Secretary of Defense for Policy David J. Trachtenberg, Press Briefing on US Department of Defense's Response to Turkey Accepting Delivery of the Russian S-400 Air and Missile Defense System, 17 July 2019

Turkey's relations with the United States have been gradually deteriorating since the end of the Cold War. A NATO member since 1952, Turkey was a vital hub for US operations in the Middle East via the Incirlik air base. Turkey was also long considered by the US as a modern, secular nation and as such an important model for other nations in the region (despite the regular interference of the Turkish military in politics). But the decision not to allow US forces to move through Incirlik for the invasion of Iraq in 2003 was a sign that Turkey was beginning a re-alignment away from Western interests and towards a more assertive independent position of its own. Much of this shift has taken place under the leadership of Recep Erdogan and the Justice and Development party (AKP), with Erdogan serving as prime minister from 2003–2014 and president from 2014. During this period Erdogan has also played down membership of the EU, a Turkish foreign policy interest since the 1960s, and instead embarked on a divisive strategy of courting support among the large Turkish diaspora within the EU (and particularly in Germany).

Under Erdogan, contentious issues in relations with the United States have escalated. The residence in the US of Erdogan's political adversary, the Sunni cleric Fethullah Gülen, has long been a bone of contention, particularly following the attempted coup in July 2016 that Erdogan claimed was Gülen's work (with US support). Concerns over Erdogan's promotion of Turkey as a Muslin nation have also drawn criticism from US Christian organisations on the grounds of undermining religious freedoms in a secular state. With the outbreak of the Syrian civil war in 2011, relations have been further strained. US military support for Kurdish forces in the north-east of the country clashed with long-held Turkish enmity towards any form of Kurdish autonomy in the region, and the designation of Kurdish groups such as the PKK as terrorist organisations. But the most contentious issue concerns the purchase by Turkey of the Russian S-400 air defence system, which had been flatly rejected by the US as being incompatible with Turkish involvement with the F-35 Joint Strike Fighter project. Since Turkey was a key partner in the F-35 programme, the US cancellation of cooperation on this one issue due to the S-400 purchase upset supply lines and threatened a potential loss in revenue for Turkey of $1bn in immediate contracts and $9bn in long-term commitments. The US also threatened sanctions under the Countering America's Adversaries Through Sanctions Act (CAATSA), which allows action to be taken against those who do business with the Russian arms sector. The F-35 decision marked the most serious rift between the two NATO allies and raised questions as to how far Erdogan's wish for strategic independence would actually go, including in terms of NATO membership.

DOI: 10.4324/9781003159551-67

[This document includes the full statements but excludes the Q&A session that followed]

STAFF: Good afternoon, ladies and gentlemen. Thank you for joining us today. This afternoon, Under Secretary of Defense for Acquisition and Sustainment Ellen Lord and Deputy Under Secretary for Policy David Trachtenberg will provide a Department of Defense update on Turkey's accepting of the Russian S-400 system and what that means for the F-35 program moving forward.

The purpose of this briefing is to focus on the F-35 and Turkey, so please limit your questions to that. Both leaders have an opening statement and then we'll take your questions. We do have a hard stop at 3:30, so please be respectful with your questions so everyone will have a chance.

Before we start, the department would like to offer our condolences for the individuals Turkey lost during an attack today. Our hearts go out to their friends and families during this difficult time and the U.S. reaffirms its commitments to support the government and the people of Turkey.

UNDER SECRETARY OF DEFENSE ELLEN LORD: Thank you, Mike. Thank you all for being here this afternoon. Last Friday, the United States learned that Turkey accepted delivery of a Russian S-400 air and missile defense system. I'm here today to highlight three things.

One, the U.S. has full confidence in the F-35 program and supply chain. Two, the U.S. and other F-35 partners are aligned in this decision to suspend Turkey from the program and initiate the process to formally remove Turkey from the program. Three, as President Trump said in his statement today, the U.S. still values our strategic partnership with Turkey.

The Department of Defense, and the U.S. government more broadly, have worked very hard to chart an alternative path that would enable Turkey to acquire air defense systems within NATO alliance standards for interoperability and still allow Turkey to remain within the F-35 partnership.

The United States has been actively working with Turkey over the sale of the Patriot air and missile defense systems to satisfy its legitimate air defense needs. Since early 2017, when Turkey began publicly discussing its interests in the Russian-made S-400 system, all levels of the U.S. government have consistently communicated that the F-35 and the S-400 are incompatible.

As other U.S. officials and I have clearly said, Turkey cannot field a Russian intelligence collection platform in proximity to where the F-35 program makes, repairs and houses the F-35. Much of the F-35's strength lies in its stealth capabilities, so the ability to detect those capabilities would jeopardize the long-term security of the F-35 program.

We seek only to protect the long-term security of the F-35 program. In early June, the acting secretary of defense communicated to Minister Akar that unless Turkey canceled acceptance of this system, Turkey would be removed from the F-35 program in an orderly, respectful and deliberate manner.

All actions to wind down were reversible and this was done to allow sufficient time for Turkish personnel associated with the F-35 program to be reassigned and depart the United States by July 31, 2019. Please understand we cannot answer any questions on the matters of intelligence.

Turkey's purchase of the S-400 is inconsistent with its commitments to NATO and will have detrimental impact on Turkish interoperability with the alliance. Regardless of Turkey's decision to proceed with the procurement of the Russian system, the F-35 international partnership is strong and resilient.

I have regularly engaged with our partners as we sought a better outcome and began charting a path forward without Turkey's participation in the program. Our partnership regrets that we have arrived at this moment, but I and the F-35 Joint Program Office will continue to engage fully with our F-35 partners as we work to expeditiously complete the unwinding of Turkey's participation in the partnership.

We have been working in earnest to develop and implement changes to our supply base and supply chain to accommodate the potential for Turkish removal from the program. To bridge the gap initially to mitigate Turkey's removal, the program will use primarily U.S. sources for Turkey's work share, but this will gradually open up to program partners for first, second and third sources.

Because of this planning, Turkey's removal from the F-35 program will have minimal impact on the larger F-35 partnership. We have also worked closely with our industry partners throughout this process and I have notified F-35 industry leaders of Turkey's suspension to ensure the supply chain continues to stay closely informed and involved.

Turkey will certainly, and regrettably, lose jobs and future economic opportunities from this decision. It will no longer receive more than $9 billion in projected work share related to the F-35 over the life of the program.

Turkey made more than 900 parts for the F-35 and had been assigned more than $1 billion in industrial participation across 10 Turkish suppliers. All Turkish F-35 students and instructor pilots currently in the United States have firm plans to leave the country.

Roughly 20 Turkish personnel at the Joint Program Office will no longer retain access to JPO spaces. These actions to remove Turkey from the F-35 program are intended to mitigate risks to the F-35 and are separate from any congressionally-mandated, Russia-related sanctions under the Countering America's Adversaries Through Sanctions Act, or CAATSA. I will defer all CAATSA questions to my colleagues at the State Department.

In closing, and before Deputy Under Secretary Trachtenberg speaks, let me reiterate that Turkey remains a close NATO ally and our military-to-military relationship remains strong. We continue to honor our commitment to ensure the safety of our NATO ally, and support missions benefiting regional security and stability. Thank you.

David?

DEPUTY UNDER SECRETARY OF DEFENSE DAVID TRACHTENBERG: Good afternoon, everyone. And thank you all for being here today. I will be brief in my comments.

As Under Secretary Lord said, this is a rather unfortunate development and one the U.S. government has worked tirelessly to avoid. But let me be clear, the United States greatly values our strategic relationship with Turkey. That remains unchanged. As long-standing NATO allies, our relationship is multilayered and extends well beyond the F-35 partnership.

We will continue our extensive cooperation with Turkey across the entire spectrum of our security relationship. We have been clear and consistent that Turkey can choose to acquire the S-400 or the F-35. It cannot have both. Our decision to unwind Turkey's participation in the F-35 program is no surprise as our concerns have repeatedly been communicated to the Turkish government.

Our reaction today is a specific response to a specific event. It is separate and distinct from the broader range of security interests where the United States and Turkey work together against common threats. Our military-to-military relationship remains strong. And we will continue to participate with Turkey in multilateral exercises to improve readiness and interoperability, including upcoming exercises in Georgia, Germany and Ukraine, as well as engage with Turkey on a broad range of NATO issues.

While Turkey's decision is unfortunate, ensuring the security and integrity of the F-35 program and the capabilities it will provide to our partners remains our top priority. Thank you.

Questions

Why is it valuable – politically, economically, strategically – for the United States if NATO allies use US-manufactured equipment such as the F-35 Strike Fighter?

What are the advantages of having Turkey a member of NATO?

Reference

https://www.defense.gov/Newsroom/Transcripts/Transcript/Article/1908442/under-secretary-of-defense-for-acquisition-and-sustainment-ellen-m-lord-and-dep

Document 21

General Intelligence and Security Service [AIVD], Insight into Targets: Fifteen Years of Jihadist Attacks in the West, The Netherlands, 29 July 2019

Although terrorism is not a new phenomenon, the background and motivation of terrorists, their targets and their methods have changed considerably over time. Jihadist terrorism – based on a belief system that sanctions violence against non-Muslims – in particular has become a well-known phenomenon since the 1980s, and especially since "9/11". The Netherlands faced its first example of this threat with the killing of Dutch film-maker and journalist Theo van Gogh on an Amsterdam street in November 2004, although the AIVD had arrested several members of the radicalized "Hofstadgroep" already in October 2003. The budget of the AIVD would grow substantially from 67.3m Euro in 2002 to 175m Euro in 2008. In 2019 the Dutch security service drew up a report to examine the changing threat assessment and patterns of violence across the West. In the early 2000s the main threat was seen as coming from the Al Qaeda network and its sympathisers, who declared allegiance to Osama bin Laden. The rise of Islamic State (ISIS) in the 2010s provided an additional focus for radicalized discontent, especially as several hundred European Muslims went to join its "caliphate" in Syria and Iraq after 2011. The report provides a useful insight into the perception of these types of threat by the Dutch service.

As in all Western nations, the terrorist threat from radical groups further sharpened the debate regarding immigration from non-Western countries, and this would in turn fuel the rise of parties on the populist right during the 2000s. The pressure on security services to prevent further attacks also led to increased media attention for their activities and, primarily through Edward Snowden, the exposure of the extent of surveillance across all societies. US-EU disagreements on the exchange of passenger name records (PNRs) for transatlantic flights would rumble on through the 2000s before an agreement was reached in 2011. The AIVD was a valued ally of US organisations such as the National Security Agency (NSA) but was not a core partner (the so-called Five Eyes group).

[This is an excerpt from the full document]

Introduction

The jihadist terrorist threat is characterised by a great diversity of potential targets. The aim of this publication is to provide insight in the targets of jihadist terrorism by studying the jihadist terrorist attacks in the West of the past fifteen years. This publication therefore does not focus on the perpetrators of jihadist terrorist attacks, but on their targets.

This publication offers an insight into the actual attacks of the past fifteen years and is not intended to offer insight into the current or future threat on these (or other) targets.

DOI: 10.4324/9781003159551-68

Jihadist terrorist aims

Terrorists carry out attacks for a variety of reasons. This publication relates to violent acts and attacks carried out for jihadist terrorist aims. The definitions of the terms 'jihadism' and 'terrorism' are open to discussion, which consequently has a bearing on the criteria for classifying an attack as jihadist terrorism. For that reason it is important to give clear descriptions of the definitions on which this target analysis is based.

The AIVD defines terrorism as the ideologically motivated actual or threatened violence against persons, property, or the fabric of society, with the aim of bringing about social change, creating fear amongst the population, or influencing the political decision-making process.

In selecting terrorist attacks for this publication, the determining factor has been whether the motivation for the violent act stemmed from (aspects of) radical Islamist or jihadist Salafist ideology. Examples are: (contributing to) the (violent) struggle against the West, the defence of Islam against (perceived) enemies, the countering of Western influence and (military) interventions in Islamic countries, the striving for the establishment of a 'caliphate' and/or the introduction of the Sharia.

In everyday language, such attacks are generally referred to as 'jihadist attacks' or 'terrorist attacks'. For the sake of readability, this publication will simply refer to these as 'attacks'.

Although attacks are and were carried out all over the world, this publication specifically looks at attacks in Western countries, i.e. Western Europe, North America, and Australia, in the period from January 2004 until December 2018.

Targets

The jihadist terrorist threat in the West is predominantly constituted by the activities of the groups Islamic State in Iraq and al-Sham (ISIS) and al-Qaeda (AQ), and networks and individual sympathisers affiliated with these groups. Attacks by ISIS as well as al-Qaeda can be divided into three categories: leadership-directed attacks, attacks encouraged by members of ISIS or AQ, and attacks inspired by these groups. In the past few years, inspired attacks have become an increasingly substantial part of the jihadist terrorist threat in the West.

ISIS in particular has been successful at mobilising and inspiring sympathisers in the West to carry out attacks in its name. From 2014 on, the ISIS leadership began to issue calls for such attacks. The major attacks in Paris (November 2015) and Brussels (March 2016) were still planned, prepared and directed by ISIS leadership, but since then ISIS has been less and less capable of carrying out centrally directed and coordinated attacks in the West. The group has instead become more dependent on relatively small-scale attacks by sympathisers.

Attacks by al-Qaeda and its affiliated networks and sympathisers can also be categorised as directed, encouraged, or inspired attacks. The last successful attack in the West that can be attributed to (one of the 'branches' of) al-Qaeda attack was the attack on the Charlie Hebdo offices in Paris (January 2015). Al-Qaeda has proven to be much less successful than ISIS at mobilising sympathisers for attacks, but it does call upon sympathisers to carry out attacks in the same manner as ISIS. Al-Qaeda also still harbours the intention of carrying out large-scale attacks against symbolic Western targets.

Number of attacks

There have been 112 radical Islamist and jihadist Salafist terrorist attacks in the West in the past fifteen years. The timeline shows the rise and fall of the number of attacks in the past fifteen years. Of all the attacks, 80% was committed by a single perpetrator.

The first ten years of this period show that each year a relatively small number of attacks took place in the West, with a slight peak in 2009/2010. The past five years show a steep rise in the number of attacks in the West, followed by a strong decline in 2018. Of all attacks carried out in the past fifteen years, no less than three-quarters occurred in the past five years. This coincides with the rise of ISIS and the fact that from 2014 onward ISIS leadership began to call on its sympathisers in the West to carry out attacks. The strong decline in the number of attacks in 2018 follows the fall of the caliphate proclaimed by ISIS, and the fact that the organisation had lost much of its strength.

It is not merely the higher number of attacks in the past five years that distinguishes this period from the preceding ten years. The geographical distribution, the choice of targets, and the methods used have also changed in the past five years. In what follows, this publication will therefore at various points differentiate between the attacks of the first ten years and those of the last five.

The 112 attacks in the West occurred throughout the entire year, although the number of attacks carried out from May to September 2018 was relatively higher than in the period from October to April (54% as opposed to 46%). The past fifteen years have not seen a rise in the number of attacks surrounding Christian holidays.

Of the 112 attacks that took place in the West, 13% occurred during Ramadan. In the first ten years, only one attack took place during Ramadan (the murder of Theo van Gogh in the Netherlands on 2 November 2004), against 16% of attacks taking place during Ramadan in the past five years. This shift of the past five years coincides with the rise of ISIS. From 2015 onwards, ISIS called on its sympathisers each year to carry out attacks during Ramadan. Still, of only one attack that was carried out during Ramadan (the attack on a police officer and his family in France in 2016) do we know that the perpetrator explicitly planned the attack to take place in the month of Ramadan. Furthermore, the main share of attacks in the West occurred outside of Ramadan.

Outcome of the attacks

Succeeded versus failed

Of the 112 attacks in the West in the past fifteen years, 76% can be considered succeeded, meaning that they were actually carried out and resulted in casualties and/or damage. The other 24% can be deemed failed; these attacks did not obtain the intended effect (damage or casualties), for example because explosives failed to detonate. In this regard too there has been a shift in the past fifteen years. During the first ten years of that period, half of all attacks succeeded, and half failed. In the past five years, however, the percentage of success has risen to 84%. So, not only have there been more attacks in the West in the past five years (three-quarters of all attacks of the past fifteen years), but these attacks also succeeded more often.

Casualties

There is a general perception that jihadist terrorists primarily strive to inflict as many casualties as possible. However, this is just one of their goals, and there is no consensus within jihadist terrorist circles about the question whether it is permitted to claim as many (innocent) victims as possible, or which casualties would be legitimate. ISIS propaganda mentions public locations where crowds of people are gathered (such as events) as suitable targets. AQ on the other hand explicitly advises against attacks in public locations, because that might cause Muslim casualties as well.

In the past fifteen years there have been several attacks in the West that were plainly intended to cause large numbers of casualties, and the impact of such attacks is enormous. Still, these kinds of attacks are fairly rare: in the past fifteen years there have been seven attacks (6% of the total) that caused over a hundred casualties. The vast majority of attacks (70%) caused fewer than fifty casualties, 6% involved between fifty and a hundred casualties, and in 18% of attacks in the West there were no casualties at all.

Geographical distribution

In the past fifteen years, fourteen Western countries have had to deal with attacks: Australia, Belgium, Canada, Denmark, Germany, Finland, France, Italy, the Netherlands, Austria, Spain, the United Kingdom, the United States, and Sweden. Of these countries, France has had to bear the brunt of jihadist terrorism: 27% of all attacks in the West took place there. France is followed by the United States (20%), and then the United Kingdom (13%), and Germany (10%). In total, 70% of all attacks of the past fifteen years in the West took place in these four countries.

The geographical distribution of attacks has shifted significantly in the course of those fifteen years. During the first ten years, the United Kingdom was targeted the most in attacks; in that period, a quarter of attacks occurred there. After the UK comes the United States with 18%, followed by France and Germany (11% each). This distribution is quite different when one considers the past five years, in which three-quarters of all attacks of the past fifteen years occurred. Of these attacks, no less than 32% took place in France. This means that the number of attacks in France strongly increased in the past five years both in terms of absolute numbers and in a relative sense. France's 'leading position' for the past fifteen years is to a large extent due to the great number of attacks that this country had to face in the last five years (the first jihadist terrorist attack in France did not occur until 2012). In the United States 20% of all attacks took place in the past five years, followed by Germany (10%), and the United Kingdom (8%), which in the preceding ten years had to deal with a quarter of all attacks.

Not just capital cities

Although in recent years a number of large attacks took place in capital cities (Madrid, London, Paris, Brussels), the majority of the attacks occurred outside of the Western capitals. Of the 112 attacks in the past 15 years, 41% took place in the capital of the country in question, and in 59% the attack site was outside of the capital.

Attacks in the country in question

On the basis of the attacks in the West in the past fifteen years it is possible to conclude that when jihadists intend to strike a country by means of an attack (and wish to do so in the West itself, and not in a conflict zone) they will practically always carry out the attack in the country in question. There are almost no instances of attacks on targets of a Western country that take place in a different Western country. Only one attack out of 112 fits this description: the shooting of US military personnel at Frankfurt airport in 2011. The targeted country in this attack was the United States, whereas the attacksite was Germany. But, as mentioned, this is an exception. One could argue that although the attack at Zaventem airport in 2016 took place at a Belgian airport, the explosives were intentionally detonated next to the desks of two American airlines. In addition, the suspect of the 2015

Thalys attack has stated that the members of the US military on the train were the target, but it has not (yet) been established whether this was indeed the case.

Blasphemers

The murder of the Dutch film maker Theo van Gogh in 2004 was the first attack in the West that targeted an alleged blasphemer. At the time this was still uncommon. Following the Danish 'cartoon crisis' of 2005/2006, attacks targeting those who have offended the prophet have become more frequent. Remarkably, in all cases the targets could be related to the fact of making or publishing cartoons of the prophet. Of the attacks on blasphemers, 37% succeeded and 63% failed. This can partially be explained by the fact that in a number of cases the individuals in question were under protection. After 2015, when three attacks against alleged blasphemers took place, there were no further attacks against this target category. There was an attack in the Netherlands in 2018 in which there was a link to Mohammed cartoons, in this case the Mohammed cartoon contest announced by Geert Wilders. The perpetrator of this attack stated that he travelled to the Netherlands specifically to avenge this affront to the prophet.

Differences between countries

There are also geographical differences in jihadist terrorist target selection, with jihadists in one country selecting targets different from those selected in other countries. In the United States, 41% of all attacks in the past fifteen years were directed at public locations, 18% at police officers and 14% at the military. In the United Kingdom, on the other hand, public transport together with public locations were the targets hit most often (both 29%), followed in third place by political targets, with 21%.

Western politicians have been mentioned explicitly in the past in publications by terrorist groups and by jihadist leaders calling for attacks. To jihadists, they are legitimate targets as they bear the political responsibility for, for example, military interventions in Islamic countries. Still, only two countries have suffered attacks against political or government targets in the past fifteen years, namely the United Kingdom and Canada.

Strikingly, military personnel and police officers were targeted much less often in the United Kingdom than in other countries in the top 4. In France, police officers and military personnel were the targets most often hit (30% and 27% respectively), followed by public locations (20%). In Germany, public transport was hit most often (27%), followed by police officers, public locations, and – remarkably – events (18% each). The question which targets were most often targeted in jihadist terrorism is therefore answered differently for each Western country.

If we look at where the most attacks on uniformed personnel took place, then most attacks by far against this target category occurred in France (41%), followed at some distance by the United States (17%). In the United Kingdom, Germany, Belgium, Canada, and Italy too uniformed personnel was a target, but to a much lesser extent. In the majority of cases of attacks against uniformed personnel the victims were military staff and police officers recognisable as such because of their uniform, and in a public location at the time of the attack.

In the past fifteen years, Denmark has had to contend with the most attacks – half of the total number of attacks in this category – against blasphemers. This can be explained: most of these attacks were related to the publication of Mohammed cartoons in the Danish daily newspaper *Jyllands-Posten* in 2005 and the artist behind the most infamous cartoon

(Kurt Westergaard) lives in Denmark. Other attacks against blasphemers occurred in the United States, France, Sweden, and the Netherlands.

Means of attack

In the 112 attacks carried out in the West in the past fifteen years, five different means of attack were used: explosives, firearms, stabbing weapons, striking weapons, and vehicles. In a few instances, the attacks involved arson, hostage taking and decapitation as method of operation.

In the past fifteen years, 41% of all attacks was committed with a stabbing weapon, such as a knife. For 26% of attacks, explosives, such as IEDs (improvised explosive devices), and pipe bombs were used. In a quarter of cases, a firearm was the means of attack.

The method of operation for attacks in the West has also changed in the course of these fifteen years. During the first ten years, explosives were by far the most frequent means of attack. No less than 54% of all attacks in that period were carried out with the use of explosives. Firearms came second (29%) and stabbing weapons were in third place (18%).

This has changed considerably in the past five years. Stabbing weapons have become the preferred means of attack: 48% of all attacks of the past five years were carried out with a stabbing weapon. In 24% of cases a firearm was used, and in 17% of the attacks a vehicle was used as the attack means. Over the past five years the percentage of attacks in which explosives were used, fell from 54% to 17%. This observed shift in attack means correlates with the changing threat perspective of the past five years, in which the focus came to lie on inspired attacks by sympathisers.

Vehicles

A relatively new development that occurred in the past five years is the use of vehicles as means of attack. Attacks using vehicles are carried out not only by jihadists, but also for example by those on the far right (London, Charlottesville) and people who are not motivated by any specific ideology in their attack (the 2009 Queen's Day attack in the Netherlands).

The first time a jihadist used a vehicle to carry out an attack was in the United States in 2006. It was not until 2014 that the second attack with a vehicle took place, but in 2016 and 2017 the number of attacks by vehicle increased greatly. In 2016, there were four instances of the use of a vehicle to carry out attacks, and in 2017 there were nine. This sharp increase in the use of vehicles as a means of attack correlates with the sharp increase in the number of attacks of the past five years. The fact that the number of attacks using a vehicle has fallen to a single attack in 2018, also fits this trend.

Hostage-taking and decapitation

The second development is that in 11% of the attacks of the past five years, hostages were taken; all cases of hostage-taking by jihadist terrorists in the West occurred during the last five years. Decapitation as a method of attack hardly ever occurs in the West: in the past fifteen years only two attack plots featured plans to decapitate people, but actual decapitation took place in only one case, in June 2015 in France. This was the first (and so far only) successful decapitation by jihadists in a Western country.

CBRN and drones

Jihadist terrorists have not used any chemical, biological, radiological, or nuclear (CBRN) means for attacks in the West. The AIVD does hold information that in certain cases jihadists have expressed an interest in such unconventional means of attack. The same applies to the use of UAVs (unmanned aerial vehicles) or drones as a means of delivery (strictly speaking a drone is not a means of attack in itself). Jihadists have never carried out attacks in the West in which a drone was used.

Questions

What trends in jihadist attacks does the document establish?

Do you think that terrorism represents a shared, common threat to the transatlantic region?

Reference

https://english.aivd.nl/publications/publications/2019/07/29/publication-aivd-insight-into-targets---fifteen-years-of-jihadist-attacks-in-the-west

Document 22

US Bureau of Energy Resources, Fact Sheet: Nord Stream 2, 27 December 2019

Nord Stream 2, the second gas pipeline for the large-scale export of natural gas from Russia to Germany across the Baltic Sea, became an increasingly controversial issue between the Trump administration and participating European governments and businesses. It was the latest episode in a long-running feud between the US and Europe as to Europe's potential reliance on Russian energy supplies, dating back to the Cold War 1970s and 1980s. The Russian state-owned company Gazprom is the majority shareholder of the parent company, and many European companies, including German, Dutch and French energy giants, are playing an active role in the construction of the pipeline and the distribution of the imported natural gas. Some Central European governments opposed the plan for fear of being bypassed as an energy transit corridor and therefore facing a loss of income. In 2018 the EU Commission also refused to back the project, arguing that it went against EU proposals for diversifying gas supply. The EU had already been through a heated diplomatic disagreement with Russia before 2009 regarding the Transit Protocol to the Energy Charter Treaty, which was meant to prevent political interference in energy supplies. From the US, concerns focused on the potential danger of European dependence on Russian energy being used as a political tool by Moscow. From this perspective, energy replaces the Russian nuclear arsenal as a coercive diplomatic instrument, only this time there is no balance in the form of a US nuclear deterrent. As a result, Nord Stream 2 has laid bare the very different attitudes towards Russia (security threat or economic partner?) on both sides of the Atlantic. Respective European governments have repeatedly put forward the opinion that Nord Stream is only a commercial project and that the gas pipelines will reinforce the economic interdependence among all countries involved, which can only have a positive effect on international relations. Already in 2017, Germany relied on Russia for 40% of its total gas consumption, around 53bn cubic meters, and Nord Stream 2 would increase supply by an additional 55bn. The controversy recalls the 1982 dispute between the Reagan administration and (West) Germany concerning the Siberian gas pipeline to Western Europe. At that time, too, the US feared that Western Europe would become dependent on the Soviet Union's energy supply.

On December 20, 2019, President Trump signed the National Defense Authorization Act (NDAA) for Fiscal Year 2020, including Section 7503(d), also known as the Protecting Europe's Energy Security Act (PEESA) of 2019.

Related parties must ensure that vessels involved in Nord Stream 2 "immediately cease construction-related activity" in a "good-faith wind-down," as indicated by the Office of Foreign Assets Control (OFAC). That includes "involved parties that have knowingly sold, leased, or provided vessels that are engaged in pipe laying at depths of 100 feet or more below sea level for the construction of Nord Stream 2." Parties that do not comply will face sanctions as described in PEESA.

DOI: 10.4324/9781003159551-69

Nord Stream 2 is a tool Russia is using to support its continued aggression against Ukraine. Russia seeks to prevent it from integrating more closely with Europe and the United States. Nord Stream 2 would enable Russia to bypass Ukraine for gas transit to Europe, which would deprive Ukraine of substantial transit revenues and increase its vulnerability to Russian aggression. Nord Stream 2 would also help maintain Europe's significant reliance on imports of Russian natural gas, which creates economic and political vulnerabilities for our European partners and allies. For these reasons, the United States Government and a plurality of European countries oppose Nord Stream 2.

The United States Government strongly supports diversification of energy supplies because options help diminish the role of geopolitics in energy markets, reduce consumer prices, and enhance a country's energy security. For instance, it has been estimated that the availability of U.S. LNG saved European consumers $8 billion by enabling them to negotiate lower prices with existing suppliers.

The U.S. State Department will follow the letter of the law of the new NDAA legislation. It provides the Secretary up to 60 days to issue a report to Congress to identify violating entities. The Secretary will issue that report expeditiously. The United States will impose sanctions unless related parties *immediately* demonstrate good faith efforts to wind-down. Related parties need to finish wind-down within 30 days. Any company involved in Nord Stream 2 needs to look carefully at what that means for their operations.

The United States' intention is to stop construction of Nord Stream 2. Congress acted, and the President signed the bill. The U.S. position opposing Nord Stream 2 has been consistent across multiple administrations, as part of a longstanding practice to promote energy security through diversification of energy supplies by country of origin, path of delivery, and fuel types, including renewables. Anyone engaged in the energy trading business ought to do it under fair terms, which are transparent, and operate according to market principles.

Questions

Explain the German position on Nordstream. Do you agree that it is merely a "commercial project"?

Was the Trump administration correct in applying sanctions on an issue of European energy supply?

Reference

https://www.state.gov/fact-sheet-on-u-s-opposition-to-nord-stream-2

Document 23

Cybersecurity of 5G Networks: EU Toolbox of Risk Mitigating Measures, European Parliament, January 2020

Communications and data transfer have been a problematic field in US-EU relations, with the US geared more towards ensuring system security and the Europeans towards protecting privacy. In July 2020 the European Court of Justice ruled against the US-EU Privacy Shield, which had enabled transatlantic data exchange, on the grounds that American privacy standards were inadequate. The development of the 5G wireless network communications infrastructure caused further high-level tension between the United States and Europe due to security concerns related to who would provide the technical hardware. 5G, which was first introduced in the USA and elsewhere in 2018, means faster speeds and greater bandwidth, as well as an expansion of connectivity with 'the internet of things'. Since it requires the use of new radio frequencies, the arrival of 5G involves major contracts for tech companies to upgrade existing infrastructure. Control of 5G networks has become a vital issue of national security.

The rejection of Chinese tech giant Huawei as a 5G supplier by the United States placed it in direct opposition to certain allies, including the UK, leading President Trump to claim that Huawei involvement could lead to the US no longer sharing sensitive intelligence. In 2019–2020 both the EU and the UK acknowledged that the political context of 5G was as important as the technology, with the UK asserting that Huawei would be considered a "high risk vendor" due to its close association with the Chinese government. Such a designation would mean that a supplier would be excluded from the "core" (critical or sensitive) of a network, but some cybersecurity experts dispute whether "core" activities and infrastructure could be sufficiently protected once a supplier was anyway part of the network. As a result, 5G is forcing difficult trade-offs between security concerns and the need for competitiveness. The EU Toolbox was an attempt to map out a way forward, matching EU and member state interests in a common approach to ensure "technological sovereignty". Yet the EU was divided between those rejecting Huawei involvement (such as Romania and Poland), those reducing it (France and Spain), and those undecided (Germany). A divided EU left it open to US pressure and unable to prioritise its own tech suppliers such as Ericsson and Nokia. As a result, 5G will continue to be a major transatlantic issue.

[This is an excerpt from the full document]

Introduction

5G networks will play a central role in achieving the digital transformation of the EU's economy and society. Indeed, 5G networks have the potential to enable and support a wide range of applications and functions, extending far beyond the provision of mobile communication services between end-users. With worldwide 5G revenues to reach an

DOI: 10.4324/9781003159551-70

estimated €225 billion in 2025, 5G technologies and services are a key asset for Europe to be able to compete in the global market.

The cybersecurity of 5G networks is therefore essential to protect our economies and societies and to enable the full potential of the important opportunities they will bring. It is also crucial for ensuring the technological sovereignty of the Union.

Following the support expressed by the European Council on 22 March, 2019 for a concerted approach to the security of 5G networks, the European Commission adopted its Recommendation on the cybersecurity of 5G networks (hereafter 'The Recommendation') on 26 March, 2019. The Recommendation called on Member States to complete national risk assessments and review national measures, to work together at EU level on a coordinated risk assessment and to prepare a toolbox of possible mitigating measures.

Each Member State completed its own national risk assessment of its 5G network infrastructures and transmitted the results to the Commission and ENISA – the European Union Agency for Cybersecurity.

Based on these national risk assessments, on 9 October, 2019 Member States – with the support of ENISA and the Commission – published a report on the EU Coordinated Risk Assessment on Cybersecurity in 5G Networks. This report identifies the main threats and threat actors, the most sensitive assets, the main vulnerabilities (including technical ones and other types of vulnerabilities, such as the legal and policy framework to which suppliers of information and communications technologies equipment may be subject to in third countries), and the main associated risks. To complement this report and as a further input for the toolbox, ENISA carried out a dedicated threat landscape mapping, consisting of a detailed analysis of certain technical aspects, in particular the identification of network assets and of threats affecting these.

The Council Conclusions of 3 December, 2019 endorsed the work of the Member States' Cooperation Group on Network and Information Security (NIS Cooperation Group), supporting the findings of the coordinated risk assessment. In particular, the Council welcomed 'the ongoing joint European efforts on safeguarding the security of 5G networks based in particular on the Commission Recommendation on Cyber Security of 5G Networks and stressed 'the importance of a coordinated approach and effective implementation of the Recommendation in order to avoid fragmentation in the Single Market'. To this effect, the Council called upon Member States, the Commission and ENISA, to 'take all necessary measures within their competences to ensure the security and integrity of electronic communication networks, in particular 5G networks and to continue to consolidate a coordinated approach to address the security challenges related to 5G technologies.'

The EU coordinated risk assessment report highlights a number of important security challenges which are likely to appear or become more prominent in 5G networks. These security challenges are mainly linked to:

−Increasing security concerns related to the availability and integrity of the networks, in addition to the confidentiality and privacy concerns;
−Key innovations in the 5G technology (which will also bring a number of specific security improvements), in particular the increased important role of software and the wide range of services and applications enabled by 5G networks; and
−The role of suppliers in building and operating 5G networks, the complexity of the interlinkages between suppliers and operators, and the degree of dependency on individual suppliers.

The report further concludes that these challenges create a new security paradigm, making it necessary to reassess the current policy and security framework applicable to the sector and its ecosystem, and making it essential for Member States to take the necessary mitigating measures.

Conclusions and way forward

The EU toolbox sets out a range of measures and actions that – if appropriately combined and effectively implemented – form the basis for a coordinated approach in this area. Indeed, given the wide range of risk areas identified in the EU coordinated risk assessment and their different nature, no single type of measure will be sufficient and instead a range of measures used in an appropriate combination, will be necessary in order to address all key risk areas.

Based on the assessment of possible mitigation plans and the identification of the highest effectiveness measures, this toolbox recommends that:

1   All Member States should ensure that they have measures in place (including powers for national authorities) to respond appropriately and proportionately to the presently identified and future risks, and in particular ensure that they are able to restrict, prohibit, and/or impose specific requirements or conditions, following a risk-based approach, for the supply, deployment, and operation of 5G network equipment on the basis of a range of security-related grounds.

They should in particular:

- Strengthen security requirements for mobile network operators (e.g. strict access controls, rules on secure operation and monitoring, limitations on outsourcing of specific functions, etc.);
- Assess the risk profile of suppliers; as a consequence, apply relevant restrictions for suppliers considered to be high risk – including necessary exclusions to effectively mitigate risks – for key assets defined as critical and sensitive in the EU coordinated risk assessment (e.g. core network functions, network management and orchestration functions, and access network functions);
- Ensure that each operator has an appropriate multi-vendor strategy to avoid or limit any major dependency on a single supplier (or suppliers with a similar risk profile), ensure an adequate balance of suppliers at national level and avoid dependency on suppliers considered to be high risk; this also requires avoiding any situations of lock-in with a single supplier, including by promoting greater interoperability of equipment;

2   The European Commission, jointly with Member states, should contribute to:

- Maintaining a diverse and sustainable 5G supply chain in order to avoid long-term dependency, including by: Making full use of the existing EU tools and instruments, in particular through the screening of potential foreign direct investments (FDIs) affecting 5G key assets and by avoiding distortions in the 5G supply market stemming from potential dumping or subsidies; and
- Further strengthening EU capacities in the 5G and post-5G technologies, by using relevant EU programmes and funding.

    – Facilitating coordination between Member states regarding standardisation to achieve specific security objectives and developing relevant EU-wide certification scheme(s) in order to promote more secure products and processes.

3   To ensure that this coordinated approach stands the test of time, the mandate of the NIS Cooperation Group Work Stream should be extended, as well as the cooperation with other relevant bodies and entities, in order, in particular, to:

    – Review periodically – with the support of the Commission and ENISA – the national and EU risk assessments on the security of 5G and post-5G networks, further elaborating and aligning the assessment methodology followed and adapting to the evolving 5G technology.
    – Perform a detailed and regular monitoring and evaluation of the implementation of the toolbox based on a structured reporting by Member States;
    – Coordinate and support the implementation of supporting actions, which require cooperation at EU level, in particular regarding the elaboration of guidance and exchange of best practices on the various measures.
    – Support further possible coordination at EU-level where appropriate, in particular to bring further convergence as regards technical and organisational security requirements for network operators.

Questions

How would you contrast the US attitude towards Huawei with the activities of the US National Security Agency (see Part III, Document 4)?
Should the EU be able to determine the ICT decisions of its member states, and if so on what grounds?

Reference

https://ec.europa.eu/digital-single-market/en/news/cybersecurity-5g-networks-eu-toolbox-risk-mitigating-measures

Document 24

Speech by Prime Minister Boris Johnson, Old Naval College, Greenwich, 3 February 2020

On 24 July 2019 Boris Johnson became prime minister of the UK. A Conservative member of parliament for Henley from 2001–2008, he was elected twice as mayor of London before re-entering parliament in 2015. From then on he took a prominent role in the Brexit campaign, campaigning successfully for a "Leave" vote in the June 2016 referendum and serving as foreign secretary under prime minister Theresa May before resigning in July 2018 in response to her attempts to forge a deal with the EU.

Johnson had a mixed relation with the Trump administration prior to this speech. As foreign secretary he had admired Trump's forthright style as a possible model for forcing an exit from the EU, and had supported some of Trump's decisions such as recognition of Jerusalem as Israel's capital in December 2017. He also developed a close working relation with Trump's advisor Stephen Miller, the two of them discussing speechwriting tactics. Miller was also important for "talking up" Johnson in a period when Trump himself seemed more interested in Nigel Farage, the founder of the UK Independence Party (UKIP). Trump saw the Brexit referendum result as a positive harbinger for his own subsequent election success in November 2016. Nevertheless, major differences existed between Johnson and Trump. Both were populists and had nationalist platforms that could easily clash. Johnson believed in the continuing importance of NATO, whereas Trump continuously attacked the US's European allies for failing to invest in the alliance as they should, and questioned its use for US foreign policy interests. Johnson supported the Iran nuclear deal and the Paris climate accords against Trump's rejection of both. But the main obstacles to relations were the possible conditions for a post-Brexit US-UK trade agreement. US hardline interests regarding pharmaceuticals, health care, and agriculture made it clear that Britain would have to lessen some of its regulatory controls if it was to secure a trade deal. Given the essential response of the National Health Service to the Corona virus pandemic during 2020, protecting national interests in health care provision was an issue of great importance. The reference to this issue in the speech below indicated that while Johnson was prepared to go against widespread anti-Trump feeling in Britain, he was also aware that he could not simply accept any deal, despite the great significance of such a move for a post-Brexit Britain to balance the potential loss of EU markets and establish itself internationally.

[This is an excerpt from the speech]

We are re-emerging after decades of hibernation as a campaigner for global free trade.

And frankly it is not a moment too soon because the argument for this fundamental liberty is now not being made.

We in the global community are in danger of forgetting the key insight of those great Scottish thinkers, the invisible hand of Adam Smith, and of course David Ricardo's more

DOI: 10.4324/9781003159551-71

subtle but indispensable principle of comparative advantage, which teaches that if countries learn to specialise and exchange then overall wealth will increase and productivity will increase, leading Cobden to conclude that free trade is God's diplomacy – the only certain way of uniting people in the bonds of peace since the more freely goods cross borders the less likely it is that troops will ever cross borders.

And since these notions were born here in this country, it has been free trade that has done more than any other single economic idea to raise billions out of poverty and incredibly fast.

In 1990 there were 37 percent of the world's population in absolute poverty – that is now down to less than ten per cent.

And yet my friends, I am here to warn you today that this beneficial magic is fading.

Free trade is being choked and that is no fault of the people, that's no fault of individual consumers, I am afraid it is the politicians who are failing to lead.

The mercantilists are everywhere, the protectionists are gaining ground.

From Brussels to China to Washington tariffs are being waved around like cudgels even in debates on foreign policy where frankly they have no place – and there is an ever growing proliferation of non-tariff barriers and the resulting tensions are letting the air out of the tyres of the world economy.

World trading volumes are lagging behind global growth.

Trade used to grow at roughly double global GDP – from 1987 to 2007.

Now it barely keeps pace and global growth is itself anaemic and the decline in global poverty is beginning to slow.

And in that context, we are starting to hear some bizarre autarkic rhetoric, when barriers are going up, and when there is a risk that new diseases such as coronavirus will trigger a panic and a desire for market segregation that go beyond what is medically rational to the point of doing real and unnecessary economic damage, then at that moment humanity needs some government somewhere that is willing at least to make the case powerfully for freedom of exchange, some country ready to take off its Clark Kent spectacles and leap into the phone booth and emerge with its cloak flowing as the supercharged champion, of the right of the populations of the earth to buy and sell freely among each other.

And here in Greenwich in the first week of February 2020, I can tell you in all humility that the UK is ready for that role.

We are ready for the great multi-dimensional game of chess in which we engage in more than one negotiation at once and we are limbering up to use nerves and muscles and instincts that this country has not had to use for half a century.

Secretary of State Liz Truss tells me she has the teams in place:

She has the lawyers, top dollar I've no doubt, the economists, trade policy experts and if we don't have enough, or if they don't perform, believe me we will hire some more.

We will reach out to the rest of the Commonwealth, which now has some of the fastest growing economies in the world.

It was fantastic at the recent Africa summit to see how many wanted to turn that great family of nations into a free trade zone, even if we have to begin with clumps and groups, and we will take these ideas forward at Kigali in June.

We will engage with Japan and the other Trans-Pacific agreement countries, with old friends and partners – Australia, New Zealand, Canada – on whom we deliberately turned our backs in the early 1970s.

We will get going with our friends in America and I share the optimism of Donald Trump and I say to all the naïve and juvenile anti-Americans in this country if there are any – there seem to be some – I say grow up – and get a grip.

The US already buys one fifth of everything we export.

And yes of course there are going to be difficulties:

Our shower trays seem to fall foul of US rules Liz, and if you want to sell insurance across America, Mr Ambassador, you still have to deal with 50 separate regulators, and it is high time I think we all agree that they cut their punitive tariffs on Scotch whisky.

And it goes without saying to all those conspiracy theorists who may still be in existence, all those believers in the Bermuda Triangle or who think that Elvis will be found on Mars. It goes without saying that of course the NHS is not on the table and no we will not accept any diminution in food hygiene or animal welfare standards.

But I must say to the America bashers in this country if there are any that in doing free trade deals we will be governed by science and not by mumbo-jumbo because the potential is enormous.

Questions

Do you think a strong US-UK relationship is essential for strong transatlantic relations in general? Is free trade such an essential element for the transatlantic economy?

Reference

https://www.gov.uk/government/speeches/pm-speech-in-greenwich-3-february-2020
Permission: Open Government License (OGL)

Document 25

President Donald J. Trump, "Suspension of entry as immigrants and nonimmigrants of certain additional persons who pose a risk of transmitting 2019 novel coronavirus," Proclamation 9993, 11 March 2020

In December 2019 the Chinese government confirmed that health authorities were treating several dozen infections of a flu-like virus in the city of Wuhan. This turned out to be the Corona virus, or COVID-19 (short for "Coronavirus disease 2019"). The first death was reported on 11 January, a 61 year old man who was a regular customer to the market that is widely regarded as the epicentre for the outbreak. The first case in the United States was identified on 21 January – a man in his 30s who had returned from Wuhan. By the end of that month, the World Health Organisation (WHO) had declared a "public health emergency of international concern." Cases spread rapidly in Europe, with northern Italy being a particular hotspot. By the end of October 2020 there were 42 million cases and 1.1 million deaths worldwide, with almost a fifth of those, 228,000, in the United States alone.

The economic effects of COVID-19 have been stark, with lockdowns having a devastating effect on the service and travel sectors and unemployment rising everywhere. But the virus pandemic also exposed the weakness of international cooperation. The WHO, the only global authority designed to respond to such an outbreak, faced accusations of partisanship from the US that it had reacted slowly and softly to China's inability to control the virus sooner. President Trump announced on 30 March that he would be withdrawing the US from the Organisation, a move that further escalated his pursuit of "America First" ahead of the norms of liberal internationalism.

The document below marked another low point in transatlantic relations, when President Trump announced a ban on travel of those wanting to enter the US from the Schengen area of the EU (those member states that operated a borderless travel space for their citizens). Comments made at the time of the announcement effectively accused the EU of failing to respond adequately to the virus, leading the region to be declared a health hazard for Americans. Additionally, the UK and Ireland were excluded from the ban, which some pointed out was perhaps due to them both hosting Trump-owned golf courses. EU Commission president Ursula von der Leyen and EU Council president Charles Michel jointly criticized the move as occurring "without consultation" against a threat that "requires cooperation rather than unilateral action." Following his arrival in the White House, President Trump made no secret of his disdain for the EU as an economic rival and regulatory nuisance. In turn, the EU has sought greater rapprochement with China on trade, technology, Iran, and climate change.

On January 31, 2020, I issued Proclamation 9984 (Suspension of Entry as Immigrants and Nonimmigrants of Persons Who Pose a Risk of Transmitting 2019 Novel Coronavirus and Other Appropriate Measures To Address This Risk). I found that the potential for widespread transmission of a novel (new) coronavirus (which has since been renamed

DOI: 10.4324/9781003159551-72

"SARS-CoV-2" and causes the disease COVID-19) ("SARS-CoV-2" or "the virus") by infected individuals seeking to enter the United States threatens the security of our transportation system and infrastructure and the national security. Because the outbreak of the virus was at the time centered in the People's Republic of China, I suspended and limited the entry of all aliens who were physically present within the People's Republic of China, excluding the Special Administrative Regions of Hong Kong and Macau, during the 14-day period preceding their entry or attempted entry into the United States, subject to certain exceptions. On February 29, 2020, in recognition of the sustained person-to-person transmission of SARS-CoV-2 in the Islamic Republic of Iran, I issued Proclamation 9992 (Suspension of Entry as Immigrants and Nonimmigrants of Certain Additional Persons Who Pose a Risk of Transmitting 2019 Novel Coronavirus), suspending and limiting the entry of all aliens who were physically present within the Islamic Republic of Iran during the 14-day period preceding their entry or attempted entry into the United States, subject to certain exceptions.

The Centers for Disease Control and Prevention (CDC), a component of the Department of Health and Human Services, has determined that the virus presents a serious public health threat, and CDC continues to take steps to prevent its spread. But CDC, along with State and local health departments, has limited resources, and the public health system could be overwhelmed if sustained human-to-human transmission of the virus occurred in the United States on a large scale. Sustained human-to-human transmission has the potential to cause cascading public health, economic, national security, and societal consequences.

The World Health Organization has determined that multiple countries within the Schengen Area are experiencing sustained person-to-person transmission of SARS-CoV-2. For purposes of this proclamation, the Schengen Area comprises 26 European states: Austria, Belgium, Czech Republic, Denmark, Estonia, Finland, France, Germany, Greece, Hungary, Iceland, Italy, Latvia, Liechtenstein, Lithuania, Luxembourg, Malta, Netherlands, Norway, Poland, Portugal, Slovakia, Slovenia, Spain, Sweden, and Switzerland. The Schengen Area currently has the largest number of confirmed COVID-19 cases outside of the People's Republic of China. As of March 11, 2020, the number of cases in the 26 Schengen Area countries is 17,442, with 711 deaths, and shows high continuous growth in infection rates. In total, as of March 9, 2020, the Schengen Area has exported 201 COVID-19 cases to 53 countries. Moreover, the free flow of people between the Schengen Area countries makes the task of managing the spread of the virus difficult.

The United States Government is unable to effectively evaluate and monitor all of the travelers continuing to arrive from the Schengen Area. The potential for undetected transmission of the virus by infected individuals seeking to enter the United States from the Schengen Area threatens the security of our transportation system and infrastructure and the national security. Given the importance of protecting persons within the United States from the threat of this harmful communicable disease, I have determined that it is in the interests of the United States to take action to restrict and suspend the entry into the United States, as immigrants or nonimmigrants, of all aliens who were physically present within the Schengen Area during the 14-day period preceding their entry or attempted entry into the United States. The free flow of commerce between the United States and the Schengen Area countries remains an economic priority for the United States, and I remain committed to facilitating trade between our nations.

NOW, THEREFORE, I, DONALD J. TRUMP, President of the United States, by the authority vested in me by the Constitution and the laws of the United States of America, including sections 212(f) and 215(a) of the Immigration and Nationality Act, 8 U.S.C.

1182(f) and 1185(a), and section 301 of title 3, United States Code, hereby find that the unrestricted entry into the United States of persons described in section 1 of this proclamation would, except as provided for in section 2 of this proclamation, be detrimental to the interests of the United States, and that their entry should be subject to certain restrictions, limitations, and exceptions. I therefore hereby proclaim the following:

Section 1. Suspension and Limitation on Entry. The entry into the United States, as immigrants or nonimmigrants, of all aliens who were physically present within the Schengen Area during the 14-day period preceding their entry or attempted entry into the United States is hereby suspended and limited subject to section 2 of this proclamation.

Sec. 2. Scope of Suspension and Limitation on Entry.

a   Section 1 of this proclamation shall not apply to:

   i   any lawful permanent resident of the United States;

   ii   any alien who is the spouse of a U.S. citizen or lawful permanent resident;

   iii   any alien who is the parent or legal guardian of a U.S. citizen or lawful permanent resident, provided that the U.S. citizen or lawful permanent resident is unmarried and under the age of 21;

   iv   any alien who is the sibling of a U.S. citizen or lawful permanent resident, provided that both are unmarried and under the age of 21;

   v   any alien who is the child, foster child, or ward of a U.S. citizen or lawful permanent resident, or who is a prospective adoptee seeking to enter the United States pursuant to the IR-4 or IH-4 visa classifications;

   vi   any alien traveling at the invitation of the United States Government for a purpose related to containment or mitigation of the virus;

   vii   any alien traveling as a nonimmigrant pursuant to a C-1, D, or C-1/D nonimmigrant visa as a crewmember or any alien otherwise traveling to the United States as air or sea crew;

   viii   any alien

A   seeking entry into or transiting the United States pursuant to one of the following visas: A-1, A-2, C-2, C-3 (as a foreign government official or immediate family member of an official), E-1 (as an employee of TECRO or TECO or the employee's immediate family members), G-1, G-2, G-3, G-4, NATO-1 through NATO-4, or NATO-6 (or seeking to enter as a nonimmigrant in one of those NATO categories); or

B   whose travel falls within the scope of section 11 of the United Nations Headquarters Agreement;

   ix   any alien whose entry would not pose a significant risk of introducing, transmitting, or spreading the virus, as determined by the Secretary of Health and Human Services, through the CDC Director or his designee;

   x   any alien whose entry would further important United States law enforcement objectives, as determined by the Secretary of State, the Secretary of Homeland Security, or their respective designees, based on a recommendation of the Attorney General or his designee;

   xi   any alien whose entry would be in the national interest, as determined by the Secretary of State, the Secretary of Homeland Security, or their designees; or

   xii   members of the U.S. Armed Forces and spouses and children of members of the U.S. Armed Forces.

b   Nothing in this proclamation shall be construed to affect any individual's eligibility for asylum, withholding of removal, or protection under the regulations issued pursuant to the legislation implementing the Convention Against Torture and Other Cruel, Inhuman or Degrading Treatment or Punishment, consistent with the laws and regulations of the United States.

Sec. 3. Implementation and Enforcement. (a) The Secretary of State shall implement this proclamation as it applies to visas pursuant to such procedures as the Secretary of State, in consultation with the Secretary of Homeland Security, may establish. The Secretary of Homeland Security shall implement this proclamation as it applies to the entry of aliens pursuant to such procedures as the Secretary of Homeland Security, in consultation with the Secretary of State, may establish.

b   Consistent with applicable law, the Secretary of State, the Secretary of Transportation, and the Secretary of Homeland Security shall ensure that any alien subject to this proclamation does not board an aircraft traveling to the United States.

c   The Secretary of Homeland Security may establish standards and procedures to ensure the application of this proclamation at and between all United States ports of entry.

d   An alien who circumvents the application of this proclamation through fraud, willful misrepresentation of a material fact, or illegal entry shall be a priority for removal by the Department of Homeland Security.

Sec. 4. Termination. This proclamation shall remain in effect until terminated by the President. The Secretary of Health and Human Services shall recommend that the President continue, modify, or terminate this proclamation as described in section 5 of Proclamation 9984, as amended.

Sec. 5. Effective Date. This proclamation is effective at 11:59 p.m. eastern daylight time on March 13, 2020. This proclamation does not apply to persons aboard a flight scheduled to arrive in the United States that departed prior to 11:59 p.m. eastern daylight time on March 13, 2020.

Sec. 6. Severability. It is the policy of the United States to enforce this proclamation to the maximum extent possible to advance the national security, public safety, and foreign policy interests of the United States. Accordingly:

a   if any provision of this proclamation, or the application of any provision to any person or circumstance, is held to be invalid, the remainder of this proclamation and the application of its provisions to any other persons or circumstances shall not be affected thereby; and

b   if any provision of this proclamation, or the application of any provision to any person or circumstance, is held to be invalid because of the lack of certain procedural requirements, the relevant executive branch officials shall implement those procedural requirements to conform with existing law and with any applicable court orders.

Sec. 7. General Provisions. (a) Nothing in this proclamation shall be construed to impair or otherwise affect:

i   the authority granted by law to an executive department or agency, or the head thereof; or

ii   the functions of the Director of the Office of Management and Budget relating to budgetary, administrative, or legislative proposals.

b   This proclamation shall be implemented consistent with applicable law and subject to the availability of appropriations.

c   This proclamation is not intended to, and does not, create any right or benefit, substantive or procedural, enforceable at law or in equity by any party against the United States, its departments, agencies, or entities, its officers, employees, or agents, or any other person.

IN WITNESS WHEREOF, I have hereunto set my hand this eleventh day of March, in the year of our Lord two thousand twenty, and of the Independence of the United States of America the two hundred and forty-fourth.

DONALD J. TRUMP

Questions

Why did President Trump react so negatively to the Schengen countries in particular?
Consider this ban in the context of the US role as a principal provider of "global public goods" (i.e. leading effective global governance).

References

https://www.federalregister.gov/References/2020/03/16/2020-05578/suspension-of-entry-as-immigrants-and-nonimmigrants-of-certain-additional-persons-who-pose-a-risk-of

Document 26
EU-China Relations Fact Sheet, 20 June 2020

Formal relations between the then European Community and the People's Republic of China (PRC) were established in 1975, in the wake of the seminal diplomatic recognition of the PRC by the United States three years before. Despite interest in commercial opportunities, by 1989 two-way trade amounted to $13bn, a mere 1% of the EC's total foreign trade and 13% of China's. Developments speeded up after the end of the Cold War. In 1993 Germany put forward an Asian strategy that sought to "strengthen economic relations with the largest growth region in the world," and the European Commission followed up with A Long-Term Policy for China-Europe Relations in July 1995. Alongside the interest in Chinese production and markets, the EU also aimed at integrating a rising China into the existing frameworks of US-led global governance. In 2003 China and the EU confirmed their 'strategic partnership' and a year later China became the EU's second-biggest trading partner (after the US). The partnership had two aspects that caused problems for EU-US relations: Chinese participation in the Galileo global navigation system, and the potential lifting of the EU's arms embargo that was initiated in the wake of the Tiananmen Square massacre of June 1989. Since then China has gradually caused increasing strains in the transatlantic relationship, with the United States expecting a reluctant Europe to join its efforts to "contain" the great power ambitions of Beijing.

In the 2010s China increasingly became an active player within the space of European governance itself, complicating the US expectation of a common approach. The transcontinental Belt and Road Initiative launched in 2013 revolutionised China-EU trade, with the long-term potential difficult to judge as of 2020. Investments in the wake of the 2008 financial crisis, in particular the Greek port of Piraeus, solidified China's presence in Europe's infrastructure networks. Joint military exercises with Russia in the Mediterranean in 2015 and the Baltic in 2017 brought the Chinese military to Europe's vicinity, while ambitious Arctic strategies saw China also demanding a say in the governance of Europe's high north. Even within the EU itself, Beijing's close involvement with Central and Eastern European countries via the '17+1' arrangement was seen by some critics as a means to split the EU and prevent a united front against China's growing economic power. The signing of a major EU-China trade deal at the end of 2020 confirmed the trend that the EU, driven in particular by the sizeable German stake in China as an export market, was not going to follow Washington's line. While the Factsheet below presents a picture of a forthright EU requiring Beijing to change course on key issues such as human rights and the South China Sea, there is no doubt that Brussels is prepared to accommodate a powerful China more easily than Washington.

The EU's approach towards China was set out in a Strategy adopted in 2016 and updated in March 2019 in a Joint Communication of the European Commission and the High Representative. The balance of challenges and opportunities presented by China has shifted

DOI: 10.4324/9781003159551-73

over time. For the EU, China is simultaneously (in different policy areas) a cooperation partner, a negotiation partner, an economic competitor and a systemic rival. The EU pursues realistic, effective and coherent engagement with China, based on our values and interests.

TRADE

In 2019 the EU was China's biggest trading partner while China was the EU's second largest trading partner.

Trade in goods between the EU and China was worth over €1.5bn a day in 2019.

The EU exported to China €198bn and imported €362bn in 2019.

In 2018 the EU exported €46bn of services to China, while China exported €30bn to the EU.

COMPREHENSIVE AGREEMENT ON INVESTMENT

Under negotiation, to create:

– a more level playing field for business
– new market opportunities for both sides

And encourage China to:

– advance its economic reforms
– give the market a more decisive role

COVID-19, A GLOBAL CHALLENGE THAT REQUIRES GLOBAL ACTION

The EU and China agree on the need to address global health threats through international cooperation, and on the role of the World Health Organisation in ensuring an efficient and coordinated response. At the height of the outbreak in China, the EU coordinated the delivery to China of personal protective equipment and medical supplies from its member states. China later reciprocated with supplies to EU member states. In May 2020 the EU led a crucial resolution of the World Health Assembly on the international response, including an independent and comprehensive evaluation into the response to COVID-19. The EU and China are working on possible joint support to African countries.

HUMAN RIGHTS

The EU consistently speaks out about the deteriorating human rights situation in China – in particular, Xinjiang, Tibet and the treatment of human rights lawyers and defenders.

- The EU holds a regular human rights dialogue with China, with a view to promoting human rights, fostering the rule of law and supporting civil society.
- The EU has a strong stake in the continued stability and prosperity of Hong Kong under the 'One Country, Two Systems' principle. It attaches great importance to the preservation of Hong Kong's high degree of autonomy, in line with the Basic Law and with China's international commitments, and raises these issues at political level with Beijing.

WTO REFORM

- The EU and China both strongly support the WTO. The EU wants to work closer with China on WTO reform, including to strengthen industrial subsidies rules.

OCEAN GOVERNANCE

- The EU-China Ocean Partnership, signed in 2018, aims at improving international ocean governance and promote a sustainable blue economy. The EU expects China to engage more actively in the areas of sustainable fisheries and marine resources.

CLIMATE CHANGE, ENERGY AND RESOURCE EFFICIENCY

China, with 28% of global greenhouse gas emissions, is a crucial partner for the EU on implementing the Paris Agreement.

The EU is encouraging China to show greater ambition and assume greater responsibility on climate action, commensurate with its international influence and its economic strength.

Based on the Paris Agreement, the EU and China are reinforcing their cooperation to advance the international climate negotiations process and in areas like carbon markets, long-term development strategies, clean energy and energy efficiency, low emission transport and cities.

CYBER SECURITY

The annual EU-China Cyber Taskforce offers the opportunity to exchange views including in the context of international security and as regards the economic aspects of cyber security.

The EU expects China to engage more against malicious cyber activities and on the protection of intellectual property.

FOREIGN POLICY AND DEVELOPMENT COOPERATION

EU-China cooperation was a major factor in first securing the Iran nuclear agreement and now in working together to ensure its full and effective implementation.

In the South China Sea, the EU supports the peaceful settlement of disputes in accordance with UNCLOS and maintaining freedom of navigation and overflight.

The EU and China should work more closely to tackle global challenges and international security issues, including in Afghanistan, the Middle East, Libya, and counter-piracy.

The EU wants to further build on cooperation with China on African issues, in full respect of the principle of African ownership.

EU-CHINA CONNECTIVITY

The EU's Strategy on Connecting Europe and Asia provides a strong basis for engagement, including with China, on the basis of international norms and standards.

The key principles driving the EU's engagement on connectivity are sustainability, transparency, open procurement and level playing field.

The EU-China Connectivity Platform aims at promoting sustainable transport corridors based on the principles of the Trans-European Transport networks policy.

Questions

Do you think the EU is justified in trying to influence China on issues such as basic freedoms and human rights?

Should the EU pursue its own China policy or should it always team up with the United States to have a greater chance of forcing China's compliance?

References

https://eeas.europa.eu/sites/eeas/files/eu-china_factsheet_06_2020_0.pdf

Document 27

"United for a New Era": Analysis and Recommendations of the Reflection Group Appointed by the Secretary General of NATO, 25 November 2020

In an interview in The Economist *(7 November 2019), the French President Emmanuel Ma-cron described the Alliance as "brain dead". With this remark he deliberately escalated the widespread sense of unease surrounding a lack of political and strategic cohesion within the transatlantic alliance. At the time of the interview Turkey was at serious odds with its NATO allies due to the purchase of Russian S-400 anti-aircraft missiles (see Part III Document 20), its disagreement with Greece over the exploitation of energy reserves in the Eastern Mediter-ranean, and general concerns about Turkish-Russian cooperation on the Syrian crisis. Tur-key's flirt with Russia and President's Trump blatant indifference to NATO were among the main incentives for the Organisation to install a Reflection Group to consider future options. This approach had been used before, most notably with the Harmel report of 1967, named after the Belgian Minister of Foreign Affairs, Pierre Harmel, which laid out NATO's strategy in an era of increasing Détente with the Soviet Union. On the basis of a strategic assessment of NATO's security environment, the 2020 Reflection Group came up with almost 140 recom-mendations, of which the main findings are listed below. Interestingly, for the first time China is seen as a potential strategic rival.*

[This is an excerpt from the full document]

Main Findings: Moving Toward NATO 2030

NATO must adapt to meet the needs of a more demanding strategic environment marked by the return of systemic rivalry, persistently aggressive Russia, the rise of China, and the growing role of EDTs [Emerging Disruptive Technologies], at the same time that it faces elevated transnational threats and risks. The overarching political objective for NATO must be to consolidate the transatlantic Alliance to ensure that it possesses the tools, co-hesion, and consultative attributes to provide collective defence in this more challenging landscape. NATO's political dimension must adapt in order to maintain and strengthen its efficiency as well as ensuring its relevance for all Allies. To this end, this report offers 138 recommendations, of which the following are some of the main takeaways:

1 The starting point must be to update the 2010 Strategic Concept. This should be seen as an opportunity to solidify cohesion by confronting new strategic realities and bringing together the various strands of recent adaptations into one coherent stra-tegic picture. When updating the Concept, Allies should seek to preserve NATO's three core tasks and enhance its role as the unique and essential transatlantic forum for consultations; it should update content related to the principles undergirding the NATO Alliance, changes to the geostrategic environment (including both Russia and China), and the need to incorporate terrorism more fully into NATO's core tasks.

DOI: 10.4324/9781003159551-74

2 NATO should continue the dual-track approach of deterrence and dialogue with Russia. The Alliance must respond to Russian threats and hostile actions in a politically united, determined, and coherent way, without a return to 'business as usual' barring alterations in Russia's aggressive behaviour and its return to full compliance with international law. At the same time, NATO should remain open to discussing peaceful co-existence and to reacting positively to constructive changes in Russia's posture and attitude. NATO should evolve the content of its dual-track strategy to ensure its continued effectiveness by raising the costs for Russian aggression and develop a more comprehensive response to hybrid forms of Russian aggression, while at the same time supporting increased political outreach to negotiate arms control and risk reduction measures.

3 NATO must devote much more time, political resources, and action to the security challenges posed by China – based on an assessment of its national capabilities, economic heft, and the stated ideological goals of its leaders. It needs to develop a political strategy for approaching a world in which China will be of growing importance through to 2030. The Alliance should infuse the China challenge throughout existing structures and consider establishing a consultative body to discuss all aspects of Allies' security interests vis-à-vis China. It must expand efforts to assess the implications of China's technological development and monitor and defend against any Chinese activities that could impact collective defence, military readiness, or resilience in the Supreme Allied Commander Europe's (SACEUR) Area of Responsibility.

4 Emerging and disruptive technologies are a challenge but also opportunity for NATO. Competing with the efforts underway by large authoritarian states to achieve dominance in key EDTs must be a strategic priority for the Alliance and its members. NATO should serve as a crucial coordinating institution for information-sharing and collaboration between Allies on all aspects of EDTs that have a bearing on their security.

5 Terrorism poses one of the most immediate, asymmetric threats to Allied nations and citizens. NATO should more explicitly integrate the fight against terrorism into its core tasks. This fight should be given a place within NATO structures, supported by necessary resources, commensurate with the threat that it poses. NATO should enhance the fight against terrorism as part of the hybrid and cyber conversation and ensure that the threat from terrorism figures in exercises and lessons learned. NATO should strive to improve current practices of intelligence-sharing among Allies to achieve better, common situational awareness in key areas including emerging safe havens and terrorists' use of EDTs, as well as hybrid tactics.

6 NATO must articulate a consistent, clear, and coherent approach to the South, addressing both traditional threats like terrorism, and the growing presence of Russia and to a lesser extent China. NATO must maintain political focus on building up military preparedness and response for the southern/Mediterranean flank, in particular by revising and delivering its Advance Plans and strengthening the Hub for the South at JFC Naples. NATO should strengthen ties and cooperation, especially with the EU, in the framework of a coordinated approach. It should increase the frequency of political consultations, including at the NAC level, on the South.

7 NATO should reaffirm its support for arms control while maintaining an effective nuclear deterrence. It should play an enhanced role as a forum to debate challenges to existing arms control mechanisms and consult on any future arrangements. NATO should continue to support the strengthening of effective verification regimes and enable monitoring capabilities and enforcement mechanisms. It should develop an agenda for international arms control in key areas of EDT with military application.

NATO should further adapt its defence and deterrence posture in the post-Intermediate-Range Nuclear Forces (INF) Treaty setting to take into account the threat posed by Russia's existing and new military capabilities. It should continue and revitalise the nuclear-sharing arrangements that constitute a critical element of NATO's deterrence policy.

8   Climate change will continue to shape NATO's security environment. While modulating emissions is primarily a national competency, NATO has a role to play in increasing situational awareness, early warning, and information sharing, including by considering the establishment of Centre of Excellence on Climate and Security. It should build on efforts to include climate change and other non-military threats such as pandemics in NATO planning on resilience and crisis management, with an emphasis on making energy and telecommunications grids better able to withstand weather events. NATO should revise its 2014 Green Defence framework and make more strategic use of the Science for Peace and Security programme in order to develop and implement better green military technology.

9   Maintaining political cohesion and unity must be an unambiguous priority for all Allies. Allies on both sides of the Atlantic must reaffirm their commitment to NATO as the principal institution for the defence of the Euro-Atlantic area. Allies should pledge themselves to a code of good conduct to abide by the spirit as well as the letter of the North Atlantic Treaty. Allies should maintain and meet agreed burden-sharing requirements. NATO should reassert its core identity as an Alliance rooted in the principles of democracy, and Allies should consider establishing a Centre of Excellence for Democratic Resilience dedicated to providing support to individual Allies, upon their request, for strengthening societal resilience to resist interference from hostile external actors in the functioning of their democratic institutions and processes.

10   The Group calls for transatlantic consultation to be strengthened in a systematic, credible, and powerful manner. Allies must reaffirm the role of the North Atlantic Council as a genuine forum for consultation on major strategic and political issues. Allies should strive to hold national policies to the line of policy developed at NATO. The Alliance should institute a practice whereby Allied Foreign Ministers make a periodic appraisal of the Alliance's political health and development. NATO should hold more frequent Ministerials and, when appropriate, expand their format. It should resume the practice whereby the number of annual Foreign Ministerials matches the number of Defence Ministerials, with meetings alternating between NATO HQ and Allied capitals. It should hold more informal meetings and institute regular consultations on issues beyond the traditional agenda, including meetings of NATO Political Directors or other senior officials for e.g., Middle East, African, and East Asian affairs as well as cyber and other topics as appropriate.

11   ATO and the EU should seek to reinvigorate trust and understanding at the highest levels. At the next NATO Summit or the next available opportunity, it would be useful for NATO and EU Heads of State and Government to meet in a special formal session to review the current state of the relationship and examine areas for greater cooperation. The two organisations should create an institutionalised staff link through a permanent political liaison element in NATO's International Staff (IS) and the European External Action Service (EEAS). NATO should welcome EU efforts towards a stronger and more capable European defence capacity insofar as these strengthen NATO, contribute to a fair transatlantic burden-sharing, and fully involve non-EU Allies. Ongoing European efforts should be better used to increase the share of European Allies in support of NATO capability targets.

12   NATO should outline a global blueprint for better utilising its partnerships to advance NATO strategic interests. It should shift from the current demand-driven approach to an interest-driven approach and consider providing more stable and predictable resource streams for partnership activities. NATO's Open Door Policy should be upheld and reinvigorated. NATO should expand and strengthen partnerships with Ukraine and Georgia, seek to heighten engagement with Bosnia and Herzegovina, and counter destabilisation across the Western Balkans. NATO should energise the Mediterranean Dialogue (MD) and the Istanbul Cooperation Initiative (ICI) through strengthened political engagement, capacity building, and resilience enhancement. It should deepen cooperation with Indo-Pacific partners, including by strengthening information-sharing and creating regularised dialogues on technological cooperation and pooling of R&D in select fields.

13   The principle of consensus is a cornerstone of the Alliance, but NATO must be diligent in ensuring that it remains capable of reaching and implementing decisions in a timely fashion. NATO should strengthen measures to ensure that consensus-based decisions are implemented and not diluted in follow-on work. It should consider bolstering the Secretary General's chief executive role in order to make decisions on routine matters and to bring difficult issues into the open at an early stage. NATO should create a more structured mechanism to support the establishment of coalitions inside existing Alliance structures and should examine ways to time-limit decision making in crisis. To deal with the growing frequency of single-country blockages involving external bilateral disputes, it should consider raising the threshold for such blockages to the Ministerial level.

14   With regard to political structure, staffing, and resources, NATO needs a strong political dimension to match its military adaptation. NATO should consider increasing the delegated authorities of the Secretary General to make meaningful decisions on personnel and certain budgetary matters.

NATO should establish a centre of higher learning to cultivate future talent outside of NATO and launch a scholarship program, tentatively called the Harmel Fellowship Programme, under which each Ally would fund a scholarship programme for at least one individual every year from another NATO Ally to undertake postgraduate study at one of its leading universities.

Questions

The document lays out a wide agenda, both transatlantic in focus and global in ambition. Is it a credible agenda, given the state of transatlantic relations in 2020?
Should NATO concentrate more on China as a "strategic threat"?

Reference

https://www.nato.int/nato_static_fl2014/assets/pdf/2020/12/pdf/201201-Reflection-Group-Final-Report-Uni.pdf 2030

Index